The Private World of Soviet Scientists from Stalin to Gorbachev

The Private World of Soviet Scientists from Stalin to Gorbachev sheds new light on the complex transition of Soviet society from Stalinism into the post-Stalin era. Using the case study of Chernogolovka, one of dozens of scientific towns built in the USSR under Khrushchev, Rogacheva explains what motivated the scientific intelligentsia to participate in the late Soviet project and what it contributed to the stability of the USSR. Rogacheva traces the history of this scientific community from its creation in 1956 through the early Gorbachev period to paint a nuanced portrait of the living conditions, political outlook, and mentality of the local scientific intelligentsia. Utilizing new archival materials and an extensive oral history project, she argues that Soviet scientists were not merely bought off by the Soviet state, but that they bought *into* the idealism and social optimism of the post-Stalin regime. Many shared the regime's belief in the progressive development of Soviet society on a scientific basis, and embraced their increased autonomy and privileged status.

MARIA A. ROGACHEVA is a Visiting Assistant Professor of Global Studies at the College of William and Mary.

The Private World of Soviet Scientists from Stalin to Gorbachev

Maria A. Rogacheva

College of William and Mary

CAMBRIDGE
UNIVERSITY PRESS

CAMBRIDGE
UNIVERSITY PRESS

University Printing House, Cambridge CB2 8BS, United Kingdom

One Liberty Plaza, 20th Floor, New York, NY 10006, USA

477 Williamstown Road, Port Melbourne, VIC 3207, Australia

4843/24, 2nd Floor, Ansari Road, Daryaganj, Delhi – 110002, India

79 Anson Road, #06–04/06, Singapore 079906

Cambridge University Press is part of the University of Cambridge.

It furthers the University's mission by disseminating knowledge in the pursuit of education, learning, and research at the highest international levels of excellence.

www.cambridge.org
Information on this title: www.cambridge.org/9781107196360
DOI: 10.1017/9781108164696

First published 2017

Printed in the United States of America by Sheridan Books, Inc.

A catalogue record for this publication is available from the British Library.

ISBN 978-1-107-19636-0 Hardback

To my Parents, with much love

Contents

List of Figures   *page* viii
Acknowledgments   ix

   Introduction   1

1 An Unusual Testing Ground: Building a Town in the Marshes,
   1955–1962   23

2 Children of the Great Patriotic War: The Formation of Soviet
   Scientists, 1930–1955   49

3 "We Were Building a Town for Ourselves": Everyday Life in
   Chernogolovka in the 1960s and 1970s   75

4 Scientists, Ideology, and the Communist Party in Chernogolovka   108

5 Chernogolovka Scientists between Loyalty and Dissent:
   The Soviet Invasion of Czechoslovakia and the Liubarskii Affair   131

6 Scientists behind the Iron Curtain: Traveling Abroad in the 1960s
   and 1970s   152

   Conclusion   175

Biographical Notes   181
Bibliography   188
Index   203

Figures

1.1 First Street (*Pervaia ulitsa*) in Chernogolovka, 1962   *page* 24
1.2 Nikolai Semenov (right) and Fedor Dubovitskii (left)   33
3.1 Chernogolovka under construction, 1964   82
3.2 First Street (*Pervaia ulitsa*) in the mid-1960s   83
3.3 Vladimir Enman (right) at his garden plot, 1960   88
3.4 Vsevolod Gantmakher (second from the right), Chernogolovka ca. 1964   97
4.1 Evgenii Poniatovskii, Yuri Osipyan, and Veniamin Shekhtman (left to right) at the Presidium of the Soviet Academy of Sciences, 1971   125
4.2 Chernogolovka scientists at the November 7th Demonstration, 1986   127

Acknowledgments

A number of people and institutions have made this book possible, and it is my pleasure and honor to thank them for their support, patience, encouragement, and generosity. First, I want to thank Jim McAdams, whose passion for learning, deep knowledge of Soviet and Eastern European politics and history, and friendship proved instrumental to completion of this project. Jim has been a great mentor over the last ten years, challenging me to address major issues, to work through difficult questions, and to understand Soviet scientists on their own terms. I can never thank him enough for the hundreds of hours of inspirational conversations, intellectual guidance, care, and support. I am also grateful to my graduate advisor, Semion Lyandres, who introduced me to the field of Soviet studies, encouraged me to think critically about my evidence, and successfully guided me through my doctoral research and writing. To Semion, I largely owe my general perspective on Soviet history. His deep understanding of the nature of the Russian Revolution has benefited my own work. My other dissertation committee members, Wilson Miscamble and Alexander Martin, provided valuable feedback on the project during its formative stage. Father Bill welcomed me to the University of Notre Dame back in 2006 and, in his witty Australian way, helped me to transition to the American educational system. His dedication to scholarship and teaching has substantially shaped my own research and teaching. He has been a true friend, too. Alexander Martin set high academic standards for my scholarship and created a stimulating intellectual environment for studying modern European history at Notre Dame. I also owe a vast intellectual debt to the late Sabine MacCormack, who was a model scholar.

This book has also benefited from the generous feedback of other scholars. Vladimir Shlapentokh advised me to focus on a small scientific community in the late Soviet era. Denis Kozlov read multiple conference papers on Chernogolovka scientists and provided first-rate feedback. Vladislav Zubok helped me discern the idealism of the postwar Russian intelligentsia. Ethan Pollock and Paul Josephson provided the highly valuable perspective of historians of Soviet science. I would also like to thank Lynne Viola, David Shearer, Abbott Gleason, Francine Hirsch, Andy Bruno, Kathryn Ciancia, David

McDonald, Kate Brown, Asif Siddiqi, Thomas Remington, Michael David-Fox, and Alexander Rabinowitch for sharing their expertise on Soviet and East European history.

Most of all, I am indebted to members of the first generation of Chernogolovka scientists, who agreed to be interviewed for this project and spent many hours of their time helping me better understand one of the most exciting, yet controversial, periods of Soviet history. Talking to these highly educated and accomplished people about their lives was one of the most enjoyable parts of my research. I am thankful for the opportunity to get to know all "my scientists," but especially Rimma Liubovskaia and Rustem Liubovskii, Vladimir Enman, Oleg Efimov, Georgii Manelis, Ernest Suvorov, and Vera Sedykh. I also want to thank the staff of the archives I worked in, and especially Lidiia Sergeevna Naumova at the Central Archive of Social and Political History of Moscow (TsAOPIM), Irina Georgievna Tarakanova at the Archive of the Russian Academy of Sciences, and Nadezhda Nikolaevna Naumenko at the Archive of the Institute of Solid State Physics. Their interest in my research and their assistance, as well as their endless tea supplies, made my work in the Russian archives much more pleasant.

My research in Russia was made possible by the generous financial support of a number of institutions. At Notre Dame, the Institute for Scholarship in the Liberal Arts gave me a grant to begin my oral history project with Chernogolovka scientists. The Kellogg Institute for International Studies supported me during my most labor-intensive research year in Russia. The Graduate School not only made my studies at Notre Dame possible, but also provided additional funding that allowed me to undertake research trips to Russia in 2010 and 2012. Yet I am most indebted to the Nanovic Institute for European Studies, which supported essentially every research project I undertook during my time at Notre Dame. The Nanovic Institute funded my research at the Hoover Institution in summer 2008. It also funded me during the sixth year of my graduate studies, which allowed me to focus on writing when I needed it the most. I would like to thank Sharon Konopka for welcoming me at the Nanovic Institute, and John Tomasi and Dina Egge for providing me office space at the Political Theory Project at Brown University. I am also grateful to Jennifer Tishler at the University of Wisconsin-Madison for inviting me to be a Fellow at the Center for Russia, East Europe, and Central Asia. Finally, receiving the Robert C. Tucker/Stephen F. Cohen Dissertation Prize in 2014 proved crucial during the last stretch of my work on this project.

My thanks also go to my gifted editors at Cambridge University Press, Lewis Bateman and Lucy Rhymer, for masterfully guiding my manuscript to publication. I am indebted to their talented staff, too, especially Melissa Shivers, Chloé Harries, and Ian McIver. I also want to thank Jeevitha Baskaran and my copy-editor for their hard work preparing my book for publication.

In South Bend, Indiana, I was fortunate to enjoy the friendship and support of Alexander and Alla Mukasyan and Promit and Monali Das, for which I am truly grateful.

My family has been a constant source of inspiration and support as I worked on this project. My parents, Alexander Rogachev and Galina Rogacheva, have been the most loving and supportive parents one could ever imagine. They taught me to strive for intellectual excellence, and gave me the confidence to move forward. My brother, Sergei, facilitated the technical side of the project, making sure that my digital recorder kept working during all interviews. My mother-in-law, Cheryl Bandoch, believed in me when I needed it most. Above all, Joshua Bandoch has been a truly amazing husband, friend, and intellectual companion. His love, patience, understanding, sense of humor, and analytical mind have kept me going all these years. He helped me to "see the forest behind the trees" and encouraged me to keep working on this project, providing critical feedback on multiple drafts of each chapter. It would not be an exaggeration to say that without his love and support this book would never have been written. For this, and so much else, I will always be grateful.

Introduction

"If we managed to use the power of modern science to its full capacity, we
could provide for each and every person according to their needs."

Nikolai Semenov, 1958

On February 28, 1956, the Council of Ministers of the USSR adopted a
resolution obligating the Soviet Academy of Sciences to establish a research
testing ground for the Institute of Chemical Physics (ICP). The ICP had
actively participated in the Soviet nuclear project since 1946. So, when
Nikolai Semenov, the institute's director and the first Soviet scientist to be
awarded the Nobel Prize, requested a testing ground to promote research on
new powerful explosives, the Soviet government quickly approved the construction. Several months later, construction began in a sparsely populated area
located thirty-five miles to the northeast of Moscow, not far from the tiny
village of Chernogolovka. By 1959, the testing ground had a twelve-apartment
residential house, a two-storied hotel, and a cafeteria.

That same year, the first employees arrived in Chernogolovka. Almost all of
them were young men and women, in their mid-twenties, with science and
engineering degrees from the best Soviet universities. Some of them came directly
from their undergraduate studies; others were finishing up graduate work. The vast
majority of newcomers were physicists and chemists. In the early 1960s, once
Semenov began to transform the testing ground into a scientific center, he also
employed biologists and mathematicians. Originally, the lack of material comfort
made Semenov worry that no one would want to come to this nascent settlement in
the marshes. However, the testing ground grew rapidly. By August 1962, when the
Academy decreed to establish a scientific center in Chernogolovka, more than
800 people had been successfully working at the Branch of the Institute of
Chemical Physics (or the ICP Branch, for short). Of this number, 423 were
scientists conducting pioneering research at the intersection of physics and chemistry. A decade later, Chernogolovka's population reached 8,000, making it one of
the most vibrant centers for fundamental research in the USSR.

The establishment of the testing ground in Chernogolovka went unnoticed
in the Soviet Union. Stalin's death on March 5, 1953, and the process of

de-Stalinization unleashed by the new collective leadership, threw Soviet society into disarray. The release of Gulag prisoners, the end of the Doctors' Plot, and the arrest of Lavrentii Beria, Stalin's notorious head of the secret police, all signaled the beginning of a new era. On February 25, 1956, Nikita Khrushchev, the First Secretary of the Communist Party of the Soviet Union, publicly denounced Stalin's crimes at the Twentieth Party Congress. The world that Soviet people had known for nearly three decades, with its rigid ideological control and cult of Stalin, was rapidly falling to pieces.

Soviet accomplishments in the scientific sphere were much less ambiguous, yet even more impressive. The launch of Sputnik into space on October 4, 1957, produced a hugely enthusiastic popular response, inaugurating the first triumphant decade of Soviet space exploration.[1] The construction of Akademgorodok, an interdisciplinary scientific center in the heart of Siberia, also received wide publicity in the Soviet press. From early on, Akademgorodok enjoyed steady support from the Soviet government, which saw science and technology as the key to constructing Communism and surpassing the economic production of the capitalist world. Khrushchev himself was involved in the project, making sure that Mikhail Lavrentiev, the founder of the Siberian city of science, received the best human and financial resources.[2]

Unlike Akademgorodok, Chernogolovka never really became a recognized symbol of de-Stalinization. The original budget allocated for Chernogolovka's construction was limited. So was its stated purpose: research on new powerful explosives. In contrast to Lavrentiev, Semenov did not rely on Khrushchev's personal support to get his project off the ground; nor did he promise the creation of an urban utopia that would contribute to Soviet economic development. Despite this, in six short years Semenov's military-oriented testing ground transformed into a full-fledged scientific center dedicated to fundamental research. Hundreds and then thousands of young scientists came to live and work in Chernogolovka in the 1960s and early 1970s. Many of them were put in charge of cutting-edge groups and laboratories, developing new directions of scientific research. They established research facilities and organized daily life in the town. The input of the first generation of Chernogolovka scientists was crucial for the success of Semenov's daring enterprise, which would have been unthinkable under late Stalinism.

What does it mean that a town like Chernogolovka emerged at that particular moment of Soviet history? What made it possible, and what does it contribute to our understanding of how Soviet society changed and

---

[1] James T. Andrews and Asif A. Siddiqi, eds., *Into the Cosmos: Space Exploration and Soviet Culture* (Pittsburgh: University of Pittsburgh Press, 2011), pp. 4–5.

[2] Paul R. Josephson, *New Atlantis Revisited: Akademgorodok, the Siberian City of Science* (Princeton: Princeton University Press, 1997), p. xvi.

how it functioned after Stalin's death? What can we learn from this case study about the stability and longevity of the late Soviet system? This book sets out to answer these questions by placing the history of Chernogolovka in the context of the complex transition of Soviet society from Stalinism into the post-Stalin era. I argue that the revitalization of socialism through scientific development was at the very core of Khrushchev's reforms, popularly known as the Thaw. In stark contrast to his predecessor, the First Secretary recognized that the Soviet Union needed to stop stifling innovation in order to progress. The regime also acknowledged that to build a modern, affluent society and to compete with the capitalist world in the economic and military spheres, it had to bring the scientific intelligentsia on board. Under Khrushchev, scientists became elite members of Soviet society and leading figures in the future construction of Communism. They regained the professional autonomy they had lost during Stalin's rule.[3] Prominent scientists such as Semenov initiated, and headed, the construction from scratch of dozens of scientific towns across the USSR. By the mid-1960s, many of these towns came to represent the best of what the late Soviet model of socialism, or mature socialism, had to offer. Residents of these towns enjoyed generous and consistent state funding of their research, as well as privileged material conditions, including modern housing, free health care and education for their children, and better food supplies. They could travel abroad for scholarly exchanges and scientific conferences. They also enjoyed relative professional and personal autonomy, as long as scientists avoided openly dissenting against the system. While the Khrushchev regime failed to deliver Communism to the majority of the Soviet population, it was more successful in producing "a happy society of creative and highly educated people"[4] within strictly limited boundaries.

Khrushchev's promise to reinvigorate socialism through science provoked an enthusiastic response among the first Cold War generation of Soviet scientists. Hundreds of thousands of Soviet citizens who had joined the ranks of the scientific intelligentsia in the late 1950s and the 1960s were not merely bought off by the Soviet state. They bought *into* the idealism and social optimism of the late Soviet regime that claimed science would play a crucial role in the construction of Communism. Scientists did not manipulate the post-Stalin system. They lived and functioned successfully within this system, and were eager to contribute to the country's scientific and technological development. Privileged and isolated from the outside world, Chernogolovka offered

---

[3] In the field of genetics, the Soviet regime continued to interfere in scientific affairs throughout the Khrushchev era. On scientists' struggle to free biology from Lysenkoism, see Josephson, *New Atlantis Revisited*, pp. 82–119.

[4] Vladislav Zubok, *Zhivago's Children: The Last Russian Intelligentsia* (Cambridge: The Belknap Press of Harvard University Press, 2009), p. 123.

outstanding opportunities to the first Cold War generation of Soviet scientists who had flocked into the profession after World War II. It allowed scientists to escape the miserable conditions of their youth, which was scarred by mass repressions and the Great Patriotic War. More importantly, it allowed them to have fulfilling lives under Khrushchev and Brezhnev.

Far from being in opposition to the system, many Chernogolovka scientists were proud of their closeness to a powerful state. Some of them contributed to building up the Soviet military–industrial complex, creating solid rocket propellant and new powerful explosives. The vast majority, though, worked on non-military topics in materials science, combustion science, organic chemistry, and polymer production. Many shared the regime's belief in the progressive development of Soviet society on a scientific basis – one of the key tenets of Marxism – and saw their work for the Party-state as a necessary part of that effort.

Remarkably, Chernogolovka scientists' idealism and professional autonomy did not come to an end after Khrushchev's ouster in 1964. The early Brezhnev era oversaw the rapid expansion of the local scientific community, including the establishment of new research institutes, the emergence of informal cultural organizations, and lively residential development. Although by the late 1970s some scientists had grown critical of the economic failings of the Soviet system, most members of Chernogolovka community continued to identify with the regime's proclaimed goal of building a "just and egalitarian" society with the help of science and technology. Surprisingly, rather than undermining their core beliefs, the collapse of the Soviet Union made them even stronger.

My aim in writing this book has been to provide a human face to the story of late Soviet science, and in particular to explain how scientists in closed academic communities such as Chernogolovka managed to have fulfilling lives under Khrushchev and Brezhnev. Relying on newly available archival materials and an extensive oral history project, I set out to reconstruct the outlooks of an idealistic cohort of scientists who enjoyed the rare privilege of living in a closed community dedicated to scientific research. Chernogolovka scientists' personal stories run through the narrative. I track the histories of individual people from their coming of age during late Stalinism to their decision to join the ranks of the scientific elite in the mid- to late 1950s. I examine scientists' everyday lives, and the transformation of their political outlook during the Khrushchev and the early Brezhnev years. I also explore scientists' experiences traveling abroad in the 1960s and 1970s, trying to shed light on how and why the scientific intelligentsia came to identify with the late Soviet project. But what *was* the Soviet project after 1953? What would take the place of Stalinism?

The Soviet Project After Stalin

The legacy of the Stalin era, both domestic and foreign, was terrifying. Rapid postwar reconstruction and the stunning success of the Soviet nuclear program masked the fact that entire areas of the economy had been woefully neglected. Heavy industry and the military–industrial complex continued to dominate the Soviet command economy during the last decade of Stalin's rule, while consumer-oriented industries and housing remained in short supply. By the early 1950s, most sectors of the population, especially the party elite and the intelligentsia, had been terrorized and paralyzed by fear, expecting a new wave of repressions. Several million prisoners were still languishing in the Gulag, many of them serving sentences based on false accusations. The international situation was equally dire. As the Cold War kept escalating, the ageing, and increasingly paranoid, dictator came to alienate both Soviet enemies and friends.

Yet, when Stalin died, abandoning socialism could not have been further from the minds of the new collective leadership. From 1953 to 1956, a furious power struggle unfolded in the Kremlin among Politburo members. Nikita Khrushchev, who emerged victorious, saw the revitalization of socialism uncorrupted by Stalinist excesses as his main priority. He made this clear at the Twentieth Congress of the CPSU in February 1956, when he attempted to disconnect Stalin's crimes from Leninism, the Communist Party and the Soviet regime. "We are fully confident," the First Secretary claimed at the end of the secret speech, "that our party, guided by the historical decisions of the Twentieth Congress, will lead the Soviet people down the Leninist path to new successes and new victories."[5]

Born in 1894, Khrushchev was a child of the Russian Revolution and had fully embraced its creed and its values, including the promise of economic liberation and unending progress. A true Communist believer, he was convinced that socialism was superior to capitalism because it provided a better life for ordinary men and women. The Soviet model, Khrushchev preached, could produce "a happy society of creative and highly educated people." The Soviet people would naturally follow his lead, once he showed them what genuine socialism, purified of its Stalinist distortions, had to offer.[6] In hindsight, it might appear that the return of Gulag inmates, the "Thaw" in literature and arts, and the re-opening of Soviet society to the West were inevitable, since many members of the collective leadership acknowledged the need for reforms. Still, Khrushchev's personality, with his distinctive blend

---

[5] *Doklad Pervogo sekretaria TsK KPSS tov. N.S. Khrushcheva XX s'ezdu Kommunisticheskoi Partii Sovetskogo Soiuza "O kul'te lichnosti i ego posledstviiakh"* (Moskva: Novaia gazeta, 2008), p. 71.

[6] For a comprehensive portrait of Nikita Khrushchev, see William Taubman, *Khrushchev: The Man and His Era* (New York: W.W. Norton, 2003).

of pragmatism and utopian faith in Marxist–Leninist ideology, significantly shaped the contours and pace of de-Stalinization.

While Khrushchev believed that the sacrifices of collectivization and industrialization were necessary to transform the Soviet Union into a modern industrial power, he also was convinced that after Stalin's death Soviet society entered a new stage of socialist construction. The revolutionary struggle, he argued, was in the past. Satisfaction of people's material needs should become the main priority of the Soviet government. In his memoirs, recorded several years after his fall, Khrushchev wrote that it pained him that workers in the Soviet Union were worse off than workers in tsarist Russia before 1917: "The idea of socialism and communism, developed by Marx, Engels and Lenin, is correct. But it is only an idea, and you cannot make soup out of it."[7] Socialism was meaningless if it could not provide people with basic material comforts, such as sufficient food and adequate housing. After forty years of deprivation, struggle, and suffering, the First Secretary promised, Soviet people could finally reap the fruit of their labor.

Khrushchev's "New Deal" soon produced impressive results. Beginning in 1953, the Soviet government carried out a massive housing program that allowed millions of people to move into new, separate apartments for the first time in their lives. The regime also significantly increased investment in education, pensions, health care, and consumer-oriented industries. These new policies laid the foundations for "a better-off society with social safety nets and of a state with greater responsibility for material standards of its citizens."[8] The initial success of Khrushchev's reforms was facilitated by the rapid economic growth that had begun in the USSR during the last several years of Stalin's rule.

Repudiation of mass violence marked Khrushchev's second major break with Stalinism. In 1959, the First Secretary solemnly proclaimed that the Soviet Union had completed the "full and final construction of socialism."[9] This led him to reconsider the relationship between the Soviet regime and society, rejecting the use of mass violence. One major accomplishment of socialist construction, Khrushchev stated, was a growing consensus within society. Since the new generation of Soviet citizens had come of age under socialism, the time had come to extend trust to all major groups of the population and to build relations between the regime and society on the basis of greater mutual confidence.[10] Rehabilitation of the victims of

---

[7] N.S. Khrushchev, *Vospominaniia: Vremia. Liudi. Vlast'. T. 4* (Moskva: Moskovskie novosti, 1999), p. 161.

[8] Zubok, *Zhivago's Children*, p. 124.

[9] N.S. Khrushchev, *O kontrol'nykh tsifrakh razvitiia narodnogo khoziaistva SSSR na 1959–1965 gody* (Moskva: Gospolitizdat, 1959), p. 7.

[10] Alfred B. Evans, Jr., *Soviet Marxism-Leninism: The Decline of an Ideology* (Westport: Praeger, 1993), p. 59.

Stalinism was one important consequence of this new policy. Equally exciting was Khrushchev's belief that mobilizing the Soviet people and rekindling their revolutionary enthusiasm could work miracles. The new Soviet leader had especially high expectations of Soviet youth, which he assumed was not only ideologically pure, but also better trained and educated. The Virgin Lands campaign,[11] launched in 1954, was a potent symbol of Khrushchev's attempts to reinvent the relationship between Soviet rulers and the ruled on a more reciprocal basis.

Khrushchev was no liberal, of course. Neither was commitment to liberalization a central hallmark of his rule.[12] To some extent, he was forced to become a reformer by the political struggle, social unrest, and raised popular expectations in the wake of Stalin's death. At the same time, as a true believer in socialism, Khrushchev was convinced that once the Soviet system was liberated from the extremes of Stalinism, it could overtake and surpass the most advanced capitalist countries. At the 1959 Party Congress, which proclaimed the complete victory of socialism, the First Secretary stated that Soviet economic development had achieved such a high level that the country was now ready for the full-scale construction of Communism.[13] "It is very likely that in the near future we will be able to fully satisfy the needs of the Soviet people in food, housing, and clothes within reasonable limits," he told the Congress delegates.[14] The transition from socialism to Communism soon became the crux of the Twenty-Second Party Congress that took place in October 1961. The Third Party Program, adopted at the Congress, confirmed the imminent crisis of the capitalist system and the inevitable, peaceful victory of socialism around the globe. The program defined Communism as a classless society in which all people would be equal and jointly own the means of production. It stated that under Communism "labor for the common good would become the first necessity," and the great principle of Communism would finally come true: "from everyone according to his abilities, to everyone according to his needs."[15] The party pledged to complete the construction of Communist society in the Soviet Union within two decades.

---

[11] On the Virgin Lands campaign, see Michaela Pohl, "From White Grave to Tselinograd to Astana: The Virgin Lands Opening, Khrushchev's Forgotten First Reform," in Denis Kozlov and Eleonory Gilburd, eds., *The Thaw: Soviet Society and Culture during the 1950s and 1960s* (Toronto: University of Toronto Press, 2013), pp. 269–307.

[12] See, for example, Polly Jones, ed., *The Dilemmas of De-Stalinization: Negotiating Cultural and Social Change in the Khrushchev Era* (London: Routledge, 2006), p. 12; Stephen V. Bittner, *The Many Lives of Khrushchev's Thaw: Experience and Memory in Moscow's Arbat* (Ithaca: Cornell University Press, 2008), pp. 9–11.

[13] Khrushchev, *O kontrol'nykh tsifrakh*, p. 15.   [14] Khrushchev, *O kontrol'nykh tsifrakh*, p. 110.

[15] *XXII s'ezd Kommunisticheskoi Partii Sovetskogo Soiuza (17–31 oktiabria 1961 goda). Stenograficheskii otchet.* T. 3 (Moskva: Gospolitizdat, 1962), p. 274.

Scientific Intelligentsia and the Thaw

From early on in his rule, Khrushchev viewed the scientific intelligentsia as his natural ally in the struggle to revitalize socialism and infuse new life into the Soviet project. The First Secretary found scientists and engineers to be less intimidating than members of the cultural intelligentsia who, he worried, would put their own interests over the collective good.[16] Scientists were self-motivated, yet they were willing to work with the Soviet regime to advance their shared goals. The scientific intelligentsia was also more likely to provide practical payoffs for the economy.[17] Not only would scientists help build up Soviet military superpower; the new leader believed that science would also play a crucial role in solving Soviet economic and social problems, and eventually secure the USSR's economic superiority in the escalating Cold War.[18]

Khrushchev's support of scientists was hardly a new paradigm. Russian rulers had relied on science and technology to modernize Russia's economy since the time of Peter the Great. After the October 1917 Revolution, the Bolsheviks claimed they would build a modern industrial socialist state on the basis of science. In May 1918 Vladimir Lenin warned that socialism could not be achieved without the scientific data and help of technical and scientific specialists of the pre-Revolutionary era.[19] Despite the fact that the Bolsheviks distrusted many scientists and engineers educated prior to 1917, they enthusiastically relied on their knowledge and expertise. It is revealing, for example, that in the first several years of their rule, with the bloody Civil War under way, the Bolsheviks sanctioned, and supported financially, the creation of more than forty new research institutes in applied science and technology.[20] In the absence of a national science policy at the time, the initiatives to create research institutes often came from scientists themselves, and were not a result of a grand master plan.[21] By the mid-1930s, however, scientists' professional autonomy came to an end.[22] Stalin's

---

[16] Sergei Khrushchev, *Nikita Khrushchev: Trilogiia ob ottse*. Tom 1: *Reformator* (Moskva: Vremia, 2010), pp. 567–568.

[17] On Khrushchev's reliance on the scientific intelligentsia, see, for example, Taubman, *Khrushchev*, p. 130; Vladimir Shlapentokh, *Soviet Intellectuals and Political Power: The Post-Stalin Era* (Princeton: Princeton University Press, 1990), p. 106.

[18] Paul R. Josephson, "Atomic-Powered Communism: Nuclear Culture in the Postwar USSR," *Slavic Review* 55.2 (1996), p. 298; Josephson, *New Atlantis Revisited*, p. xvii; Taubman, *Khrushchev*, p. 378.

[19] V.I. Lenin, *Polnoe sobranie sochinenii*. T. 36 (Moskva: Gosizdatel'stvo politicheskoi literatury, 1962), p. 381.

[20] Kendall E. Bailes, *Technology and Society under Lenin and Stalin: Origins of the Soviet Technical Intelligentsia, 1917–1941* (Princeton: Princeton University Press, 1978), p. 53.

[21] Paul R. Josephson, *Physics and Politics in Revolutionary Russia* (Berkeley: University of California Press, 1991), p. 71.

[22] Interestingly, Douglas Weiner argues that some autonomous social organizations survived even during the Stalin period. See Douglas R. Weiner, *A Little Corner of Freedom: Russian Nature Protection from Stalin to Gorbachev* (Berkley: University of California Press, 1999), pp. 2–3.

assault on "bourgeois specialists" aimed to create a new, loyal Soviet intelligentsia and to put science under rigid ideological control. Hundreds of scientists were fired and arrested; some were executed. While World War II and the success of the Soviet nuclear project improved the relationship between scientists and the state, the late Stalinist regime remained highly suspicious of the scientific elite.[23]

Khrushchev rejected some key features of Stalin's science policy, even though he readily embraced others, including the nuclear program and the regime's reliance on large-scale technologies. Crucially, the new government recognized that the Stalinist view of science, with its focus on tight ideological control and narrow utilitarianism, was detrimental to Soviet economic development. The Soviet Union needed to stop stifling innovation in order to progress. Under Khrushchev, for the first time since the 1920s, the Soviet government allowed, and even encouraged, the input and autonomous actions of the leaders of the scientific community. This provoked an incredibly enthusiastic response from many talented and ambitious people, who saw the Thaw as an opportunity to implement their scientific visions and to fulfill themselves professionally. Nikolai Semenov, whose own scientific career had blossomed in the late 1920s and early 1930s, skillfully maneuvered in this new environment to expand the research carried out at the ICP.

The emergence of dozens of scientific towns in the late 1950s and early 1960s should be viewed in the context of this shifting national science policy, which I discuss in Chapter 1. Scientific settlements had existed in Soviet Russia since the late 1930s. Zhukovskii, Korolev, Dzerzhinsk, and Friazino came into being as a result of a specific state assignment, such as the creation of the Soviet aviation industry.[24] After the launch of the Soviet nuclear project in 1943–1945, the Stalin regime invested extensively in building scientific towns that were tightly integrated into the Soviet military–industrial complex and were dedicated to building up the military potential of the emerging superpower. Arzamas-16, or present-day Sarov, where the Soviet nuclear bomb was created, was at the epicenter of the "white archipelago" of atomic institutes and plants scattered around the country.[25] Ozersk, a secret nuclear town established in the southern Urals in 1945, became a pioneer in plutonium production.[26]

---

[23] David Holloway, *Stalin and the Bomb: The Soviet Union and Atomic Energy, 1939–1956* (New Haven: Yale University Press, 1994), p. 366; Ethan Pollock, *Stalin and the Soviet Science Wars* (Princeton: Princeton University Press, 2006), p. 6.

[24] G.M. Lappo, P.M. Polian, "Naukograrody Rossii: vcherashnie zapretnye i poluzapretnye goroda – segodniashnie tochki rosta," *Mir Rossii* 17.1 (2008), p. 2.

[25] Holloway, *Stalin and the Bomb*, p. 202.

[26] Kate Brown, *Plutopia: Nuclear Families, Atomic Cities, and the Great Soviet and American Plutonium Disasters* (New York: Oxford University Press, 2013), pp. 83–91.

Under Khrushchev, a new generation of scientific towns came into existence. Their main purpose was to spur Soviet economic growth, facilitate modernization, and, in the long run, contribute to building a Communist society – Khrushchev's most cherished and ambitious goal. The construction of Akademgorodok, for example, was broadly advertised as part of a larger national plan to develop the productive forces of Siberia and the Far East.[27] It became a major scientific success of Khrushchev's rule. The establishment of the physics centers in Dubna and Troitsk, a biological center in Pushchino, and a center of microelectronics in Zelenograd were all part of the Soviet government's efforts to mobilize the scientific intelligentsia and to put science in the service of building "the material-technological basis of Communism."[28]

Chernogolovka belonged to this new type of scientific town. Although the initial funding for the testing ground came from the Ministry of Medium Machine-Building, which was in charge of the Soviet nuclear industry, by the early 1960s the town transformed into a burgeoning center for fundamental research, financed by the Soviet Academy of Sciences. In addition to research on combustion and detonation, young scientists at the ICP Branch worked on advancing materials science, organic chemistry, biomedical research, and polymer production. In 1963, the Institute of Solid State Physics (ISSP) was founded in Chernogolovka. It quickly became a leading national center for research on solid state physics, a field that had been previously neglected in the USSR, but that held much promise for creating new, advanced materials for Soviet industry. Two years later, the Landau Institute of Theoretical Physics (ITP) was established. It employed dozens of the most capable theoretical physicists from across the USSR. In the 1960s and 1970s, their research on superconductors, magnetism, and the theory of phase transition received wide recognition, both in the Soviet Union and in the international arena.

Chernogolovka's first residents enthusiastically embraced the regime's promise to reinvigorate socialism through scientific development and innovation. Born in the 1930s, a decade of rapid industrialization, many grew up with a strong faith in the progressive development of the Soviet economy and society on a technological basis. The vast majority of them were too young to remember the human costs of Stalin's industrialization. They had vague recollections of the Great Terror, which their parents did their best to conceal from them. Chernogolovka scientists' tender age also spared them from direct participation in the Great Patriotic War. Having survived the hardships and deprivations of wartime and the immediate postwar years, the town's young

---

[27] Josephson, *New Atlantis Revisited*, p. 11.

[28] See, for example, Paul R. Josephson, "'Projects of the Century' in Soviet History: Large Scale Technologies from Lenin to Gorbachev," *Technology and Culture* 36.3 (1995), p. 540; Steven T. Usdin, *Engineering Communism: How Two Americans Spied for Stalin and Founded the Soviet Silicon Valley* (New Haven: Yale University Press, 2005), pp. 189–209.

residents believed that the worst was behind them. Their grandparents sacrificed their lives in the name of the Revolution. Their parents saved the USSR from the Nazi invasion. Building a scientific town from scratch, in the middle of forests and marshes, and conducting pioneering research there was their chance to be heroic and serve the Soviet state. Working in the name of science was their contribution to the Soviet project.

This sentiment resonated with the widespread patriotic feelings among postwar Soviet youth.[29] It also fit readily into the idealism and optimism of young intellectuals who aspired to build a better socialist society, purified of Stalinist excesses. Despite the shocks of de-Stalinization, many members of this generation continued to believe in the legacy of the Russian Revolution, as Zubok correctly observed.[30] For them, Communism still represented the wave of the future, just like it did for Nikita Khrushchev.

Soviet intellectuals had long subscribed to Communism's core agenda of creating a modern social order. Indeed, many saw themselves as agents of the enlightenment and civilization promised by the Soviet state.[31] Since the first post-Revolutionary decade, the scientific intelligentsia in particular worked to find common ground with Soviet power, hoping to promote their professional goals by working through the system.[32] Khrushchev's Thaw provided scientists with exactly such an opportunity. After years of humiliation and uncertainty, the scientific community finally encountered "a better tsar," to borrow Douglas Weiner's term, who was not only willing to listen, but also genuinely hoped to be enlightened.

Scientists' idealism and their improved relationship with the Soviet regime overlapped with one of the most dynamic and exciting periods of Soviet scientific development. First, the Cold War led to the tremendous expansion of the scientific enterprise in the USSR. In 1949, the Soviet atomic bomb was tested. Four years later, the world witnessed the explosion of the first hydrogen bomb, developed in the USSR. In 1954, the Soviet Union launched the world's first power-generating nuclear reactor, demonstrating its achievement in the peaceful uses of atomic energy. In its efforts to catch up with the United States, especially in the military sphere, the late Stalinist regime adopted a policy that committed the Soviet government to virtually unlimited financial investments in science.[33]

---

[29] On the patriotism of the postwar generation in the USSR, see Juliane Fürst, *Stalin's Last Generation: Soviet Post-war Youth and the Emergence of Mature Socialism* (Oxford: Oxford University Press, 2010), p. 62; and Andrew L. Jenks, *The Cosmonaut Who Couldn't Stop Smiling: The Life and Legend of Yuri Gagarin* (DeKalb: NIU Press, 2012), p. 93.

[30] Zubok, *Zhivago's Children*, pp. 36, 170.

[31] Benjamin Tromly, *Making the Soviet Intelligentsia: Universities and Intellectual Life Under Stalin and Khrushchev* (New York: Cambridge University Press, 2014), pp. 5–8.

[32] Weiner, *A Little Corner of Freedom*, pp. 10, 19, 30.

[33] Alexander Vucinich, *Empire of Knowledge: The Academy of Sciences of the USSR (1917–1970)* (Berkeley: University of California Press, 1984), p. 274.

Equally important, Stalin's successor viewed himself as a major patron of science. Although the defense needs of the country remained his key priority, Khrushchev recognized the importance of fundamental research in the nuclear age.[34] Unlike their teachers and mentors, who often had no choice but to work for the military–industrial complex, young scientists gained more autonomy in their professional lives. Many employees of Chernogolovka research institutes were encouraged to establish new directions of fundamental research that had no immediate industrial application but that held promise for future scientific breakthroughs. Finally, by the mid-1950s a great sense of optimism about science and technology, especially nuclear energy, became widespread not only in the Soviet Union but throughout the Western world. In the USSR, this optimism translated into a peculiar cult of science, when average citizens came to believe that scientific achievements would help improve people's quality of life.[35] Prominent scientists enthusiastically promoted this popular belief. "Most people cannot even imagine how incredibly powerful modern science will become by the end of this century," Nikolai Semenov bragged in 1958. "If we managed to use the power of science to its full capacity, we could provide for each and every person according to their needs."[36] This veneration for science, without a doubt, had a profound impact on the first generation of Chernogolovka scientists, influencing their political outlook and professional choices.

Over the past 25 years, scholars have studied the final three decades of the Soviet Union with an eye to explaining the sudden collapse of the USSR. This book, by contrast, aims to shed light on the stability and longevity of the Soviet system by looking at one of the most influential and populous professional groups in late Soviet society: scientists. It builds on the recent surge of work on the Thaw, especially the fate of the Soviet intelligentsia after Stalin's death in 1953. It also contributes to the growing literature on closed scientific cities in the postwar USSR, as well as the cultural history of the Soviet scientific community more generally.

Given the prominent place that scientists occupied in Soviet society during the Khrushchev and Brezhnev eras, it is surprising that few scholars have

---

[34] Crucially, both Khrushchev's and Brezhnev's regimes continued to invest extensively in the Soviet military–industrial complex. According to Loren Graham, in the late Soviet era the military was given about 75 percent of all resources. See Loren Graham and Irina Dezhina, *Science in the New Russia: Crisis, Aid, Reform* (Bloomington: Indiana University Press, 2008), pp. 2–3.

[35] Paul R. Josephson, "Rockets, Reactors and Soviet Culture," in Loren R. Graham, ed., *Science and the Soviet Social Order* (Cambridge: Harvard University Press, 1990), p. 170. On the technological arrogance of scientists in the postwar USSR, see Josephson, "Atomic-Powered Communism," pp. 297–298.

[36] N.N. Semenov, *Izbrannye trudy*. T. 4: *O vremeni i o sebe* (Moskva: Nauka, 2006), p. 39.

attempted to write a cultural and social history of the post-Stalin scientific intelligentsia. The transition of Soviet society from Stalinism into the post-Stalin era became the focus of rigorous scholarly investigation in the early 2000s. Since then, historians have examined various aspects of the Thaw, including such important topics as Khrushchev's personality and inner-party struggle,[37] the return of Gulag inmates,[38] and social unrest and dissent.[39] They have recognized the significance of gender, consumption, and the mass urban housing program,[40] as well as the re-opening of Soviet society to the West.[41] Scholars have also focused on the cultural dimensions of the Thaw, especially the experiences of the Soviet cultural and political intelligentsia, namely writers, artists, poets, and enlightened apparatchiks.[42]

Scientists generally are placed within the broad category of the Soviet intelligentsia. Some scholars have argued, in fact, that it would be too restrictive to divide the intelligentsia into "subgroups such as the *technical, creative,* or *Party* intelligentsias," because such division would obscure "the unofficial interests and concerns shared by scientists, writers, economists, and historians."[43] Drawing parallels between Soviet intellectuals and their

---

[37] Taubman, *Khrushchev*; Aleksandr Pyzhikov, *Khrushchevskaia "ottepel'"* (Moskva: Olma-Press, 2002).

[38] Nanci Adler, *The Gulag Survivor: Beyond the Soviet System* (New Brunswick: Transaction Publishers, 2002); Miriam Dobson, *Khrushchev's Cold Summer: Gulag Returnees, Crime, and the Fate of Reform after Stalin* (Ithaca: Cornell University Press, 2009); Stephen Cohen, *Victims Return: The Survivors of the Gulag after Stalin* (London: I.B. Tauris, 2011).

[39] Vladimir A. Kozlov, *Mass Uprising in the USSR: Protest and Rebellion in the Post-Stalin Years,* transl. and ed. by Elaine McClarnand MacKinnon (New York: M.E. Sharpe, 2002); Philip Boobbyer, *Conscience, Dissent and Reform in Soviet Russia* (London and New York: Routledge, 2005); Vladimir A. Kozlov, Sheila Fitzpatrick, and Sergei Mironenko, eds., *Sedition: Everyday Resistance in the Soviet Union under Khrushchev and Brezhnev* (New Haven: Yale University Press, 2011); Robert Hornsby, *Protest, Reform and Repression in Khrushchev's Soviet Union* (New York: Cambridge University Press, 2013).

[40] Susan E. Reid, "Cold War in the Kitchen: Gender and De-Stalinization of Consumer Taste in the Soviet Union under Khrushchev," *Slavic Review* 61.2 (2002), pp. 211–252; Melanie Ilic, Susan E. Reid, and Lynne Attwood, eds., *Women in the Khrushchev Era* (London: Palgrave Macmillan, 2004); Deborah Field, *Private Life and Communist Morality in Khrushchev's Russia* (New York: Peter Lang, 2007); Mark B. Smith, *Property of Communists: The Urban Housing Program from Stalin to Khrushchev* (DeKalb: Northern Illinois University Press, 2010); Steven E. Harris, *Communism on Tomorrow Street: Mass Housing and Everyday Life After Stalin* (Washington DC: Woodrow Wilson Center Press, 2013).

[41] Robert English, *Russia and the Idea of the West: Gorbachev, Intellectuals, and the End of the Cold War* (New York: Columbia University Press, 2000); Zubok, *Zhivago's Children*; Kozlov and Gilburd, eds., *The Thaw*.

[42] Jones, ed., *The Dilemmas of De-Stalinization*; Bittner, *The Many Lives of Khrushchev's Thaw*; Zubok, *Zhivago's Children*; Denis Kozlov, *The Readers of Novyi Mir: Coming to Terms with the Stalinist Past* (Cambridge: Harvard University Press, 2013); Polly Jones, *Myth, Memory, Trauma: Rethinking Stalinist Past in the Soviet Union, 1953–1970* (New Haven: Yale University Press, 2013); Tromly, *Making the Soviet Intelligentsia*; Ann Komaromi, *Uncensored: Samizdat Novels and the Quest for Autonomy in Soviet Dissidence* (Evanston: Northwestern University Press, 2015).

[43] English, *Russia and the Idea of the West*, p. 77.

pre-Revolutionary predecessors, these studies usually characterize the intelligentsia as a group defined by a deep concern about the country's social and political problems, a moral and civic agenda, and a commitment to reforms. Many describe Khrushchev's Thaw as the period of the rebirth of the Russian intelligentsia, "the time of awakening," and of spiritual and intellectual emancipation.[44] Some highlight the liberal, "Westernizing" identity of the newly awakened intelligentsia.[45] Others emphasize their idealism, arguing that a lot of educated Russians maintained a strong faith in socialist values and hoped for "a reformist evolution of the Soviet project."[46] At the same time, both groups point to the growing alienation between intellectuals and the state in the late 1960s and 1970s. The dissident trials of the mid-1960s and the Soviet invasion of Czechoslovakia in 1968 are usually considered to be a critical turning point in the intelligentsia's relationship with the Soviet regime. The gradual disillusionment of the postwar idealistic cohort of intellectuals, these historians have maintained, contributed to the eventual collapse of the Soviet Union.[47]

The focus on the cultural over the scientific intelligentsia is natural, since the former left behind voluminous written records, including diaries, memoirs, and private correspondences. Yet, scientists and engineers did not travel the same intellectual roads as members of the cultural and political intelligentsia: that is, from Communist idealism and social optimism under Khrushchev to gradual disillusionment and loss of faith in the Soviet project by the end of the Brezhnev rule. Scientists were much more integrated into the post-Stalin system than writers or artists. Their idealism and faith in the progressive development of Soviet society were more intense and did not fade as quickly, since the regime continued to explicitly rely on the scientific intelligentsia to advance the Soviet project. Scientists' disappointment with the failure of the government to reform also came much later, if at all, since the Brezhnev regime did not drastically change the established science policy. According to the

---

[44] Ludmilla Alexeyeva and Paul Goldberg, *The Thaw Generation: Coming of Age in the Post-Stalin Era* (Pittsburgh: University of Pittsburgh Press, 1993), p. 4; English, *Russia and the Idea of the West*, p. 77; Boobbyer, *Conscience, Dissent and Reform*, 57; Zubok, *Zhivago's Chidren*, p. 20.

[45] English, *Russia and the Idea of the West*, pp. 2–3, 80; Shlapentokh, *Soviet Intellectuals*, p. 148; Elena Zubkova, *Russia After the War: Hopes, Illusions, and Disappointments, 1945–1957*, transl. and ed. by Hugh Ragsdale (New York: M.E. Sharpe, 1998), p. 88. Stephen Bittner, by contrast, questions the "liberal pedigree" of the Thaw. See Bittner, *The Many Lives of Khrushchev's Thaw*, pp. 9–12.

[46] For a valuable analysis of the idealistic aspirations of the postwar Soviet youth, see Zubok, *Zhivago's Children*, pp. 25–37, 261. Zubok's argument challenges Juliane Fürst's contention about "the decline of ... commitment to socialist values and ideology" among the postwar Soviet youth. See Fürst, *Stalin's Last Generation*, pp. 2–6.

[47] Zubkova, *Russia After the War*, p. 95; Zubok, *Zhivago's Children*, p. 345; Kozlov, *The Readers of Novyi Mir*, p. 9.

unspoken compromise reached between scientists and the state, party officials usually did not directly interfere into scientific affairs – but only as long as scientists agreed to avoid demands for greater individual rights and political freedom. In Chernogolovka steady state funding continued throughout the Brezhnev era, while scientists' professional autonomy survived the political crackdown of the late 1960s.

For members of the scientific intelligentsia, the Thaw was not only about intellectual emancipation, political awakening, or "saving socialism through culture."[48] In fact, many Chernogolovka scientists did not think about the Thaw in these terms, either during or after the Khrushchev era. Much more tangible was Khrushchev's promise to build a fair and economically advanced society on the basis of scientific development and innovation – a goal that many young scientists could readily identify with. At the end of the day, the scientific community interpreted the Thaw as a time when they could finally promote their own professional interests in close cooperation with the Soviet state.

Overall, my findings confirm Benjamin Tromly's recent argument that Soviet intellectuals who came of age after the war were "far more reconciled to the existing system."[49] I demonstrate that this was especially true for the scientific intelligentsia. The scientific community in Chernogolovka was indeed tightly integrated into the late Soviet system. Even though by the early 1970s there existed a broad spectrum of political opinions among residents of the town, the vast majority of scientists continued to believe in the progressive nature of the Soviet project throughout the Brezhnev era. At the end of the day, their idealism contributed to the longevity of the late Soviet system by lending support to the ruling political elite.

This book also seeks to offer a fresh perspective on the rapidly growing scholarship on Soviet science. Historians of science have long noted the intimate relationship between the Soviet state and the scientific intelligentsia. During the Cold War, David Joravsky and Loren Graham emphasized the important relationship between ideology and Soviet science.[50] Kendall Bailes challenged the image of state-persecuted science, promoted in earlier works, arguing that the relationship between Soviet political and technical elites was not limited to coercion.[51] The archival revolution of the 1990s allowed historians to overturn the image of scientists as pure victims of the Soviet state and return agency to the scientific community.[52] Yet, historians' focus has mostly

---

[48] Tromly, *Making the Soviet Intelligentsia*, p. 22.
[49] Tromly, *Making the Soviet Intelligentsia*, pp. 11–12.
[50] David Joravsky, *Soviet Marxism and Natural Sciences, 1917–1932* (New York: Columbia University Press, 1961); Loren Graham, *Science, Philosophy, and Human Behavior in the Soviet Union* (New York: Columbia University Press, 1987).
[51] Bailes, *Technology and Society under Lenin and Stalin*, p. 8.
[52] Josephson, *Physics and Politics in Revolutionary Russia*; Loren Graham, *The Ghost of the Executed Engineer: Technology and the Fall of the Soviet Union* (Cambridge: Harvard

been on scientific institutions, programs, and disciplines – not *scientists*, their daily lives, political outlook, and mentality. Most of these studies examined the development of Soviet science under Lenin and Stalin. Only recently have historians begun to shift focus to the Khrushchev period.[53] Paul Josephson's important study of Akademgorodok, a city of science in Siberia, is a good example.[54] It sheds light on the extraordinary opportunities scientists enjoyed during Khrushchev's rule, including increased professional autonomy and intellectual freedom. Still, the focus of Josephson's book is on the development of research institutes, not on the cultural history of the Akademgorodok scientific community. His account follows the conventional interpretation of the Thaw as a "decade of academic freedom," followed by the crackdown under Brezhnev in the late 1960s. My research demonstrates that academic freedom did not come to an end everywhere in 1968, pointing to significant continuities between the Khrushchev and Brezhnev eras.

Finally, my work seeks to capitalize on the recent surge of interest in "secret cities" that were part of the Soviet military–industrial complex.[55] Recently, Kate Brown published a comparative study of Ozersk, one of the ten secret nuclear cities in the Soviet Union.[56] Shifting the focus from science to nuclear families, she demonstrates convincingly that residents of Ozersk – mostly from working-class backgrounds – were content to live in a closed but affluent community and "to exchange their civil rights for consumer rights" under Khrushchev and Brezhnev. Chernogolovka, however, was a different kind of town. It was neither secret nor affluent. Scientists, not workers, lived there.

University Press, 1993); Holloway, *Stalin and the Bomb*; Nikolai Krementsov, *Stalinist Science* (Princeton: Princeton University Press, 1997); Weiner, *A Little Corner of Freedom*; Slava Gerovitch, *From Newspeak to Cyberspeak: A History of Soviet Cybernetics* (Cambridge: The MIT Press, 2002); Alexei Kojevnikov, *Stalin's Great Science: The Times and Adventures of Soviet Physicists* (London: Imperial College Press, 2004); Pollock, *Stalin and the Soviet Science Wars*.

[53] Asif A. Siddiqi, *Sputnik and the Soviet Space Challenge* (Gainesville: University Press of Florida, 2000); Slava Gerovitch, "Stalin's Rocket Designers' Leap into Space: the Technical Intelligentsia Faces the Thaw," in Michael Gordin, Karl Hall, and Alexei Kojevnikov, eds., *Intelligentsia Science: The Russian Century, 1860–1960, Osiris* 23 (Chicago: University of Chicago Press, 2008); Andrews and Siddiqi, eds., *Into the Cosmos*; Jenks, *The Cosmonaut Who Couldn't Stop Smiling*.

[54] Josephson, *New Atlantis Revisited*.

[55] Viktoriia Glazyrina, "Krasnoiarsk-26: A Closed City of the Defence-Industry Complex," in John Barber and Mark Harrison, eds., *The Soviet Defence-Industry Complex from Stalin to Khrushchev* (London: Macmillan Press; New York: St. Martin's Press, 2000); Ekaterina Emeliantseva, "The Privilege of Seclusion: Consumption Strategies in the Closed City of Severodvinsk," in *Ab Imperio* 2 (2011), pp. 1–21. See also conference papers by Stefan Guth, "Oasis of the Future? The Atomic City of Shevchenko/Aktau, 1959–2019," and Anna Veronika Wendland, "Inside the Atomgrad: Nuclear Technology, Professional Pride, and Urban Space in the late Soviet Union," presented at the 45th ASEEES Annual Convention, November 21–24, 2013, Boston.

[56] Brown, *Plutopia*.

Many remained loyal supporters of the state not because they enjoyed privileged consumer rights, but because they continued to believe in the progressive development of Soviet society and saw science as the crucial pillar of that development.

Sources, Methodology, and Structure

This book is not about Khrushchev, Brezhnev, their science policies, or the development of scientific disciplines in the late USSR. It is about the first Cold War generation of Soviet scientists and the way in which the scientific intelligentsia contributed to the transition of Soviet society away from Stalinism and into the post-Stalin era. Who were these people, and what factors influenced their early formation? How did they live and why did they identify with Khrushchev's promise to revitalize socialism through scientific development and innovation? Did scientists' political views change once they began traveling to the West or witnessed, firsthand, the state persecution of a dissident scientist living next door in their community? Did they grow disillusioned and lose faith in the Soviet project?

These questions guided me as I embarked on the research for this book back in 2009. I soon discovered that finding sources on the daily lives, political outlook, and mentality of Soviet scientists would be a challenging task. Unlike writers, artists, poets, and enlightened apparatchiks, who published numerous memoirs and diaries in the 1990s and 2000s, members of the scientific intelligentsia left few written records behind. The vast majority of them did not keep diaries. The collections of speeches by prominent scientists, as well as personal reminiscences of their colleagues and family members, were readily available. Yet they were highly subjective, often nostalgic for earlier days, and, as a rule, revealed little about the private world and thoughts of these intellectuals.[57] This was mostly true of the few memoirs published by leading members of the Chernogolovka scientific community, which highlighted these figures' roles in establishing new research directions and organizing the scientific center, but conveyed little information about their authors' lives beyond the lab.[58]

---

[57] See, for example, N.N. Semenov, *Nauka i obshchestvo: Stat'i i rechi* (Moskva: Izdatel'stvo "Nauka," 1973); *Vospominaniia ob akademike Nikolae Nikolaeviche Semenove*, ed. by A.E. Shilov (Moskva: Nauka, 1993); Vitalii I. Gol'danskii, *Essays of a Soviet Scientist: A Revealing Portrait of a Life in Science and Politics* (Woodbury: American Institute of Physics, 1997); *Kapitsa, Tamm, Semenov: v ocherkakh i pis'makh*, ed. by A.F. Andreev (Moskva: Vagrius, 1998). The latter volume contains valuable excerpts from diaries and private correspondences of Petr Kapitsa, Igor' Tamm, and Nikolai Semenov.

[58] F.I. Dubovitskii, *Institut Khimicheskoi Fiziki (Ocherki istorii)* (Chernogolovka: Tipografiia IKhFCh RAN, 1992); F.I. Dubovitskii, *Nauchnyi Tsentr RAN v Chernogolovke* (Chernogolovka: Izdatel'skii otdel IPKhF RAN, 1999); A.G. Merzhanov, *"Luchshe byt' nuzhnym, chem svobodnym..."* (Chernogolovka: Territoriia, 2005); Yu. A. Osipyan, *Moi*

The memoirs written by prominent dissident scientists such as Andrei Sakharov, by contrast, offered valuable insights into the dissidents' world. However, the degree of dissident scientists' alienation from the Soviet state is hardly representative of the political outlook and lifestyle of hundreds of thousands of ordinary scientists who worked enthusiastically within the system.[59]

Oral history thus provided a unique opportunity to explore the private world of the Soviet scientific intelligentsia before these people, in their late seventies and eighties, passed away. Over the course of 2009–2013, I conducted, recorded, and transcribed more than sixty in-depth interviews with the first generation of Chernogolovka scientists to bring their testimonies to bear on my analysis. During the interviews, I focused on the scientists' private lives and personal experiences, both before and after they moved to Chernogolovka, as well as the events that were central to the formation and evolution of their identities. Most scientists agreed to meet with me at least two times; the average length of an interview was two to three hours. While I conducted each interview with a set questionnaire in hand, I encouraged my interviewees to take the freedom to reflect on their experiences and to talk about topics that they found important. This allowed me to establish a trusted and respectful relationship with them, and helped direct my research in a number of ways that proved both enlightening and productive.

Recently, historians have come to rely more and more on oral history.[60] Still, like many sources of a personal nature, oral history presents a number of methodological difficulties. First, there is a problem concerning the accuracy of interviewees' accounts. How do scientists' present-day experiences affect their memories of the past, and what is it about the past that is relevant to remember? Second, there is the problem of collective memory and self-censure. How does the fact that most interviewees are still members of the same community influence what they remember and how they remember it? Being aware of the drawbacks of oral history, I have made a significant effort to check the evidence of the interviews against the written materials from the local and

vospominaniia (Moskva: "Mezhdunarodnye otnosheniia," 2006); I.M. Khalatnikov, *Dau, Kentavr i drugie (Top nonsecret)* (Moskva: Fizmatlit, 2009).

[59] See, for example, R.I. Pimenov, *Vospominaniia* (Moskva: "Panorama," 1996); V.F. Turchin, *The Intertia of Fear and the Scientific Worldview* (New York: Columbia University Press, 1981); A.D. Sakharov, *Vospominaniia*. T. 1, 2 (Moskva: Vremia, 2006); Yuri Orlov, *Opasnye mysli: memuary iz russkoi zhizni* (Moskva: Zakharov, 2008).

[60] See, for example, Catherine Merridale, *Night of Stone: Death and Memory in Twentieth-Century Russia* (New York: Viking, 2000); Anne Applebaum, *Gulag: A History* (New York: Doubleday, 2003); Catherine Merridale, *Ivan's War: The Red Army, 1939–1945* (London: Faber, 2005); Orlando Figes, *The Whisperers: Private Life in Stalin's Russia* (New York: Metropolitan Books, 2007); Donald Raleigh, *Soviet Baby Boomers: An Oral History of Russia's Cold War Generation* (New York: Oxford University Press, 2012); Tromly, *Making the Soviet Intelligentsia*.

central archives of the Communist Party of the Soviet Union,[61] as well as the archives of the Russian Academy of Sciences.[62] This cross-examination proved crucial, as the written documents usually supported, but sometimes challenged, scientists' private memories. For example, many of my interviewees claimed that they enjoyed privileged food supplies in the early 1960s. To prove their point, scientists recounted walking into a local grocery store and seeing a big barrel of red caviar. This would be considered nothing short of a luxury throughout the USSR; and it was affordable, even to junior scientists. But when I mined the records of the ICP Branch's party organization, I saw a very different picture. In 1964, the party organization identified the local grocery store as the most troublesome issue. According to one party record, "every morning, before the store opens, almost one hundred people gather by its entrance, among them soldiers and janitors. By noon, there is barely anyone in the store, but there is no food there either. When scientists arrive, there is absolutely nothing for them to buy, except stale black bread." Before a large grocery store opened in the town in late 1964, basics such as bread were in short supply, to say nothing of caviar. In many other cases, however, archival evidence confirmed scientists' oral testimonies. This was true for the surviving records on building the town and organizing cultural life there. Archival evidence also supported scientists' memories about their traveling abroad and their participation in the local Communist Party organizations.

In the TsAOPIM, I was the first scholar to examine the proceeding of the meetings of the party organizations of the Branch of the ICP and the ISSP – the two research institutes at the center of my inquiry. These materials shed light on scientists' daily lives (housing, food supplies, and cultural institutions and sports facilities), their travel abroad, as well as their relationship with the Communist Party. Papers in the Russian State Archive of Contemporary History (RGANI) and the Archive of the Russian Academy of Sciences (ARAN) were instrumental in tracking the shift in Khrushchev's science policy in the late 1950s, as well as Semenov's maneuvering to transform the testing ground into a scientific center. The records of the Presidium of the Soviet Academy of Sciences also allowed me to reconstruct the conditions under which scientists were allowed to travel abroad. Finally, I examined the local archives of Chernogolovka research institutes: the Institute of Problems of Chemical Physics (the former ICP Branch and

---

[61] Central Archive of Social and Political History of Moscow (TsAOPIM) and Russian State Archive of Contemporary History (RGANI); both archives are located in Moscow.

[62] I conducted research at the Archive of the Russian Academy of Sciences (ARAN), the Archive of the Institute of Problems of Chemical Physics (former Archive of the Branch of the Institute of Chemical Physics), and the Archive of the Institute of Solid State Physics; ARAN is located in Moscow, while the other two archives are in Chernogolovka.

the ISSP. I worked through the previously unavailable archival collections, including the records of administrative meetings and local trade union committees, personal files of researchers and institutes employees, institutes' newsletters (*stengazety*), and the repositories of photo and video materials.

This book is divided into six thematic and chronological chapters. Chapter 1 explores the unusual conditions under which Chernogolovka came into existence and developed from 1955 to 1962. I examine how Nikolai Semenov managed to transform a military-oriented testing ground into a successful city of science and to secure its *post factum* approval from the Soviet government. Then, I turn to the first generation of scientists who came to live and work in Chernogolovka, focusing on the outstanding professional opportunities these young men and women enjoyed. I demonstrate that there was room for individual initiatives and innovation in the post-Stalin system, as long as they came from well-connected individuals and conformed to the political and ideological objectives of the state. I also argue that the enthusiasm and optimism of the town's young residents helped secure the success of Semenov's enterprise and aided him in convincing the Academy of Sciences to turn the testing ground into a full-fledged scientific center.

Chapter 2 introduces the reader to individual members of the Chernogolovka scientific community, highlighting their social backgrounds, upbringing, education, and their reasons for joining the scientific profession. I argue that it was the Great Patriotic War, not the mass terror of the 1930s, which played a more formative role in these scientists' lives. The massive destruction that they experienced during the war proved to be a very powerful motivation for choosing a scientific career: to "not let this happen again." The Cold War was another part of the story. In the later years of his rule, Stalin realized that to compete in the Cold War against the West, the Soviet Union needed thousands of first-class scientists and engineers. Overnight, physicists and chemists became the most sought-after professionals. For many of my interviewees this opened up myriad opportunities that their parents had not had. In the 1950s and 1960s, many young scientists and engineers could easily find employment, including in the scientific towns that quickly sprouted across the Soviet Union after Stalin's death. Scientists' early professional successes undoubtedly contributed to their idealism and strengthened their faith in the viability of Soviet society.

Since the town emerged out of a testing ground, it did not enjoy any special provisions or extra funding from the government, in contrast to Akademgorodok or "secret cities" of the military–industrial complex. However, Semenov and his associate, Fedor Dubovitskii, were able to create comfortable material conditions for the town's first residents. In Chapter 3,

I investigate the social and cultural life in Chernogolovka from the late 1950s to the mid-1970s. I look at the distribution of housing and food supplies, scientists' participation in landscaping the town, and organization of the cultural institutions on the ground. The picture that emerges from scientists' oral testimonies and the records of the local party organizations is intriguing. It is quite different from the usual image of the inefficient Soviet state, where everything was managed – often poorly – from above, while people on the ground remained largely indifferent and apathetic. The case of Chernogolovka demonstrates that once the Soviet government allowed room for individual initiatives and encouraged people to improve their own lives, they met enthusiastic responses on the ground. Scientists' participation in building the town also made them feel that they belonged to the larger Soviet project.

Chapter 4 examines how the scientific community in Chernogolovka reconciled their lives with the constant presence of the Communist Party. I first track the formation – and transformation – of scientists' political and ideological beliefs before they came to Chernogolovka: from their coming of age during late Stalinism to their reactions to Khrushchev's secret speech. The main part of the chapter focuses on the relationship between scientists and the party organizations on the ground. It demonstrates that Chernogolovka's scientific community largely accepted "the rules of the game" imposed on them by the Khrushchev and Brezhnev regimes. While some scientists resisted joining the party, because they were skeptical of its domestic and foreign policy, in the end they acquiesced, usually under public pressure. Becoming a party member had its benefits. It allowed scientists to have a positive impact on the life of their community. Having "their own people" in local party organizations meant that scientists could participate in distributing funding for scientific research, permitting travel abroad, and inviting semi-official artists to Chernogolovka. I describe the scientists' relationship with the party as "the privilege of passive participation."

In the next two chapters I investigate how scientists' political outlook changed, if at all, once they encountered active dissidents in their own community and once they began traveling abroad. Chapter 5 examines two politically charged episodes in the life of the local community: scientists' reactions to the Soviet invasion of Czechoslovakia in 1968 and their response to the KGB persecution of Kronid Liubarskii, a dissident scientist who resided in Chernogolovka from 1967 to 1972. I argue that Chernogolovka scientists were neither tacit dissidents nor eager conformists. In fact, there existed a wide spectrum of political opinions among the local scientific community. This spectrum ranged from die-hard Communist believers to active dissidents. Between these two opposite poles, various patterns of conformity and dissent existed. Some scientists identified with the regime's goals, but were wary of its repressive features. Others were passive dissidents: people who searched for alternative sources of information, but did not engage in overt challenges to the state. Another group aspired to ignore political matters altogether, claiming that science was above politics. There were also myriad *Weltanschauungen*, which fell in-between these broad categories. Scientists' political opinions, however, rarely translated into demands for greater individual rights and political freedom. Many believed that playing by "the rules of the game" was necessary to preserve a healthy working environment at their research institutes and protect their professional autonomy.

Chapter 6 explains why scientists' trips abroad in the 1960s and 1970s did not undermine their loyalty to the Soviet state. The fact that traveling abroad remained a privilege of a select minority, I argue, reminded scientists of their special status as one of the few "trustworthy" professional groups. Many scientists took pride in this trust, as well as in their own professional achievements, which often were on a par with the accomplishments of their Western colleagues. Ironically, scientists' trips only reinforced their loyalty to the Soviet regime. Many came to realize that they felt much more comfortable in Soviet society, with its emphasis on collective values, socialist equality, and its state support of science, than in the alien, capitalist West.

In the conclusion, I emphasize the significance of case studies like Chernogolovka for understanding the transformation of the Stalinist system and the emergence of a more humane, yet highly authoritarian, model of socialism under Khrushchev and Brezhnev. I also discuss scientists' reaction to Gorbachev's *perestroika* and reflect on their painful transition from elite members of Soviet society to the members of the underclass in post-Soviet Russia.

1 An Unusual Testing Ground: Building a Town in the Marshes, 1955–1962

"I am not giving too much significance to our work; I consider us to be merely fertilizer for the next generation that will create true science in Russia, a living science with plenty of discoveries and inventions."

Nikolai Semenov, letter to Petr Kapitsa, 1922

On March 17, 1959, a young man of medium build got off a bus which ran between Noginsk, a city thirty-six miles to the east of Moscow, and the neighboring villages. He looked around, and was somewhat surprised to find himself in the middle of a dense forest. Vladimir Enman, a thirty-one-year-old engineer, began walking through the woods, passed by a secluded small village named Chernogolovka, and suddenly came to the edge of a vast field covered with deep snow. In the distance, he noticed another forest, and next to it several brick buildings and barracks. The place looked lonely, yet peaceful and quiet.[1] Having traveled for almost half a day – he left Moscow early in the morning, took a regional train to Noginsk, and then spent another hour on a local bus – Enman was pleased to see a beautiful and spacious landscape. Vladimir and his wife, Maria, were planning to move here, since he had been offered a job as an engineer at the newly established testing ground of the ICP.

Although Enman knew little about the ICP, he decided to accept the job offer. He was appointed the head of a construction department at the testing ground, which was an impressive promotion for someone so young. Besides, there was a good chance his family would get a separate apartment at the construction site, an uncommon luxury in the postwar Soviet Union. Upon his arrival, Enman found out that the whole settlement consisted of three buildings: a two-storied red-brick hotel with white columns, a twelve-apartment residential house, and a tiny cafeteria which also served as the main production quarters of the testing ground (see Figure 1.1).[2] Apart from the Enmans, only a few other people lived there at that time. While the first laboratory building was still under construction, most employees of the ICP Branch worked at the ICP's main facility in Moscow.[3] Surrounded by dense forests and marshes, the place was securely

---

[1] *Chernogolovskaia gazeta*, June 22, 2006. [2] *Chernogolovskaia gazeta*, June 22, 2006.
[3] V.K. Enman, "Vospominania," in Dubovitskii, *Nauchnyi Tsentr*, p. 57.

Figure 1.1: First Street (*Pervaia ulitsa*) in Chernogolovka, 1962

hidden from the eyes of a passerby. Except for the sparsely populated village of Chernogolovka, the testing ground was largely uninhabited and uncivilized. There was no direct road connecting the settlement either to Moscow or to nearby towns, as well as no regular transportation. Moreover, as the first residents soon discovered, the town did not have grocery stores, sufficient health care, or an educational system.[4] In a sense, Enman unexpectedly found himself in the position of a pioneer summoned to civilize this pristine land. Despite all the hardships, he felt optimistic about his prospects for the future. Science was on the rise in the Soviet Union, and, as he soon realized, his new job offered incredible opportunities both for professional growth and for starting a family.[5]

The idea to build a testing ground belonged to Nikolai Semenov (1896–1986), one of the most distinguished and well-established scientists in the postwar USSR. An extraordinary researcher, Semenov made his major discovery of branched chain reactions in the early 1930s, for which he received the Nobel Prize in Chemistry in 1956 – the first Nobel Prize awarded to a Soviet scientist. Additionally, the ICP, established under Semenov's leadership in 1931, was deeply involved with the Soviet military. During World War II, the ICP actively contributed to the Soviet wartime effort. After the outbreak of the Cold War, it also played a central role in the Soviet nuclear weapons program. In 1946, Semenov's institute was put in charge of studying

---

[4] *Chernogolovskaia gazeta*, June 22, 2006.
[5] Interview 1 with Vladimir Enman, Chernogolovka, August 2009.

and measuring the parameters of the first nuclear explosion.[6] From 1953, the ICP also engaged in research and development of new powerful explosives designed to improve the performance of nuclear weapons. At first sight, the testing ground in Chernogolovka, established by the resolution of the Council of Ministers on February 28, 1956, was just another product of the Cold War: an emerging island in the invisible archipelago of the Soviet military–industrial complex.

Semenov, however, had his own plans for the site. Over the next six years, he worked to transform this military-oriented testing ground, located near the village of Chernogolovka, into an interdisciplinary scientific center. Along with military-oriented state assignments, Semenov promoted fundamental research and recruited hundreds of young men and women to work on "pure science." By August 1962, when the Soviet Academy of Sciences finally issued an official decree about building a scientific center in Chernogolovka, 821 people, including 423 highly qualified scientists and engineers, were already working there.[7] Graduates of the best Soviet technical universities, in their mid- to late twenties, the first generation of Chernogolovka scientists enthusiastically embraced the outstanding opportunities that Semenov's town offered. Many were put in charge of cutting-edge research groups and laboratories. All residents received separate housing shortly after their arrival.

How did Semenov manage to transform a testing ground into a successful city of science and to secure its *post factum* approval from the Soviet government? To answer this question, I explore the unusual conditions under which Chernogolovka came into existence, from 1955 to 1962. Semenov's success, I argue, points to the expansion of interest in fundamental research among top party officials during the Thaw era. It also testifies that there was room for individual initiatives and innovation in the post-Stalin system, as long as they came from well-connected individuals and conformed to the political and ideological objectives of the state. Another factor that contributed to the success of Semenov's enterprise was the idealistic enthusiasm of the "Thaw generation" of scientists who came to live and work in Chernogolovka in the late 1950s and early 1960s. The input of these young people helped the ICP director convince the Academy of Sciences to turn the testing ground into a full-fledged scientific center in August 1962. But first it is necessary to investigate the new scientific culture of the Thaw that made possible the emergence of Chernogolovka.

---

[6] "Sovet Ministrov SSSR, Postanovlenie №805–327ss ot 9 aprelia 1946 g. Moskva, Kreml', Voprosy laboratorii №2," in N.N. Semenov, *Izbrannye trudy*. T. 2: *Gorenie i vzryv* (Moskva: Nauka, 2005), p. 701.

[7] Dubovitskii, *Nauchnyi Tsentr*, p. 49.

The Thaw and the Shift in Soviet Science Policy

Khrushchev's rise to power, and the process of de-Stalinization that it unleashed, opened up a new era in the relationship between the Soviet regime and the scientific intelligentsia. It also marked a significant shift in Soviet science policy. Whereas in the 1930s and 1940s science contributed mostly to the needs of industrialization, under Khrushchev it transformed into a direct productive force, which relied more heavily on fundamental research. This transformation empowered a number of prominent scientists to take initiative and lobby for increased funding for fundamental research and more autonomy from Communist Party officials. Nikolai Semenov, whose own scientific career had blossomed in the late 1920s and early 1930s,[8] skillfully maneuvered in this new environment to expand the research carried out at his institute and, eventually, founded a scientific center in Chernogolovka.

Although Khrushchev enthusiastically embraced some key features of the Stalinist science policy – such as its fascination with large-scale technologies, the nuclear program, and the rapid growth of the scientific enterprise – he vigorously rejected others. In the late 1950s and early 1960s, disciplines such as biology, sociology, and psychology, which Stalin had banned on ideological grounds, were rehabilitated. Contact with Western scientists resumed. To stay updated on the most recent scientific developments, Khrushchev surrounded himself with the most talented Soviet scientists. The Scientific Council (*Sovet po nauke*), which he established in 1963, functioned as his unofficial advisory body and included such prominent scholars as Mikhail Lavrentiev (the founder of Akademgorodok) and Nikolai Semenov.[9] Most importantly, Khrushchev repudiated violence and fear, both rampant during the Stalinist era.[10] In stark contrast to his predecessor, who ravaged the scientific community in the late 1940s, Khrushchev encouraged increased autonomy for scientists in their respective disciplines, and worked to restore the trusting relationship between scientists and the state. As Paul Josephson correctly observed, all this allowed the academic community to loosen the rigid ideological constraints of the Communist Party and to reclaim control of the scientific enterprise.[11] As fear began to abate in Soviet society, scientists began to take initiative – for the first time since the 1920s.

Shortly after Stalin's death, leading members of the Academy of Sciences took advantage of the new environment and pushed for increasing the role of

---

[8] Josephson, *Physics and Politics*, p. 71. See also James T. Andrews, *Sciences for the Masses: The Bolshevik State, Public Science, and the Popular Imagination in Soviet Russia, 1917–1934* (College Station: Texas A&M University Press, 2003), p. 39.

[9] Khrushchev, *Reformator*, p. 516.

[10] Interview with Sergei Khrushchev, Cranston (Rhode Island), August 2013.

[11] Paul R. Josephson, "Soviet Scientists and the State: Politics, Ideology, and Fundamental Research from Lenin to Gorbachev," *Social Research* 59.3 (1992), p. 607.

fundamental research in Soviet science policy. In his 1954 letter to Khrushchev, Petr Kapitsa, a world-class physicist persecuted under Stalin, argued that science's main task was to create new directions of cultural development, and not merely to serve practical needs. If the Soviet government wanted to advance cutting-edge science, Kapitsa maintained, it had to prioritize theoretical scientific problems.[12] While Khrushchev was not especially fond of Kapitsa, he seemed to take his advice seriously. In February 1956, two prominent scientists – Aleksandr Nesmeianov (the President of the Soviet Academy of Sciences) and Igor' Kurchatov (the head of the Soviet nuclear project) – were invited to participate in the Twentieth Congress of the Communist Party. Nesmeianov used this opportunity to talk about the need to develop fundamental sciences, which he argued would become the basis of Soviet economic growth.[13]

Why did Khrushchev turn out to be more open to the advancement of fundamental research than Stalin? No evidence suggests that he either understood or supported research for the sake of "pure science." Khrushchev was convinced, however, that heavy investment in science and technology were crucial for achieving high productivity and building Communism – the ambitious goal spelled out in the Third Party Program. It was precisely this language that Nesmeianov and other academic scientists used when trying to persuade the First Secretary of the importance of fundamental research. In the modern period, they claimed, science would become an immediate productive force. While previously science had responded to the needs of technology, now technology responded to the achievements of science.[14] Khrushchev seemed to have fully embraced this argument by the Twenty-Second Party Congress, which took place in October 1961. The Third Program of the Communist Party, adopted at the Congress, stated that in the future science would become a "direct productive force."[15] The Program also identified the development of theoretical research as the most important task of the Communist Party.

The construction of dozens of scientific towns under Khrushchev was further proof of the reorientation of Soviet science policy. Discussions about the need to decentralize Soviet science and to enhance scientific research in the provinces began at the Central Committee at the very beginning of the Thaw. In fact, Nikolai Semenov was one of the first advocates of decentralization. In June 1954, Semenov and Sergei Khristianovich, a co-founder of

---

[12] "Pis'mo akademika P.L. Kapitsy N.S. Khrushchevu po voprosam organizatsii sovetskoi nauki, 12 aprelia 1954 g.," in *Akademiia Nauk v resheniiakh Politbiuro TsK RKP (b) – VKP (b) – KPSS, 1922–1991*. T. 2: 1952–1958, ed. by V.D. Esakov (Moskva: ROSSPEN, 2010), pp. 105–106.
[13] *XX s'ezd Kommunisticheskoi Partii Sovetskogo Soiuza (14–25 fevralia 1956 g.). Stenograficheskii otchet*. T. 1 (Moskva: Gosudarstvennoe izdatel'stvo politicheskoi literatury, 1956), p. 378.
[14] Semenov, *Izbrannye trudy*. T. 4, pp. 440–441.
[15] *Programma KPSS*, in *XXII s'ezd Kommunisticheskoi Partii Sovetskogo Soiuza*. T. 3, p. 283.

Akademgorodok, sent a memorandum to the Central Committee's Department of Science and Culture. They contended that continuing the concentration of scientific institutes in Moscow and Leningrad was dangerous "in view of the potential use of weapons of mass destruction by the aggressors."[16] Nesmeianov expressed similar concerns in his report at the General Meeting of the Academy of Sciences on December 28, 1956, when he stated that the exceptional concentration of science in Moscow, Leningrad, Kiev, and other capital cities was abnormal.[17] Scientists argued that the best way out of this critical situation was to follow the foreign example and to start building scientific centers outside of big cities. They looked to "numerous American scientific towns," and Oxford and Cambridge in the United Kingdom, for guidance.[18]

While security and economic considerations were a high priority for the Soviet government, leading members of the Academy used the politics of decentralization to achieve their own scientific goals. Many reasoned that geographic isolation from well-established scientific traditions would be beneficial for developing new areas of fundamental research.[19] They also argued that since many new disciplines emerged at the crossroads of established sciences, such as biophysics or physical chemistry, the most efficient way to organize research was to build new institutes close to each other, clustering them based on scientific profile.

In the mid- and late 1950s, several influential members of the Academy competed to be able to carry out their respective projects at the Central Committee and the Presidium of the Academy of Sciences. The most prominent were Aleksandr Nesmeianov, who lobbied for the construction of a biological center in Pushchino, seventy-five miles to the south of Moscow, and Mikhail Lavrentiev, who petitioned for the creation of an interdisciplinary scientific center in Siberia.[20] While Nesmeianov's project received the initial support of the Central Committee, he soon fell out of favor with Khrushchev, partly because the latter continued to support Trofim Lysenko. Nesmeianov's resignation in 1961 stalled the construction of Pushchino until after Khrushchev's fall.[21] By contrast, Akademgorodok became one of the greatest success stories of Soviet science during the Khrushchev era. Founded in May 1957, the city was conceived as part of a larger national plan to develop the productive forces of Siberia and the Far East, and as such received enthusiastic support from the Central Committee.[22] Khrushchev himself took

---

[16] *Akademiia Nauk v resheniiakh Politbiuro*, T. 2, p. 1126.   [17] RGANI, f. 5, op. 35, d. 48, l. 15.

[18] "Zapiska Prezidiuma AN SSSR o proekte plana razvitiia narodnogo khoziaistva SSSR na 1956–1960 gg., 7 ianvaria 1956 g.," in *Akademiia Nauk v resheniiakh Politbiuro*, T. 2, p. 392.

[19] Vucinich, *Empire of Knowledge*, p. 285

[20] Josephson, *New Atlantis Revisited*, pp. xvii–xviii.   [21] ARAN, f. 2, op. 6, d. 394, ll. 44–49.

[22] Its construction was widely advertised in major Soviet newspapers. See, for example, *Pravda*, April 2, 1957; *Pravda*, June 8, 1957; *Pravda*, November 29, 1957; *Pravda*, April 7, 1958. See

personal interest in the project, helping Lavrentiev to overcome the resistance of the Presidium of the Academy of Sciences and Nesmeianov. Khrushchev visited Akademgorodok twice, in 1959 and 1961, and ordered that Lavrentiev be given the full support of Novosibirsk economic planners and policy makers.[23] Lavrentiev, in turn, went out of his way to assure the Party that a world-class scientific research center would emerge in Siberia. By the mid-1960s, Akademgorodok indeed became a leading academic center in the Soviet Union – thanks largely to Khrushchev's involvement, the tremendous financial investments of the Soviet government, and Lavrentiev's exuberant energy. But where did Chernogolovka fit in this debate?

Nikolai Semenov and the Testing Ground in Chernogolovka

Nikolai Semenov had been a strong supporter of decentralization since the first days of the Thaw, and was watching the rivalry between Lavrentiev and Nesmeianov closely. He hailed Lavrentiev's initiative at the General Meeting of the Academy on November 2, 1957, making a case against the excessive centralization of Soviet science. "We are living in a wonderful time," Semenov said, referring to the popular enthusiasm after the Twentieth Party Congress. "I am sure that in the future more and more people will give their energies to building special scientific towns ... that would provide the best environment for research development."[24] In creating his own scientific center, however, Semenov decided to follow a different path. He did not draw on Khrushchev's support, like Lavrentiev, or use his high status within the Academy, like Nesmeianov. Instead, Semenov relied on his patronage network[25] among high Soviet officials and the military, as well as the unique atmosphere of the Thaw, which reminded him of his own experiences during the first decade of Bolshevik rule.

Few scientists in post-Stalin Russia could boast the prominence and author-ity of Nikolai Semenov. Born in 1896, Semenov came of age during the first

---

also V.B. Dorofeeva and V.V. Dorofeev, *Vremia, uchenye, sversheniia* (Moskva: Politizdat, 1975), p. 197.

[23] "Zapiska M.A. Lavrentieva i S.A. Khristianovicha o sozdanii AN RSFSR, 8 dekabria 1956 g.," in *Akademiia Nauk v resheniiakh Politbiuro*, T. 2, p. 645; "Postanovlenie Prezidiuma TsK KPSS 'O sozdanii Sibirskogo otdeleniia Akademii nauk SSSR,' 18 maia 1957 g.," in *Akademiia Nauk v resheniiakh Politbiuro*, T. 2, p. 750.

[24] *Vestnik Akademii Nauk SSSR*, December 1957, No. 12, p. 11.

[25] On patronage networks, see Mark B. Adams, "Networks in Action: The Khrushchev Era, the Cold War, and the Transformation of Soviet Science," in Garland E. Allen and Roy M. MacLeod, eds., *Science, History, and Social Activism: A Tribute to Everett Mendelsohn* (Dordrecht: Kluwer Academic Publishers, 2001), p. 261; Sheila Fitzpatrick, *Tear off the Masks! Identity and Imposture in Twentieth-Century Russia* (Princeton: Princeton University Press, 2005), p. 192; Gerovitch, "Stalin's Rocket Designers' Leap into Space," p. 192.

post-Revolutionary decade and benefited greatly from the relative autonomy scientists enjoyed in the 1920s.[26] A student of Abram Ioffe, and from 1921 to 1928 his deputy director at the Leningrad Physico-Technical Institute,[27] Semenov played a crucial role in the formation of Soviet science. His discovery of branched chain reactions in the early 1930s became Semenov's most significant contribution to Soviet and world science. It allowed him to establish a strong school in the physics and chemistry of explosions and detonation, and to organize the ICP in 1931. It also secured him membership in the Soviet Academy of Sciences (1932), and, more importantly, won him a Nobel Prize in Chemistry in 1956. Semenov's work on the theory of chain reactions and explosives eventually brought him in close contact with the Soviet military. In the late 1940s, two of his students, Yulii Khariton and Yakov Zel'dovich, became leading participants in the Soviet nuclear weapons program.[28] Semenov himself played a key role in choosing Semipalatinsk as a proving ground for testing atomic bombs. From 1946, the ICP participated actively in theoretical and experimental research on the bomb, responsible mostly for studying and measuring the parameters of an explosion during the first nuclear test.[29]

Despite his later conflict with the Stalinist regime,[30] Semenov was a strong supporter of the Soviet power that, he believed, made possible his remarkable professional success. "Modern science has no room for development within the Procrustean bed of capitalism, ruled by private-owner relationships, which turn science into business," he claimed in one of his public speeches in 1961. Only under socialism and forthcoming Communism can modern science thrive.[31] He expressed similar views in private conversations and correspondence. In a 1932 letter to Petr Kapitsa, who worked in England at the time, Semenov tried to

---

[26] Josephson, *Politics and Physics*, p. 71; Krementsov, *Stalinist Science*, pp. 4–6, 53; Weiner, *A Little Corner of Freedom*, p. 3; Andrews, *Science for the Masses*, p. 39.

[27] Abram Ioffe was the founder and director of the Leningrad Physico-Technical Institute (LFTI), often referred to as the "cradle" of Soviet physics.

[28] From 1939 to 1941, Khariton and Zel'dovich published a series of papers in which they calculated the conditions under which a nuclear chain reaction would take place. Neglected during the war, their work gained prominence once the regime launched a crash program to build a Soviet nuclear bomb. See Holloway, *Stalin and the Bomb*, p. 51.

[29] Istvan Hargittai, *Buried Glory: Portraits of Soviet Scientists* (New York: Oxford University Press, 2013), p. 205.

[30] In 1937, Semenov was fortunate to have avoided arrest as a member of a counter-revolutionary group that, ostensibly, included a large group of first-rate scientists, such as Matvei Bronstein, Vladimir Fock, and Lev Landau. See Hargittai, *Buried Glory*, p. 195. In the 1940s, Semenov and his school also underwent persecution from a group of physicists and chemists at Moscow State University, led by Nikolai Akulov, who questioned the authenticity of Semenov's discovery of chain reactions. Semenov actively opposed Trofim Lysenko and his acolytes at the Academy of Sciences, too, and continued to support Petr Kapitsa when in 1946 the latter was put under house arrest at Nikolina Gora.

[31] Semenov, *Nauka i obshchestvo*, p. 8; Semenov, *Izbrannye trudy*, T. 4, p. 425.

convince his friend to return to Russia and contribute to the birth of new Soviet science, bragging about the immense financial resources that the Bolsheviks allocated for the development of fundamental research.[32] What Semenov valued even more highly than funding, however, was the greater independence and autonomy that the Soviet state allowed the young researchers during the first post-Revolutionary decade. "Soviet power provided many current prominent scientists with vast opportunities to develop their initiatives and ideas from a young age," he said at a conference in Paris in November 1958. "Take me as an example: I was working on the theoretical problems of chemical reaction, and after the initial success of my work, in 1930 the state founded the Institute of Chemical Physics,[33] and appointed me as its director. I was barely 30 years old at the time!"[34]

For Semenov, the 1920s were a truly "heroic era." It was a time of unprecedented popular enthusiasm, when, after the Revolution, thousands of young researchers flocked into the scientific profession.[35] It was also a period when, in the absence of a systematic science policy, he and his colleagues could take the initiative and establish new research institutes across the Soviet Union, receiving eventual approval from the state.[36] It appears that Semenov interpreted Khrushchev's Thaw as an invitation to go back to the practices of the 1920s, when scientists enjoyed greater independence from the state. Instead of securing Khrushchev's support for building a new scientific town, like Lavrentiev and other scientists did, Semenov used his personal connections to get powerful Soviet officials to agree to start the construction of the testing ground. He did not advertise that a scientific center would be built in Chernogolovka; nor did he try to convince his colleagues in the Academy to support the founding of a new academic center. Semenov asked for a testing ground outside of Moscow, arguing that the latter was necessary for the ICP to continue working successfully on military-oriented assignments of the Soviet government.

The administration of the ICP started off carefully, with Semenov sending a letter to Mikhail Pervukhin, a deputy chairman of the Soviet Council of Ministers, in which he explained the purpose of the requested testing ground. The letter, written in early August 1955, was accompanied by a draft resolution on the issue. Since the testing ground was to serve the defense needs of the country, the initiative received enthusiastic support from the Council of Ministers and the Ministry of Medium Machine-Building. Despite the fact that it was extremely difficult at the time to get a suitable plot of land near Moscow, Semenov and his

---

[32] "Semenov – Kapitse (Ianvar' 1932 goda, Leningrad)," in *Kapitsa, Tamm, Semenov*, p. 531.

[33] The Institute of Chemical Physics was officially founded only in 1931.

[34] Semenov, *Izbrannye trudy*, T. 4, p. 41.

[35] Istvan Hargittai, *Candid Science: Conversations with Famous Chemists* (London: Imperial College Press, 2000), p. 468.

[36] Josephson, *Physics and Politics*, p. 71.

close associate, Fedor Dubovitskii, were allowed to choose from several proving grounds, all belonging to the Soviet Air Force. After a brief examination, the two scientists set their sights on territory near the village of Chernogolovka, conveniently located some thirty-five miles northeast of Moscow. The total size of the territory granted to the institute was 2,090 hectares, or eight square miles, although the original request of the ICP was for only 150–200 hectares.[37] On December 3, 1955, Semenov sent a letter to the Ministry of Medium Machine-Building, in which he confirmed that the ICP agreed to accept part of an air force proving ground in Noginsk. It took another three months before an official decree was issued.

On February 28, 1956, the Council of Ministers published a resolution about building a research testing ground for the ICP. Written in dry bureaucratic language, it instructed the Ministry of Defense to provide the ICP with a large plot of land in the Noginsk area, and put the Academy of Sciences in charge of the actual construction. According to the decree, the site had to consist of a pavilion for experimental research on explosives, a testing area, storehouses, roads, two apartment buildings with eight apartments each, power and water supply systems, sewage, and barracks for construction workers. It indicated that the construction had to begin immediately, and be finished by December 1, 1958. The total investment was estimated at as much as 25.6 million rubles, with the first 5 million coming from the funds allocated by the Soviet state to the Ministry of Medium Machine-Building. The decree put Semenov in charge of recruiting "young specialists" – fifteen junior research fellows (physicists, chemists, and physico-chemists) and eighteen engineers and technicians – to work at the testing ground.[38] Compared with Akademgorodok or Pushchino, Chernogolovka was clearly conceived as an outlet facility. The initial budget for Pushchino was estimated at 340 million rubles; its future population was to consist of 10,000 people.[39] The government allocated 1 billion rubles for the construction of Akademgorodok.[40]

However, from the very beginning Semenov aspired to exploit the testing ground to expand the ICP's research beyond the set limits. He explicitly prioritized fundamental science goals over military ones. According to one of his protégés, although Semenov did not reveal his plans until much later, for him the testing ground was a means to a different end.[41] To organize the new settlement in Chernogolovka in March 1956 he appointed Fedor Dubovitskii, one of his most

[37] Dubovitskii, *Nauchnyi Tsentr*, pp. 16, 19.   [38] Dubovitskii, *Nauchnyi Tsentr*, p. 24.

[39] "Proekt postanovleniia Soveta Ministrov SSSR 'O stroitel'stve nauchnogo gorodka Akademii nauk SSSR v Serpukhovskom raione Moskovskoi oblasti,' Aprel' 1956 g.," in *Akademiia Nauk v resheniiakh Politbiuro*, T. 2, p. 466.

[40] "Zapiska Otdela nauki, vuzov i shkol TsK KPSS o sozdanii Sibirskogo otdeleniia AN SSSR [Ne pozdnee 6 maia 1957 g.]," in *Akademiia Nauk v resheniiakh Politbiuro*, T. 2, p. 754.

[41] Interview 4 with Georgii Manelis, Chernogolovka, February 2011.

Figure 1.2: Nikolai Semenov (right) and Fedor Dubovitskii (left)

capable students and a talented administrator, to head the committee in charge of the construction (see Figure 1.2). As soon as construction began, Dubovitskii insisted that the general plan should leave space for possible further growth.

In August and September 1956, Tsentrakademstroi (the Central Academic Construction Organization), which was the main contractor of the Soviet Academy of Sciences, arrived at the site. They brought temporary housing for workers, and began building a twelve-apartment building and a canteen for fifty people. Yet construction progressed slowly and inefficiently.[42] A year later, by mid-September 1957, each building had only one floor.[43] Additionally, there were constant disagreements between Tsentrakademstroi and GIPRONII, a major research institute of the Academy of Sciences responsible for designing new facilities. To resolve this problem, Semenov and Dubovitskii appealed directly to "the comrades in the Council of Ministers," whom they knew from their cooperation during wartime years. After several months of negotiations between the Council of Ministers and the Presidium of the Academy of Sciences, the building of the research testing ground in

[42] ARAN, f. 2, op. 6, d. 249, l. 93.   [43] *Chernogolovskaia gazeta*, January 20, 2005.

Chernogolovka was commissioned to Glavspetsstroi, a construction organization subordinate to the Soviet military. This transfer played a major role in
securing the success of Semenov's enterprise. Now that the ICP had a powerful
construction organization at its disposal, Semenov could expand the testing
ground, building new research facilities and an extensive residential area.

Semenov's initiative provoked strong discontent from Aleksandr
Nesmeianov, the President of the Academy of Sciences, who correctly feared
that the testing ground would draw funds away from building a biological
center in Pushchino. Nesmeianov was also resentful of Semenov's peculiar
operating style: instead of getting his project approved by the Academy,
Semenov went directly to the Soviet government and military.[44] There is no
evidence to suggest that Semenov relied on Khrushchev's personal support to
overcome the initial hostility of the Academy of Sciences, like Lavrentiev did.
However, it is clear that the ICP director had personal access to the Soviet
leader and was in his good graces. According to Vitalii Gol'danskii, Semenov's
son-in-law and his former student, the fact that Semenov became the first
Soviet winner of the Nobel Prize fundamentally changed his relationship
with the authorities, as it was an important symbol of the international acclaim
of Soviet science.[45] Semenov also played a crucial role in preparing the report
for the Presidium of the CPSU Central Committee on the development of
chemistry.[46] Khrushchev had especially high expectations for this field and
its leading role in modernizing the Soviet economy. In spring 1957, Semenov
met with Khrushchev, for the first time, to talk about how the Soviet Union
lagged in the chemical industry and needed to develop polymer and plastic
materials production. According to Sergei Khrushchev, his father was pleased
with the scientist taking the initiative and bringing this problem to his
attention.[47]

Moreover, the First Secretary seemed to be personally fond of Semenov,
which the latter could count on as he proceeded with his plan in
Chernogolovka. In 1961, Khrushchev insisted that Semenov be elected
a candidate member of the Party's Central Committee – a position he occupied
until 1967. In 1963, he invited Semenov to participate in his personal Scientific
Council. Khrushchev had great respect for those scientists who thought first
about "state interests" (*myslili po-gosudarstvennomu*), and he clearly included
Semenov in this category.

---

[44] Khrushchev, *Reformator*, p. 642.   [45] Gol'danskii, *Essays of a Soviet Scientist*, p. 55.
[46] "No. 131 Protokol №116 ot 10 oktiabria 1957 g. 'Ob osnovnykh napravleniiakh v razrabotke
i sostavlenii piati-semiletnego plana razvitiia narodnogo khoziaistva SSSR,'" in *Prezidium TsK
KPSS, 1954–1964*. T. 1: *Chernovye protokol'nye zapisi zasedanii. Stenogrammy* (Moskva:
ROSSPEN, 2003), p. 267.
[47] Khrushchev, *Reformator*, pp. 537–539; Interview with Sergei Khrushchev, Cranston (Rhode
Island), August 2013.

Despite this, Semenov kept his plans to himself until 1961, when Mstislav Keldysh succeeded Nesmeianov as the President of the Academy of Sciences. Perhaps Semenov did not think he could convince Khrushchev that building another scientific town dedicated to fundamental research was in the best interests of the state. It is also possible that Semenov did not want the publicity of Akademgorodok, because he realized that the Soviet government had already dedicated tremendous financial resources to building Akademgorodok and was more likely to support a military-oriented settlement than another scientific center. Finally, by the early 1960s the shift in Soviet science policy – from narrow utilitarianism to wider support of fundamental research – had become more pronounced. Chernogolovka was no longer an anomaly but fit well into a new generation of scientific towns, promoted by the state, that focused on fundamental research and innovation, and included Akademgorodok, Pushchino, Dubna, Troitsk, Zelenograd, and others.

Semenov did not speak openly about the actual idea behind the creation of Chernogolovka until January 19, 1968, at the meeting of the Presidium of the Academy of Sciences that took place in Chernogolovka.[48] Explaining to his colleagues the nature of the research being done at the scientific center and its future prospects, Semenov claimed that from the very beginning his main goal in building the Noginsk Scientific Center[49] was to bring together professionals from various disciplines, in particular physics and chemistry, in order to direct their efforts toward solving "the big problems of science." One of the major challenges of modern science, he argued, was to overcome its narrow specialization. "The entire history of science in the twentieth century, starting with the revolution in physics and the discoveries about the atom, has been about returning to the idea of united, big science. Since it turned out that the atom had both physical and chemical characteristics, physicists and chemists had to work together, their preferences and habits notwithstanding."[50] To meet this challenge, Semenov contended, it was necessary to combine the depth of micro-specialists' research with the breadth of general tasks posed by science. Without it, he claimed, it was essentially impossible to succeed in securing scientific progress in the Soviet Union and in the world at large.[51] "We have to cultivate in scientists a keen interest in their colleagues' work. This can be achieved either through official scientific seminars, or through informal personal encounters." The easiest way to create these conditions, Semenov maintained, was to locate several research institutes working in separate fields in one

---

[48] ARAN, f. 2, op. 6, d. 688, ll. 21–114.

[49] The present name of the town appeared much later. From 1956 to 1962, the settlement's official title was the Noginsk Research Testing Ground in Chernogolovka, and from 1962 until the late 1980s it was known to Soviet and foreign citizens alike as the Noginsk Scientific Center of the Academy of Sciences in Chernogolovka.

[50] ARAN, f. 2, op. 6, d. 688, l. 23.   [51] ARAN, f. 2, op. 6, d. 688, l. 24.

place – outside of big cities, but not too far from them – to make sure that scientists from different disciplines worked and lived next to each other.[52] It was precisely this idea that guided Semenov when he began the construction of the unusual testing ground near the village of Chernogolovka.

Semenov's "Kindergarten": Populating Chernogolovka

When the construction of the testing ground in Chernogolovka had just begun in 1958, the eyes of Soviet political and scientific leaders were focused instead on the city of science in Siberia. Few people believed that Lavrentiev would succeed in convincing both accomplished scientists and recent university graduates to move to Akademgorodok and start their research from scratch there.[53] To overcome this challenge, Lavrentiev appealed directly to the Central Committee of the Communist Party, requesting that it facilitate the transfer of established scholars to Siberia and provide Akademgorodok with first choice of young specialists. His request was fulfilled, and on February 22, 1958, the Council of Ministers issued a resolution, which gave the Siberian division first choice of recent graduates from all higher educational institutions nationwide.[54] As a result, within several years, hundreds – and then thousands – of scientists made their way to Akademgorodok.

Semenov decided to pursue a different path in populating his settlement. He neither asked top party officials for support nor requested any special privileges for the testing ground. Instead, Semenov relied almost exclusively on the internal resources of his institute. Shortly after the publication of the original decree on the testing ground, he selected four laboratories of the ICP, which had been involved in research on new powerful explosives, as primary centers for recruiting scientific and technical personnel for the incipient testing ground. According to Semenov's initial plan, the ICP Branch in Chernogolovka would consist of four branches of these select laboratories, headed by established scientists: Fedor Dubovitskii, Al'fred Apin, Pavel Pokhil, and Aleksandr Beliaev. He hoped that, after a while, a younger generation of Chernogolovka's most promising scholars would replace the current leaders. On April 8, 1959, Semenov made his position clear at the meeting of the party bureau of the ICP. Commenting on Dubovitskii's report on the progress of the testing ground, he pointed out that recruitment of personnel should become the first priority: "Basically, all newly recruited scientific personnel of the ICP must be sent to work at Noginsk." Semenov insisted that only first-rate

[52] ARAN, f. 2, op. 6, d. 688, l. 25.   [53] Josephson, *New Atlantis Revisited*, p. 23.
[54] "Zapiska Otdela nauki, shkol i kul'tury TsK KPSS po RSFSR o podbore kadrov dlia Sibirskogo otdeleniia AN SSSS, 31 ianvaria 1958 g.," in *Akademiia Nauk v resheniiakh Politbiuro*, T. 2, p. 907.

university seniors and graduate students should be admitted, because eventually they would replace the established scientists there.[55]

Relying on the younger generation in building Chernogolovka fit nicely into the exuberant atmosphere of the Thaw and the spirit of the Twentieth Party Congress. Khrushchev believed that mobilizing the Soviet people and rekindling their revolutionary enthusiasm could work miracles. He had especially high expectations for Soviet youth, which he assumed was not only ideologically pure, but also better trained and educated. "Now that our country has embarked on the grand journey of constructing Communism," Khrushchev claimed at the Twentieth-Second Party Congress in 1961, "Soviet science is facing new, even more majestic tasks, which it can only solve by opening access to science to the young forces."[56] The First Secretary emphasized this point again in his 1963 memorandum to the Central Committee, arguing that it was necessary to "give a green light" in science to the talented youth.[57] Semenov, in fact, had been a strong advocate of the youth since the first days of the Thaw. On November 2, 1956, at the meeting of the Presidium of the Academy of Sciences that convened to congratulate him on winning the Nobel Prize, Semenov announced that the "fresh wind" blowing after the Twentieth Congress had had a wonderful effect on the development of new cadres. "I have been watching the growing initiative of the youth over the last one-two years. This is a really interesting and important process; it is a guarantee of our future success."[58] Several months later, Semenov addressed the Academy again, arguing that promoting "unlimited scientific initiative" and entrusting young scientists with new laboratories was crucial for preparing the young generation to take over.[59]

Semenov believed that the success of his enterprise in Chernogolovka depended largely on attracting talented young specialists and giving them opportunities to excel. Soon it became obvious that this was the only way to proceed. In early 1960, three out of four heads of laboratories at the ICP refused to leave their work and housing in Moscow and move their labs to the unknown settlement in the marshes. By that time, however, the construction in Chernogolovka was in full swing: the government had already invested at least 50 million rubles in the project, and expected the testing ground to start functioning as soon as possible.[60] Trying to find a way out of this quandary,

[55] TsAOPIM, f. 8099, op. 1, d. 35, l. 63.
[56] *XXII s'ezd Kommunisticheskoi Partii Sovetskogo Soiuza*, T. 1 (Moskva: Gospolitizdat, 1962), p. 91.
[57] "Proekt zapiski N.S. Khrushcheva v Prezidium TsK KPSS po voprosam nauki [Ne ranee 12 aprelia 1963 g.]," in *Nikita Sergeevich Khrushchev. Dva tsveta vremeni: Dokumenty iz lichnogo fonda Khrushcheva v 2-kh tomakh*, ed. by N.G. Tomilina, T. 2 (Moskva: Mezhdunarodnyi fond "Demokratiia," 2009), pp. 411–412, 415.
[58] ARAN, f. 2, op. 6, d. 232, l. 42.
[59] *Vestnik Akademii Nauk SSSR*, April 1957, No. 4, pp. 21–22.
[60] TsAOPIM, f. 8099, op. 1, d. 38, l. 9.

Semenov suggested that four new independent laboratories be created in Chernogolovka. He then went ahead and appointed the most talented and promising young scientists working at the ICP as their directors. Among them were Lev Vashin and Georgii Manelis, thirty-one and thirty years old respectively. For both of them, this appointment was unexpected, but they tried to make the best out of it. Crucially, Semenov promised that new laboratories would work to develop new, cutting-edge areas of science and to expand research carried out at the institute. This was the most convincing argument for young and ambitious scholars.

Lev Vashin first visited the construction site on June 6, 1956. He remembered that "there was absolutely nothing there, but a small village and a heap of tile for beginning construction." It was an insufferably hot day, and he was unpleasantly struck by the sight of never-ending marshes and clouds of mosquitos.[61] Vashin was a graduate of the Physical and Technical Department of Moscow State University (MGU). In January 1952, he had just turned twenty-three years old, and happily accepted a position as a junior research fellow at Semenov's institute in Moscow. At the time, his MGU advisor, Al'fred Apin, had just returned from a long-term sojourn in Arzamas-16, the epicenter of the Soviet nuclear project. He invited Vashin to join his group, and then his laboratory, at the ICP studying combustion and detonation of new powerful explosives.[62] Vashin was put in charge of a group researching the parameters of detonation. He defended his "candidate of sciences" dissertation in 1959, and in early 1960 was appointed head of the newly established laboratory of explosive compounds at the testing ground. Vashin moved to Chernogolovka on June 15, 1960, bringing his family with him.[63]

Georgii Manelis, on the other hand, was a complete novice at studying combustion. A chemist by training, he graduated from Central Asian State University in Tashkent in June 1953. As one of the twenty best students produced by the Uzbek Soviet Socialist Republic that year, Manelis received a recommendation to continue graduate studies in Moscow. He enrolled at Semenov's institute, captivated by its friendly, creative atmosphere and an opportunity to work side by side with "great men," including Yakov Zel'dovich and Yulii Khariton, who just gave the Soviet Union its own nuclear bomb.[64] As the term of his graduate program was coming to an end, Manelis was looking for ways to stay at the ICP, and readily accepted Dubovitskii's offer to switch his research area from polymers to explosives. He defended his dissertation in 1958, and moved to the testing ground in the summer of 1960.

[61] Interview 2 with Lev Vashin, Chernogolovka, April 2010.
[62] Lev Vashin, *Autobiography* (unpublished manuscript) (Chernogolovka, 2004), p. 20.
[63] Vashin, *Autobiography*, p. 23.
[64] Interview 4 with Georgii Manelis, Chernogolovka, February 2011.

His wife, Nina Konovalova, and their seven-year-old daughter arrived two years later, since Chernogolovka had no school system until 1962.

In the 1960s, Manelis's laboratory worked on the kinetics of thermal decomposition and combustion of explosives, contributing to the creation of solid rocket propellant for Soviet missiles. Over time, it gradually transitioned to non-military research focusing on chemical kinetics. Vashin's laboratory, by contrast, continued to study the combustion processes in rocket propellant until much later. Many of its scientific results and publications were classified. Aleksandr Merzhanov and Anatolii Dremin, both physicists by education, directed two other laboratories that were originally established at the testing ground to study powerful explosives. In the late 1960s, they began to incorporate non-military research into their work. In 1967, for example, Merzhanov's laboratory discovered a new class of combustion processes – self-propagating high-temperature synthesis (SHS) – which proved to be a highly efficient production method of new materials. Manelis, Vashin, Merzhanov, and Dremin made a significant contribution to the Soviet school of combustion science, originally established by, among others, Nikolai Semenov and Yakov Zel'dovich.

In 1960, all four appointees were among the youngest directors of laboratories in the whole Academy of Sciences.[65] It took all of Semenov's boisterous energy and authority to convince his colleagues to approve their appointments. Many senior scientists at the Academy were opposed to giving so much freedom to a group of youngsters. But Semenov, who became director of his own research institute at the age of thirty-five, was willing to take the risk. In December 1960, the Scientific Council of the ICP officially selected the four appointed scientists to serve as heads of new laboratories founded in Chernogolovka. The oldest of them, Lev Vashin, had just turned thirty-one years old. The Presidium of the Academy of Sciences reluctantly approved their appointments.

"They called us 'Semenov's kindergarten,'" Manelis recollected in his interview fifty years later.[66] For the first decade, the average age of Chernogolovka scientists was twenty-seven years old. They were, almost exclusively, recent graduates of the best Soviet higher education institutions. While Manelis, Vashin, Merzhanov, and Dremin were directly involved in military-oriented research, the majority of their peers were recruited to work in "pure science." Gennadii Bogdanov, for example, graduated from the Department of Chemistry at Moscow State University in 1958. He was conducting his dissertation research under the supervision of Nikolai Emanuel' at the ICP when

[65] Paul Josephson also references the rapid promotion of young scientists in Akademgorodok. See Josephson, *New Atlantis Revisited*, p. 26.
[66] Interview 4 with Georgii Manelis, Chernogolovka, February 2011.

his advisor arranged for him to move to the testing ground in 1962. Around that time, Semenov and Emanuel' became interested in applying the methods of organic chemistry to living organisms, and they were recruiting young specialists to work in that area. In Chernogolovka, Bogdanov joined a research group headed by Nina Konovalova, who was an eye doctor but trained in biomedical research at the ICP. Dedicated to finding a cure for cancer, the group worked on experimental chemotherapy, a pioneering field in the USSR at the time.[67] In 1973, Konovalova's group developed into a laboratory of experimental chemotherapy. Soon afterwards, Bogdanov established his own laboratory at the ICP Brach, which studied free radicals in living organisms and searched for anti-oxidants that could neutralize them.

In strict compliance with Semenov's vision, many newly arriving scientists focused on chemical research. Oleg Efimov was twenty-six years old when he accepted an invitation to join the recently established laboratory of complex catalysts at the ICP Branch in 1962. Efimov's research focused on electro-catalysis and the synthesis of conductive polymers.[68] Toward the late 1950s, polymer science was still not well developed in the Soviet Union. Semenov, in fact, played a key role in bringing this shortcoming to Khrushchev's attention during their first personal meeting in spring 1957.[69] Khrushchev asked the scientist to prepare a detailed factual report, which Semenov gave to party leaders later that year.[70] As a result, fast development of polymer science in the Soviet Union began, including at Semenov's institute and its branch in Chernogolovka.

The director of the laboratory and Efimov's supervisor, Aleksandr Shilov, was only thirty-two years old. Semenov's protégé and a gifted scientist, Shilov agreed to move from Moscow to the testing ground because it allowed him to develop his interest in the field of nitrogen fixation.[71] In Chernogolovka, he received one of the institute's buildings for his research. He was also encouraged to recruit a number of talented personnel. In his interview, Shilov maintained that the 1960s and 1970s were extremely productive years in his scientific career. By 1970, Shilov and his team had obtained their most significant results in nitrogen fixation: they discovered several compounds, which reduced nitrogen in a protic solution. Semenov was pleased, as the ICP was the only research institute in the USSR working on this problem. In 1979, Shilov's work on nitrogen fixation was registered as a discovery. He and his colleagues received a highly prestigious State Award of the USSR in 1982.[72]

---

[67] Interview 3 with Gennadii Bogdanov, Chernogolovka, August 2010.
[68] Interview 2 with Oleg Efimov, Chernogolovka, March 2011.
[69] Khrushchev, *Reformator*, pp. 538–543.   [70] Hargittai, *Buried Glory*, pp. 198–199.
[71] Interview 3 with Aleksandr Shilov, Chernogolovka, March 2010.
[72] Vadim Yu. Kukushkin, "Celebration of Inorganic Lives: Interview with A.E. Shilov," *Coordination Chemistry Reviews* 251 (207), pp. 8–9.

While Shilov's interest in the subject was purely theoretical, the problem of nitrogen fixation had direct industrial application, as it made possible the production of nitrogen fertilizers for Soviet agriculture.

That so many physicists, chemists, and biologists in Chernogolovka ended up researching fundamental scientific problems was not an accident. In the early 1960s, Semenov began to work toward expanding the scope and research agenda of the original testing ground, laying the foundation for its gradual transformation into an interdisciplinary academic community. In order to do this, he invited young scientists whose research had little to do with the original decree on the testing ground. All newly recruited employees had to interview at the Moscow part of the ICP with Dubovitskii, who talked to them as much about their personal backgrounds and views as about their qualifications. Dubovitskii's task was to make sure that all newcomers would fit well into the forming scientific community. Some interviews went on for several hours, after which Dubovitskii invited a job candidate to visit the testing ground, and made a final decision. In most cases, an interviewee was a protégé of an established Soviet scientist. Later on, when the news about the scientific town in Chernogolovka spread, some doctoral students acted independently and sought employment in Chernogolovka themselves.[73]

To make the testing ground more attractive to its inhabitants, the ICP administration paid particular attention to creating good living conditions and building comfortable modern housing, which I discuss at greater length in Chapter 3. Upon their arrival in Chernogolovka, the first four heads of laboratories, including Manelis and Vashin, each got a separate two-floor apartment, which was outstanding luxury for most Soviet citizens. According to Vashin, it was Semenov's idea to build the apartments and allocate them to the institute's leading scientists. Semenov borrowed the idea from England, which he visited as a tourist in the 1920s. "Of course, the design was Soviet, not English, and the apartments were not as comfortable. But when a person had no housing at all and was given an apartment like this, it was wonderful!"[74] Other scientists received one-, two-, or three-room apartments within a year of their arrival in Chernogolovka. Many realized that their conditions were exceptional for the Soviet Union, where an average family waited for decades to get their own housing.

Fifty years later, Chernogolovka first residents remembered the late 1950s and early 1960s as "an extraordinary and fabulous time." "All of the first inhabitants felt they were part of one united family and were eager to help each other," Vladimir Enman remembered.[75] "We could not avoid everyday

[73] Interview 2 with Rimma Liubovskaia, Chernogolovka, February 2011; Interview 2 with Oleg Efimov, Chernogolovka, March 2011.
[74] Interview 2 with Lev Vashin, Chernogolovka, April 2010.
[75] *Chernogolovskaia gazeta*, June 22, 2006.

difficulties, of course, especially those of us who had families. At first, there were neither kindergartens, nor stores, nor any health care at the place. Each time we needed groceries, we had to travel to Moscow or Noginsk."[76] However, according to Enman and other town residents, all these inconveniences were outweighed by the closeness to nature: beautiful forests around the testing ground, full of berries and mushrooms, and peace and quiet, all ideal for scientific research.[77] "We were all young and full of optimism and energy," Enman explained.[78] "It seems incredible now but back then the town was populated exclusively by people of the same age," Gennadii Bogdanov echoed. "Can you imagine yourself living in a world of peers, all of them with higher education and university degrees from the best technical schools? This is why I call this time fabulous."[79] This sentiment appears throughout many other interviews with Chernogolovka's first inhabitants, and is worth investigating. Was it really "fabulous" to live in a settlement that had no grocery stores, schools, or hospitals, and was not easily accessible by public transportation? We should take these oral testimonies with a grain of salt. Few of the interviewees remembered the hardships of the first decade, although there were plenty. At the same time, all were eager to discuss their scientific achievements. Nostalgia for their youth is part of their story. In retrospect, my respondents needed to believe that, despite the catastrophic decay of science in post-Soviet Russia, theirs was a story of success. The pitfalls of memory, however, do not explain it all. The settlement in the marshes, ironically, provided many scientists with outstanding opportunities not only to improve their material conditions, but also to have meaningful lives. It allowed them to isolate themselves from the poverty and injustice of the postwar Soviet Union and to make a living doing what they loved the most – science.

The background against which Chernogolovka came into being also influenced much of the optimism and enthusiasm of the town's first residents. Stalin's death in 1953 and Khrushchev's coming to power brought major political and ideological changes to Soviet society. Khrushchev's renunciation of Stalin in 1956, and his subsequent reforms in social and cultural spheres, raised hopes throughout the educated Russian elite for the improvement of life in the foreseeable future. "There was a wide-spread feeling in the mid-1950s and early 1960s that we could achieve and do anything," Manelis recalled. "This feeling was the leitmotif and the major focus of our interests. It was against this background that Chernogolovka was created. There is a swamp – so what? We can drain it and build a town!"[80] While accomplished senior scientists were reluctant to abandon their housing and laboratories in Moscow, the

[76] Enman, "Pro to, kak zhili my, druz'ia," in *Chernogolovskaia gazeta*, June 22, 2006.
[77] Dubovitskii, *Nauchnyi Tsentr*, pp. 54–59.   [78] *Chernogolovskaia gazeta*, June 22, 2006.
[79] Interview 1 with Gennadii Bogdanov, Chernogolovka, September 2009.
[80] Interview 1 with Georgii Manelis, Chernogolovka, December 2009.

"Thaw generation" of Soviet scientists perceived this as a challenge they were happy to tackle. "The decision to build a testing ground in the marshes was made, fine, but who would agree to go there?! Muscovites did not want to go. Many were invited to come, but they refused," Manelis remembered. "One of them told me later: 'Why would I go if I can write four articles, while you are busy uprooting trees and draining marshes.' But we were twenty-five, twenty-six, and twenty-seven years old at the time. We were decisive folk. And we did go: it all looked very interesting."[81]

Finally, in 1962, when the population of Chernogolovka had reached 821 people, Semenov decided that it was time to bring his "child" before the eyes of the Academy and obtain its official approval.

From Testing Ground to Scientific Center

In the first few years of Chernogolovka's existence, Semenov and Dubovitskii brought a wide variety of military, party, and scientific officials to the testing ground, looking for their approval and asking for additional funding. Since at first the testing ground worked on nuclear technologies, Semenov relied on Soviet officials concerned with national defense. For example, in 1959 he invited Pavel Zernov, a deputy minister of Medium Machine-Building in charge of the Soviet nuclear program and a key figure in constructing Arzamas-16, to visit Chernogolovka. Zernov allocated the testing ground an additional 12 million rubles for building roads, purportedly necessary to transport explosives.[82] In the early 1960s, as scientists' authority and prestige continued to grow in Soviet society, Semenov began to draw more heavily on the support of the Academy of Sciences. Yet it was not until 1961, when Mstislav Keldysh succeeded Nesmeianov as President of the Academy, that the real transformation took place.

Unlike his predecessor, Keldysh had no personal interest in supporting one scientific center over the other. Scientific construction was booming in the Soviet Union in the early 1960s, as dozens of scientific towns appeared from scratch across the country, and the growing academic community in Chernogolovka fit well within these lines. Keldysh visited the site in the summer of 1962. He was pleased to find that the ICP Branch already had several completed laboratory buildings and mechanical shops at the site, as well as a rapidly growing residential area with ninety new apartments available for employees. Moreover, the settlement had a kindergarten for thirty children and a recently opened school for 520 students.[83] The new President decided to

---

[81] Interview 1 with Georgii Manelis, Chernogolovka, December 2009.
[82] Dubovitskii, *Nauchnyi Tsentr*, p. 63.   [83] TsAOPIM, f. 8099, op. 1, d. 46, l. 63.

support Semenov's initiative and to expand construction in Chernogolovka further by building other research institutes of the Academy of Sciences there.

Keldysh's visit proved to be a watershed in the history of the town. On August 9, 1962, the Presidium of the Academy of Sciences issued a decree about establishing a multidisciplinary academic center in Chernogolovka, which was now officially called the Noginsk Scientific Center of the Academy of Sciences. According to the decree, in addition to the Branch of the ICP, two new institutes were to be built in the town: the Institute of Solid State Physics (ISSP) and the Institute of New Chemical Problems (INCP). The decree also established the Board of Directors, which had to coordinate scientific and organizational questions concerning the scientific center. It included Semenov, Dubovitskii, Kurdiumov (the founder and the first director of the ISSP), and several other members of the Academy. Dubovitskii was appointed "the authorized representative of the Presidium of the Academy of Sciences in Chernogolovka."[84]

Another resolution of the Presidium issued on April 19, 1963, specified that Chernogolovka's research institutes would focus primarily on fundamental problems of science and their practical application to production. Along with classified research, for example, the ICP Branch had to contribute to the development of the polymer industry through studying complex catalysts. The ISSP, in turn, would focus on solid state physics, underdeveloped in the Soviet Union, and look for ways to create new, advanced materials for Soviet industry.[85] The general plan of construction indicated that the Noginsk Scientific Center would become a modern town with a population of up to 20,000 people. The construction of the new institutes and the residential sector had to begin immediately, and finish by 1970. Its cost was estimated at 107 million rubles.[86]

While the INCP never managed to become a full-fledged research institution, the ISSP turned out to be a successful project. Initiated by a prominent Soviet scientist, Georgii Kurdiumov, it was soon taken up by Kurdiumov's young and energetic assistant, Yuri Osipyan. Just like Semenov several years earlier, Kurdiumov decided to rely on the younger generation of scientists. Osipyan and his peers were responsible for all organizational and construction matters of the ISSP, including the development of its future research agenda and the recruitment of capable personnel. On February 15, 1963, the date when the ISSP was officially founded, Osipyan turned thirty-two years old, becoming one of the youngest deputy directors in the Academy of Sciences. A graduate of the Moscow Institute of Steel and Alloys (MISiS), Osipyan relied on some of his most promising fellow students to launch new directions of scientific

[84] Dubovitskii, *Nauchnyi Tsentr*, pp. 67–69.   [85] ARAN, f. 2, op. 6, d. 445, ll. 9–10.

[86] TsAOPIM, f. 8099, op. 1, d. 46, l. 63.

research at the ISSP. Veniamin Shektman, for example, became the first senior research fellow at the newly established institute in June 1963. He headed a research group, and then a laboratory, that studied X-ray diffraction and phase transition in solid state, one of the main research areas at the ISSP.[87] Evgenii Poniatovskii, also a graduate of MISiS, was a specialist in the physics of metals. He transferred to the ISSP from the Institute of Metallurgy and Metal Physics (part of the Central Scientific Research Institute of Ferrous Metallurgy in Moscow) directed by Kurdiumov. In the mid-1960s, Poniatovskii assisted Kurdiumov and Osipyan in designing the ISSP's research facilities, purchasing the most up-to-date equipment, and hiring new personnel. He also established a laboratory of high-pressure physics, which studied various impacts on solid matter, another main research agenda of the ISSP.[88] "State funding of science was splendid back then," Poniatovskii recollected in his interview. "We were able to purchase any equipment we needed and to install it here."[89] Moreover, Poniatovskii was given a free hand to hire his own staff.[90] His laboratory focused on studying the physical characteristics of metals and alloys under high pressure.

Apart from MISiS, Osipyan recruited many young scientists from the prestigious Institute of Physical Problems (IPP), which was headed by legendary Soviet scientist Petr Kapitsa. Located in Moscow, the institute was famous for its world-class research and luminaries such as Lev Landau and Kapitsa himself. Unfortunately, it was also notorious for Kapitsa's refusal to expand his institute or to hire new scientific personnel. Vsevolod Gantmakher worked at the IPP for five years as a laboratory assistant after he graduated from the Moscow Physical-Technical Institute (popularly known as *Fiztech*). He defended his "candidate of sciences" dissertation in 1964, but, despite Gantmakher's excellent scientific results, Kapitsa refused to make him a junior research fellow. "I was almost thirty years old, I was married and had a child, and it was hard to support my family on 105 rubles a month, which was a salary of a lab assistant," Gantmakher remembered. "I was born in Moscow and was reluctant to move away, but Osipyan was searching for employees for his new institute in Chernogolovka, and he offered outstanding conditions. This is how I ended up here."[91] Gantmakher was hired as a junior research fellow in 1964. He brought his family to the town several years later. At the ISSP, Gantmakher researched, among other problems, the new type of

[87] Interview 2 with Veniamin Shekhtman, Chernogolovka, March 2010; *Institut Fiziki Tverdogo Tela: 40 let*, ed. by L.P. Mezhov-Deglin (Moskva: Nauka, 2004), pp. 90–97, 246; Dubovitskii, *Nauchnyi Tsentr*, pp. 187–191.
[88] *Institut Fiziki Tverdogo Tela*, pp. 58–63; Dubovitskii, *Nauchnyi Tsentr*, pp. 212–214.
[89] Interview with Evgenii Poniatovskii, Chernogolovka, March 2010.
[90] *Institut Fiziki Tverdogo Tela*, p. 64.
[91] Interview with Vsevolod Gantmakher, Chernogolovka, March 2010; *Institut Fiziki Tverdogo Tela*, pp. 72–74; Dubovitskii, *Nauchnyi Tsentr*, pp. 182–183.

penetration of electromagnetic waves into metals in the magnetic field, which led him to his major discovery, known as "the Gantmakher effect." In 1972, he established his own laboratory in Chernogolovka. Leonid Mezhov-Deglin had a similar story to share. Also a graduate of Fiztech, he was finishing up an internship at Kapitsa's institute when Osipyan came there looking for young and talented scientists to work at the ISSP. "It was a true blessing for me," Mezhov-Deglin admitted. "I had neither work nor registration in Moscow, nor permanent housing. I was happy to accept Osipyan's invitation, which allowed me to break out of this vicious circle, and moved to Chernogolovka."[92] Mezhov-Deglin's research focused on low-temperature physics and liquid helium. He defended his dissertation in 1967.

For the ISSP, the arrival of these young, talented, and ambitious scientists was also a blessing. It allowed the institute to begin scientific research almost immediately, even though its main facilities were still under construction. For the first few years, the ISSP's employees worked at one of the buildings of the ICP Branch, where Semenov allocated 1,500 square meters to them. In 1968, they finally moved into their own research facilities located half a mile away from Semenov's institute in Chernogolovka. Addressing the meeting of the Presidium of the Academy of Sciences, which took place in the town on January 19, 1968, Kurdiumov quoted Petr Kapitsa, who argued that solid state physics was at the cutting edge of physical sciences at the time. "The postwar period made it clear that new, advanced materials were necessary to produce new technology and equipment," Kurdiumov stated.[93] "Only fundamental research on solid state physics can allow us to make significant progress in this area." To demonstrate the importance of his newly established institute for the development of the Soviet industry, Kurdiumov referenced the rapid expansion of solid state physics institutions in the United States in the 1950s.[94]

In 1965, the Council of Ministers approved another initiative of a group of young scientists asking to establish the Institute of Theoretical Physics (ITP) in Chernogolovka. Discussions about organizing the ITP had begun at the Presidium of the Academy as early as November 1963. The ITP was a product of the school of Lev Landau, a world-renowned theoretical physicist whose scientific activity had suddenly come to a halt after a terrible car accident two years earlier. Led by Landau's students, Isaak Khalatnikov and Alexei Abrikosov, the institute attracted dozens of talented theoretical physicists from across the Soviet Union. The idea behind its creation, supported by many leading academicians, including Kapitsa, was to locate the institute in a scientific center that combined various research institutes with a strong

[92] Interview 3 with Leonid Mezhov-Deglin, Chernogolovka, March 2011.
[93] ARAN, f. 2, op. 6, d. 688, 1.79.   [94] ARAN, f. 2, op. 6, d. 688, l. 79.

experimental base.[95] In the late 1960s and 1970s, the ITP focused on such problems of theoretical physics as electric characteristics of metals and semi-conductors, superconductivity and superfluidity, magnetism, and the theory of phase transition.[96] Some of the research carried out at the ITP at the time received world recognition only decades later. For example, Alexei Abrikosov was awarded a Nobel Prize in Physics in 2003 for his "pioneering contribution to the theory of superconductors and superfluids."

Nikolai Semenov welcomed the establishment of new institutes in Chernogolovka, as it promised to transform the unknown settlement into the interdisciplinary community he had envisioned. By 1968, the Noginsk Scientific Center had emerged as the principle complex within the Academy of Sciences that carried out fundamental research at the intersection of physics and chemistry. It included six research institutes which employed 2,296 scientists.[97] The Branch of the ICP and the ISSP were the most prominent among them, shaping the contours and character of Chernogolovka's scientific community. I will introduce members of this community individually in Chapter 2, which deals with family backgrounds and the formation of Chernogolovka scientists.

On March 25, 1922, Nikolai Semenov wrote to his friend, Petr Kapitsa, who worked at the Cavendish Laboratory at Cambridge University at the time: "I am not giving too much significance to our work; I consider us to be merely fertilizer for the next generation that will create true science in Russia, a living science with plenty of discoveries and inventions."[98] Semenov's idealism, suppressed during the late 1930s and 1940s when the Stalinist utilitarian vision of science prevailed, came to the fore during the Thaw era. Unlike Stalin, who was forced to tolerate limited intellectual autonomy among a small group of nuclear scientists to get the bomb,[99] Khrushchev based his science policy on the premise that the majority of the scientific intelligentsia could be trusted. Scientists could, in fact, advance the political and ideological objectives of the state. In the late 1950s and 1960s, Khrushchev extended the autonomy that only select scientists enjoyed under his predecessor to the rest of the scientific community, empowering scientists to take initiatives and pursue their own visions. Leading members of the Academy of Sciences, such as Semenov, responded enthusiastically to the new political climate. Semenov interpreted the Thaw as an invitation to go back to the practices of the 1920s, when scientists enjoyed greater autonomy from the state, to carry out his own vision.

[95] ARAN, f. 2, op. 6, d. 471, ll. 115–116.   [96] ARAN, f. 2, op. 6, d. 688, l. 94.
[97] ARAN, f. 2, op. 6, d. 688, l. 61.   [98] *Kapitsa, Tamm, Semenov*, pp. 484–485.
[99] Holloway, *Stalin and the Bomb*, p. 366.

The unusual conditions under which Chernogolovka came into existence also point to other, equally important developments of the Thaw: the uncertain and contradictory nature of Khrushchev's reforms, on the one hand, and the heightened popular expectations, on the other hand.[100] It is highly unlikely that Semenov would have ventured to transform a military-oriented testing ground into an interdisciplinary scientific center in an earlier or later period of Soviet history. His initiative, nonetheless, seemed natural in the uneven and rapidly changing atmosphere of the Thaw. While the new Soviet leadership expected scientists to solve the economic and social problems of the Soviet Union, scientists like Semenov were not afraid to take the initiative and to test the limits of their newly gained professional autonomy. That Semenov decided to rely on his patronage network indicates that he was probably well aware of the uncertain nature of the period. An experienced administrator, he did not want to leave the realization of his project to the good graces of the Communist Party. Semenov chose, instead, to interpret the Thaw to fit his own scientific vision, and to adapt to the changing political climate along the way.

Finally, the idealistic optimism of the first generation of Chernogolovka scientists played a crucial role in the success of Semenov's enterprise. Vladimir Enman and thousands of his young peers enthusiastically embraced the outstanding opportunities that the Thaw offered to the scientific intelligentsia. Many shared the idealism of the Khrushchev regime, and were eager to participate in building some kind of socialism in the Soviet Union, cleansed of Stalin's crimes. While they did not aspire to change the political system in the USSR, "the Thaw generation" of Soviet scientists pushed the boundaries of what was allowed in a highly authoritarian and centralized Soviet state, through their daily interactions with the regime. Let us, then, meet these young and ambitious people and explore their life trajectories before they came to the town.

---

[100] Jones, ed., *The Dilemmas of De-Stalinization*, p. 14; Bittner, *The Many Lives of Khrushchev's Thaw*, pp. 3–4; Jones, *Myth, Memory, and Trauma*, p. 11; and Andrews and Siddiqi, eds., *Into the Cosmos*, p. 76.

2 Children of the Great Patriotic War: The Formation of Soviet Scientists, 1930–1955

"I was not recruited as a soldier during the war – but I felt that I was a soldier of another war, the scientific-technical war."

Andrei Sakharov, *Vospominaniia*, T. 1

It is impossible to understand the idealistic optimism of the first generation of Chernogolovka scientists without taking a close look at the miserable conditions of their childhood and adolescence. Rimma Liubovskaia, for example, lost her father during the Great Patriotic War, as World War II is often referred to in Russia. Nikolai Stepanov, a salesman in the village Aleksandrovskoe of the Stavropol' region, was drafted into the Red Army in 1942. He was killed in the Crimea one-and-a-half years later. The five-year-old Rimma, her mother, and her older brother lived under German occupation for several dreadful months. When the war ended, the family suffered so badly from famine they decided to move to Central Asia where they had some relatives. "We starved even worse there," Liubovskaia recollected in her interview. "My mother, a teacher by profession, had to take a job at an asbestos factory. The factory gave us a room in a communal apartment with no furniture except a sheet of asbestos fiber, which we used as our bed."[1] Despite this misery, Liubovskaia was confident that one day she would go study in Moscow. An exemplary student, she made her way to the Soviet capital in the summer of 1954, enrolling in the Mendeleev Institute of Chemical Technology. Back then, Liubovskaia admitted, she never thought she would become a scientist. She passionately desired to receive a higher education, however, since it was her only way out of postwar deprivation and suffering.

Liubovskaia's story was a common one for postwar Soviet youth. Like millions of other children born in the 1930s, she lost her father during World War II and was raised by her mother, who had to work long days to provide the family with basic material comfort. Like millions of others, she grew up in abject poverty, characteristic of the postwar USSR. Similar to many of her peers, Liubovskaia perceived the extreme hardship she experienced during the war and the immediate postwar years as something normal. A product of the

[1] Interview 1 with Rimma Liubovskaia, Chernogolovka, October 2010.

Stalinist education system, as a child she believed that she had been born in the most advanced country in the world and was grateful to Joseph Stalin for her "happy childhood." The Soviet victory of 1945 convinced her even further that the USSR was a country of enormous possibilities, and she was eager to work hard to capitalize on them.[2] "Since we were victorious in such a terrible war, we believed that we could do anything," another Chernogolovka scientist, Georgii Manelis, remembered. "We thought that we just had to work harder, and everything would come together. This was the leitmotif of our generation."[3]

This chapter examines the formation of Chernogolovka scientists: their upbringing in the 1930s, their wartime experiences, and their decision to join the ranks of the Soviet scientific elite. I show that it was the Great Patriotic War, not the Great Terror of the 1930s, that played the critical role in scientists' formation. When the war began, the majority of Chernogolovka scientists were too young to be drafted: the oldest were only thirteen years old. But they were old enough to remember the war as an all-encompassing tragedy. For most scientists, the war brought material deprivation, hasty evacuation, hunger, and even starvation. It interrupted their schooling and destroyed their homes. The war effectively ended their childhoods. Yet the Great Patriotic War also provided the moral framework for much of this generation.[4] Its extraordinary brutality helped shape the identities of these young Soviet intellectuals, turning them into loyal citizens and patriots of the USSR. The memories of collective pain and suffering that Chernogolovka scientists endured during the wartime years enhanced their commitment to the Soviet project, its values, and its ideology. My argument challenges Juliane Fürst's contention about the decline in ideological commitment among postwar Soviet youth.[5] There were few cynics among the town's first residents. A shared Communist outlook and a belief in the progressive development of Soviet society on a scientific basis, not consumption, remained the primary identifier for these young people.

The Great Patriotic War was also a significant factor in Chernogolovka scientists' choice of profession. Many believed that the Soviet victory was a result of the immense technical progress that the USSR underwent in the 1930s. Getting a higher technical or scientific education became these people's motto. It was their chance to fit into postwar Soviet society, to fulfill their ambitions, and to secure better lives for themselves and their children. The Cold War was another part of the story. In the late 1940s, young people's

[2] On the sparkling optimism of postwar Soviet youth, see Zubok, *Zhivago's Children*, pp. 29, 34–36.

[3] Interview 1 with Georgii Manelis, Chernogolovka, December 2009.

[4] Fürst, *Stalin's Last Generation*, pp. 61–62. Elena Zubkova argues that "the social psychology of the war years shaped all of postwar life." See Zubkova, *Russia after the War*, p. 12.

[5] Fürst, *Stalin's Last Generation*, pp. 3, 6. By contrast, Vladislav Zubok points to the socialist idealism of the postwar Soviet generation, in Zubok, *Zhivago's Children*, pp. 24, 34.

yearning for higher education coincided with the great deficit of educated professionals in the Soviet Union. Reacting to this deficit, the Stalinist state increased salaries for university professors and embarked on a massive expansion of higher learning.[6] Since the regime considered scientists to be crucial to building up the military–industrial complex and enhancing the Soviet economy, it invested heavily in training scientific personnel. In 1947, the Physical and Technical Department was founded at Moscow State University to train specialists in nuclear physics, chemical physics, radio engineering, and other critically important sciences. Four years later, this privileged department was transformed into the famous Moscow Physical-Technical Institute, or Fiztech, which soon became one the most elite institutes for scientific education in the Soviet Union.

The unprecedented prestige of science, as well as Soviet achievements in nuclear research and space exploration, ignited the imagination of postwar Soviet youth. By the early 1950s, physicists and chemists became the most sought-after professionals. For many of my interviewees, this opened up myriad opportunities that their parents had not had. Becoming a scientist allowed them to have a well-paying and highly respected job, and to advance quickly in society. It also provided a sense of purpose to these young intellectuals, eager to partake in the advances of modern science, on the one hand, and to contribute to building a just and egalitarian society, on the other. During the Thaw, thousands of scientists and engineers graduated from Soviet universities, easily finding employment, including in the scientific towns that rapidly sprouted across the Soviet Union. Chernogolovka, in this respect, was representative of a general pattern. Let us now examine the formative years of the town's first residents.

Growing Up in the Soviet Union During the 1930s

Leonid Mezhov-Deglin was born in late December 1937, ten days before his father's execution. His father, Pavel Mezhov, was an ardent supporter of the Russian Revolution and a beneficiary of the upward social mobility of the early Stalin era.[7] At thirty-seven, he occupied a leading position at the Giprokoks Trust, which supervised by-product plants construction in Soviet Ukraine. The family enjoyed luxury accommodations in one of the elite buildings in the center of Khar'kov, as well as a number of other privileges. As the Revolution began to devour its children during the mass repressions of the

[6] Tromly, *Making the Soviet Intelligentsia*, p. 3.
[7] On upward social mobility, see Sheila Fitzpatrick, *Everyday Stalinism: Ordinary Life in Extraordinary Times: Soviet Russia in the 1930s* (New York: Oxford University Press, 1999), pp. 85–87.

late 1930s, Mezhov became an immediate target for elimination.[8] He was accused of sabotaging blast-furnace production, arrested, beaten, and shot dead on January 8, 1938. "When they came to arrest my father," Mezhov-Deglin recalled in his interview, "he had a loaded gun on him. He could have defended himself, but then they would have killed my pregnant mother and my older brother. He put down the gun and opened the door, although he knew what was coming."[9] After Mezhov's arrest, his family was evicted from their apartment to the basement.[10] All their personal belongings, including furniture, were confiscated from them. Leonid's mother, a chemical engineer by profession, was fired from her job. To support the family, she took a position as a shift engineer at a chemical cooperative (*khimicheskaia artel'*), working at night to avoid further repressions.

In spite of this personal tragedy, Leonid grew up thinking that he had a wonderful, happy childhood. For one thing, his mother concealed from him the fact of his father's arrest until after the rehabilitation papers arrived in 1957. She simply told Leonid his father was killed at the front. For another, the intensive political indoctrination that took place in Soviet nurseries, kindergartens, and schools helped Mezhov-Deglin identify with the values of the Soviet state. Decades later, even after the Soviet collapse, he still genuinely believed that there was nowhere in the world where children lived as well as they did in Stalin's Russia. "As a child, I had access to various study groups and recreation facilities, including summer camps. It was all free and available to us, although my family was extremely poor."[11] Ironically, for the rest of his life Mezhov-Deglin remained grateful to the Soviet regime for these incredible opportunities. The son of an "enemy of the people," he was convinced that he owed his personal success and achievements to the benevolence of the omnipotent state.[12]

The myth of a "happy childhood" was one of the most powerful propaganda devices in the USSR. "Even those who had serious reservations about Soviet policy in other ways," Catriona Kelly argues, used the humane treatment of children "as a proof to themselves that the system was not all bad."[13] According

---

[8] On the repressions among the Bolshevik party officials, see Robert Conquest, *Great Terror: A Reassessment* (New York: Oxford University Press, 1990), pp. 227–233; and Applebaum, *Gulag*, pp. 94–98.

[9] Interview 1 with Leonid Mezhov-Deglin, Chernogolovka, March 2010.

[10] In the 1930s, it was customary for authorities to confiscate all or part of a family's living space when a member of that family was arrested. See Katherine B. Eaton, *Daily Life in the Soviet Union* (Westport: Greenwood Press, 2004), p. 157.

[11] Interview 3 with Leonid Mezhov-Deglin, Chernogolovka, March 2011.

[12] On the Stalinist "economy of the gift," see Jeffrey Brooks, *Thank you, Comrade Stalin!: Soviet Public Culture from Revolution to Cold War* (Princeton: Princeton University Press, 2000), pp. 83–84.

[13] Catriona Kelly, *Children's World: Growing up in Russia, 1890–1991* (New Haven: Yale University Press, 2007), p. 111.

to the official propaganda, the happiness of every child was guaranteed by the Soviet state itself. In return, the paternalist state expected children, and later adults, to be obedient citizens, eternally grateful to the Soviet leadership, and especially to the beloved leader, Comrade Stalin.[14] The vast majority of Chernogolovka scientists internalized this myth from an early age. Many admitted they thought they were extremely lucky to have been born in the Soviet Union, a country that allegedly offered equal opportunities to all its citizens. Scientists' oral histories abound with memories of direct and indirect participation in celebrating the cult of Stalin.[15] Some recalled walking on stage to read a poem thanking Stalin for a happy childhood. Others confessed to having decorated their shabby rooms in communal apartments with Stalin's portraits.

Did Chernogolovka scientists, born at the height of Stalin's repressions, indeed have happy childhoods, or did their memory play a trick on them, highlighting the bright episodes of their early lives and suppressing the bleak ones? First, it appears that social background and parents' occupation were critical for determining what kind of childhood one would have. For example, children of higher-up party functionaries were more likely to have suffered from persecution in the mid- to late 1930s than children of workers, peasants, or the new Soviet intelligentsia. Second, adults also seem to have put enormous efforts into protecting their children from potentially painful experiences, even though at times securing normal lives for their families came at exceedingly high cost. What did the social composition of the town's scientific intelligentsia look like?

Chernogolovka's first residents came from diverse social backgrounds. Children of party officials and military men, engineers and university professors, peasants and workers, ended up working side by side at research institutes of the emerging scientific center. In the 1920s and early 1930s, most of their parents were captivated by the transformative potential of the Russian Revolution, and strove hard to inscribe their lives into a larger revolutionary narrative.[16] Many felt inspired by the extraordinary educational and professional opportunities that the new Soviet state offered, and enthusiastically dedicated their young lives to building the world's first socialist society.[17]

---

[14] Kelly contends that "from 1936 especially, the notion that children owed their perfectly happy childhood to the Soviet leadership was to become one of the central tenets of propaganda, aimed both at the Soviet population and at potential supporters abroad"; in Kelly, *Children's World*, p. 1.

[15] For an extended analysis of scientists' relationship with the Soviet state and ideology, see Chapter 4, "Scientists, Ideology, and the Communist Party in Chernogolovka."

[16] Jochen Hellbeck, *Revolution on My Mind: Writing a Diary Under Stalin* (Cambridge: Harvard University Press, 2006), p. 9.

[17] Stephen Kotkin, *Magnetic Mountain: Stalinism as a Civilization* (Berkeley: University of California Press, 1995), pp. 6–7, 12–14.

Not all of them, however, enjoyed equal success. Among my interviewees, as well as Mezhov-Deglin, several other scientists had also lost their parents in the purges. Vladimir Enman was one of them. His father, Karl Enman, joined the ranks of the Red Army during the Civil War, and had a distinguished career as a Soviet military officer. In 1934, he was appointed head of the Department of Firing Instruction (*kafedra ognevoi podgotovki*) at the Red Army Academy of Mechanization and Motorization in Moscow. The Enmans resided in a luxury two-room apartment in one of the buildings occupied by the command staff of the People's Commissariat of Defense in Lefortovo.[18] The family's fortune, though, did not last long: on June 12, 1938, Karl Enman was arrested as part of the Tukhachevskii affair.[19] He was executed three months later, on September 27, 1938, together with seventy-seven other high-ranking officers of the Red Army.[20] Vladimir was only ten years old when this happened. The arrest and the search took place at night, when he was asleep. "I learned about my father's arrest by accident," he remembered. "I was playing outside with local boys and one of them called me 'a son of the enemy of the people.'" Shortly after his father's execution, Vladimir, his mother, grandmother, and three sisters were evicted from their housing in Lefortovo and squeezed into one room of a communal apartment located in the basement. Vladimir's older sister left high school and started working to save the family from starvation. "I don't know how we managed to survive," Enman admitted. "At least we were fortunate to have been allowed to stay in Moscow."[21]

One did not have to be a visible political, administrative, or military figure to be targeted in the Great Terror. As Catherine Merridale rightly observes, the threat of arbitrariness was integral to the Stalinist system.[22] Evgenii Poniatovskii, another scientist whose father perished in the 1930s, was born into a family of engineers. Both of his parents worked at the Central Telegraph Office in Moscow. In 1938, Evgenii's father was arrested, purportedly because of his Polish origins. His last name was Polish and this was enough for the Soviet authorities to suspect him, even though he had never left the Soviet Union. "At the time, they were purging the Poles, Estonians, Latvians, getting ready to sign the Molotov-Ribbentrop Pact," Poniatovskii explained. Unlike the other two families, Evgenii and his mother were not evicted from their apartment. Moreover, Poniatovskii's mother was allowed to continue working at the Central Telegraph Office. "After all, my father was only an ordinary

[18] Interview 1 with Vladimir Enman, Chernogolovka, August 2009.
[19] Mikhail Tukhachevskii was one of the first Marshals of the Soviet Union, and in the 1930s played a central role in modernizing the Red Army. He was arrested in May 1937 by Stalin's order, accused of espionage and high treason, and executed in June 1937.
[20] "Spravka V.K. Enmana," in Enman's family archive.
[21] Interview 1 with Vladimir Enman, Chernogolovka, August 2009.
[22] Merridale, *Night of Stone*, p. 201.

engineer. I think relatives of the higher-ups had to suffer more."[23] It was a matter of chance, of course, that Mezhov-Deglin, Enman, and Poniatovskii survived the repressions, as millions of their less fortunate peers were sent to the Gulag.[24]

The vast majority of Chernogolovka scientists, however, did not experience the Great Terror firsthand. Even though the process of mass repressions was basically unlimited, their parents were lucky enough to be spared. Children of workers and the new Soviet intelligentsia represented the two largest categories from which the first Cold War generation of Soviet scientists emerged.[25] Aleksandr Shilov, for example, was born in 1930 into the family of a prominent Soviet chemist, Evgenii Shilov. His father was a Professor of Chemistry at the Ivanovo Institute of Chemistry and Technology and a well-respected scientist, whose research on bleaching technology made an important contribution to the Soviet textile industry.[26] "I know it was a dark time for Russia," Shilov admitted. "But for me and my family it went unnoticed."[27] Shilov's future colleague at the ICP Branch, Georgii Manelis, grew up in the academic environment, too. Both of his parents were university professors in Tashkent. "Mine was a typical Soviet family," Manelis recalled. It was largely thanks to the Revolution, he was convinced, that a Ukrainian Jew from Vinnytsia and a daughter of an Ural Cossack could start a family, receive a higher education, and pursue academic careers. Yet, Manelis recognized that the only reason his parents were spared in the 1930s was that they lived in Tashkent, far away from the Soviet capital.[28] Manelis's wife, Nina Konovalova, shared many of the same experiences growing up. Her parents graduated from Tashkent University and went on to research and teach economics. The family occupied two rooms of a communal apartment in the center of Tashkent. "I cannot say that we were a well-off family. We lived a modest life, but there was always something to eat in the house. My parents always managed to give me 10 kopeks so that I could buy myself an 'Eskimo' ice-cream."[29] Just like her husband, as a child, Nina was protected by her parents from the dreadful experiences of the 1930s.

---

[23] Interview with Evgenii Poniatovskii, Chernogolovka, March 2010.

[24] On the fate of children of "enemies of the people," see Cathy A. Frierson and Semyon S. Vyslensky, *Children of the Gulag* (New Haven: Yale University Press, 2010) and Figes, *The Whisperers*. For personal accounts of the impact of the Great Terror on children, see Owen Matthews, *Stalin's Children: Three Generations of Love, War, and Survival* (New York: Walker & Company, 2008) and Inna Shikheeva-Gaister, *Deti vragov naroda: Semeinaia khronika vremen kul'ta lichnosti* (Tenafly, NJ: Hermitage Publishers, 2003).

[25] Nicholas De Witt, *Education and Professional Employment in the USSR* (Washington DC: National Science Foundation, 1961), p. 351.

[26] "Khimiia i zhizn' akademika Shilova," in *Chernogolovskaia gazeta*, January 14, 2010; Kukushkin, "Celebration of Inorganic Lives," p. 1.

[27] Interview 1 with Aleksandr Shilov, Chernogolovka, March 2010.

[28] Interview 2 with Georgii Manelis, Chernogolovka, December 2010.

[29] Interview with Nina Konovalova, Chernogolovka, March 2011.

A substantial number of Chernogolovka's first residents came from a working-class background. Many grew up in poverty, but managed to enjoy a "happy childhood" even at the height of Stalin's terror as their parents remained unscathed. Gennadii Bogdanov was born in Bryansk in 1934. His parents had no formal education, and were employed at the Bryansk Machine-Building Factory: his father as a rate-setter, his mother as a shipping agent. Before the war, the Bogdanovs occupied a room in a barrack on the outskirts of Bryansk. The barrack had neither hot water nor central heating; the bathroom was located outside.[30] Rimma Shibaeva also remembered growing up in a dreary workers' settlement outside of Murom. Both of her parents were factory workers. After Rimma's father left when she was fourteen, her mother had to raise Rimma and her younger sister by herself. "We all shared a small room in a communal apartment," Shibaeva recalled. "We lived poorly, but my mother worked extremely hard to support me and my sister and to allow us to receive a secondary education."[31] Lev Vashin's family was slightly better-off. His father came from a large and poor peasant family, but benefited greatly from the Revolution. Having graduated from special training courses organized by the Komsomol, he worked as a teacher, and then as a school director later in life. As far as Vashin could remember, his father managed to provide a decent living for the family both before and after the war.[32]

The fact that most Chernogolovka scientists did not experience the repressions firsthand does not mean that they knew nothing about them. Ernest Suvorov's grandmother lost almost all her relatives in 1937. Although she never mentioned it to her grandson, she once took him to prison to visit her sister, an elderly woman who had been arrested for one imprudent comment about Stalin. "I was barely ten then, and I could not figure out why my grandmother would take me there. I began to understand it only when I grew up: she wanted me to see this with my own eyes and to remember it for life."[33] Manelis stated that he did not hear about the Gulag as a child. But he knew that one of his uncles had been executed in 1937. "My parents did not even mention this at home. I just knew that he was 'taken away' [*ego vziali*]."[34] Konovalova grew up in a relatively secure environment, but she was well aware that both of her uncles had been repressed. Moreover, she knew that her father kept a suitcase with basic personal belongings under his bed and that "he was constantly expecting the arrest."[35] Bogdanov's parents were ordinary workers and managed to avoid repressions. However, his grandmother told him that three out of

[30] Interview 1 with Gennadii Bogdanov, Chernogolovka, September 2009.
[31] Interview 1 with Rimma Shibaeva, Chernogolovka, October 2010.
[32] Interview 1 with Lev Vashin, Chernogolovka, March 2010.
[33] Interview 1 with Ernest Suvorov, Chernogolovka, August 2010.
[34] Interview 1 with Georgii Manelis, Chernogolovka, December 2009.
[35] Interview with Nina Konovalova, Chernogolovka, March 2011.

her five sons had been arrested and shot in the mid-1930s as part of the Leningrad affair.[36] Vashin came from a peasant background, but during one of his visits to a Belorussian village he witnessed the arrest of his aunt's husband.[37]

What did the young children make of these obscure rumors back then? While most of my interviewees had only vague recollections of the Great Terror, it is important to remind ourselves that in the late 1930s fear was present in most Soviet families' lives. Parents were too afraid to talk about the purges at home, and usually kept them secret from their own children.[38] "It was dangerous to talk about politics during that dreadful time," Vladimir Zakharov explained.[39] "Our parents did not mention these topics in conversations with us. It was considered unacceptable to talk to children about repressions," Manelis echoed. "You should understand that this was a time when everyone feared for their children, and at the end of the day did not really tell them anything," Liubovskaia confirmed.[40] While some parents were too fearful to talk, others were physically unable to communicate their political views to their children. Many had barely any time to spend with their children at all, working for their families' survival. This was especially true in households where fathers perished during the repressions and mothers were forced to become the sole providers. Finally, like many ordinary people at the time, parents of many Chernogolovka scientists chose not to know, closing their eyes and ears to the depressing rumors of mass executions around them.[41]

One consequence of this was that children often did not know what their parents thought about life in the Soviet Union. "The relationship between our generation and theirs was broken," Rustem Liubovskii reflected. "We did not ask them any questions, and they were too afraid to talk anyways."[42] Even decades later, many scientists could not remember whether their parents supported the Bolshevik regime, and if so, to what degree. Most of my interviewees simply did not know what their parents thought of Stalin's leadership or how they interpreted mass disappearances of their relatives, friends, and colleagues. This lack of communication seemed normal at the time. In Stalin's Russia, it was too dangerous to voice a dissenting opinion, as all manifestations of discontent were stigmatized as "outbursts of the class

---

[36] Interview 2 with Gennadii Bogdanov, Chernogolovka, December 2009.
[37] Interview 1 with Lev Vashin, Chernogolovka, March 2010.
[38] Figes, *The Whisperers*, p. 255; Merridale, *Night of Stone*, p. 7; Alexeyeva and Goldberg, *The Thaw Generation*, p. 14.
[39] Interview 1 with Vladimir Zakharov, Chernogolovka, July 2009.
[40] Interview 1 with Rimma Liubovskaia, Chernogolovka, October 2010.
[41] For an enlightening discussion of the atmosphere against which the Great Terror came unraveled, see Merridale, *Night of Stone*, pp. 198–202.
[42] Interview 2 with Rustem Liubovskii, Chernogolovka, February 2011.

enemy."[43] Moreover, parents themselves – indoctrinated, silenced, and terrorized – usually did not know what to make of the mass arrests and executions of
the late 1930s.[44] It appears that those who did not fully support the regime kept
their doubts to themselves. Oleg Efimov, for example, remembered his mother
taking down Stalin's portrait after he had put it on the wall in his room. She did
not explain why she did it, but this incident made Efimov wonder about his
parents' political views.[45] Yet, he never thought about asking his mother
directly.

Another factor to take into account is the young age of the Chernogolovka
interviewees. Vladimir Enman, born in 1928, was only ten when his father was
executed. Lev Vashin was nine when he witnessed his uncle's arrest. The rest of
Chernogolovka scientists were even younger during the mass repressions. How
much could children make of political events that were not even part of the
official public discourse? As parents avoided dangerous discussions at home,
children were vulnerable to the propaganda that pervaded every sphere of
Soviet society, including the media, education, and culture. Many remained
oblivious to the high price their parents had to pay for preserving the myth of
a "happy childhood." Yet adults could not save their offspring from the horrors
of World War II that began to consume the Soviet Union on June 22, 1941.
The war overshadowed scientists' experiences of the 1930s, and became the
major event that shaped their identities. The war inflicted unprecedented
suffering on future scientists, and prompted them to think for the first time
about their place in Soviet society.

Suffering and Survival During the Great Patriotic War

"I became self-conscious on August 23, 1942, when the Germans began carpet
bombing the city of Stalingrad," Sergei Mileiko, a senior researcher at the ISSP,
recollected. Mileiko was born near Stalingrad in 1935. After the Nazi invasion,
both of his parents, land surveyors (*zemlemery*) by profession, were mobilized
to build defensive works around Stalingrad. The family had to stay in the
besieged city.[46] The seven-year-old Sergei and his younger brother were

[43] Sarah Davies, *Public Opinion in Stalin's Russia: Terror, Propaganda, and Dissent, 1934–1941*
      (New York: Cambridge University Press, 1997), p. 4.
[44] Stephen Lovell notes that "Russia has never had a true moral reckoning with the catastrophes of
      collectivization and terror"; in Stephen Lovell, *The Shadow of War: Russia and the USSR, 1941
      to the Present* (Chichester; Malden: Wiley-Blackwell, 2010), p. 1. Catherine Merridale argues
      that "a fifty-year public silence has left them [the survivors] without the collective framework
      that is needed to contain debate," in Merridale, *Night of Stone*, p. 189.
[45] Interview 1 with Oleg Efimov, Chernogolovka, March 2011.
[46] On the Battle of Stalingrad, see Merridale, *Ivan's War*, pp. 172–179. For a military history of the
      siege of Stalingrad, see Antony Beevor, *Stalingrad* (New York: Viking, 1998). See also Jochen
      Hellbeck, *Stalingrad: The City That Defeated the Third Reich*, transl. by Christopher Tauchen
      (New York: PublicAffairs, 2015).

enrolled in a kindergarten, while their baby sister had to go to a round-the-clock day-care, where she eventually died. "After my sister's death, my mother was unable to continue working. In early September, my father was allowed to leave work for one day to evacuate his family from Stalingrad. He had to go back, but my mother, brother and I spent the winter of 1942–1943 in Vladimirovka, a village on the other side of the Volga River." Mileiko remembered that the entire winter he and his brother carved wooden planes out of logs and put them everywhere in the house. "Why planes, you would ask? Because these two weeks under German air strikes revealed that Stalingrad was totally helpless and unable to defend itself. These two weeks defined my future choice of profession. Both my brother and I went to aeronautical institutes for higher education. Like many people of our generation, we were determined to never let this kind of catastrophe happen again."[47]

Forty thousand people were killed during the first week of German air strikes in Stalingrad, remembered so vividly by Mileiko. Among them there were thousands of civilians and refugees fleeing eastward across the Volga.[48] Within the first few days of the attack, Stalingrad was turned into rubble. "There is not a single green twig on the tree; everything has perished in the flames," a Soviet general wrote years later about the battleground.[49] While few of Mileiko's colleagues witnessed such brutality firsthand, many had their own painful recollections of their wartime experiences, and their own stories to share. For many children, Juliane Fürst argues, "the war had not been the heroic endeavor that soon emerged as the Soviet meta-narrative. Loss, injury, injustice, and brutality dominated the memory of many youngsters."[50]

It has been estimated that the Great Patriotic War destroyed about 30 percent of Soviet national wealth. When the war was over, many of the country's most developed areas lay in ruins, including 32,000 industrial enterprises, 65,000 kilometers of railway, and housing for 25 million people.[51] The Soviet human losses were even more terrifying. The war cost the Soviet Union over 27 million people, of which approximately 76 percent were men born between 1901 and 1931 – the most capable contingent of the male population.[52] It deprived millions of children of their fathers, creating a generation that grew up in extreme hardship and had to struggle for survival from an early age.

When the war began, the majority of Chernogolovka scientists were too young to be drafted. Georgii Manelis and Lev Vashin were among the oldest in June 1941, yet they were only eleven and twelve years old respectively. Some of the younger scientists, such as Leonid Mezhov-Deglin or Rustem Liubovskii, born in 1937 and 1938, had barely turned three or four years old.

[47] Interview 1 with Sergei Mileiko, Chernogolovka, August 2010.
[48] Beevor, *Stalingrad*, p. 106.   [49] Merridale, *Ivan's War*, p. 173.
[50] Fürst, *Stalin's Last Generation*, p. 34.   [51] Lovell, *The Shadow of War*, p. 2.
[52] Zubkova, *Russia after the War*, p. 20.

Most of their memories, therefore, provide evidence of how Soviet children perceived and experienced the war. The vast majority of my interviewees had to relocate with their parents to the eastern parts of the Soviet Union, while only a few were able to stay in their homes. Some had to start working in their early teenage years to provide for themselves and their families. In spite of this, they never had enough to eat, and some endured actual starvation.[53] Material deprivation, evacuation, air raids, and hunger were common themes in most scientists' memories of the war.

Those interviewees who ended up in the Nazi occupied territories naturally suffered worse that those who lived to the east of Moscow. Rimma Liubovskaia's most poignant memory of the war goes back to the winter of 1943, several months after Aleksandrovskoe was occupied by the Germans. "One day they found a dead German officer in front of our house," she recalled. "It was announced that one hundred people from our neighborhood would be shot in retaliation; my mother, brother and I among them." Liubovskaia remembered that the Germans brought all of them to the edge of the village where there was a statue of Lenin. "They dug the statue out and made a large pit in its place. They said they were going to bury people there. Everyone was terrified, of course, but then the Germans somehow found out that the officer died a natural death, and they let us go." Liubovskaia also remembered the bombing of the village, the German troops' retreating, and the burning down of houses in Aleksandrovskoe. "I guess these were very powerful memories. They have stayed with me ever since."[54]

Gennadii Bogdanov knew that the war had begun when German planes began bombing Bryansk in the summer of 1941:

I was at home, and all of a sudden a bomb exploded in a small park right next to our barrack. I was seven years old, a small kid, and the blast wave knocked me off my feet and threw me against the wall. I also remember how Soviet troops stopped in our park on their way to the front, because they had a field kitchen out there, and made buckwheat soup with canned stewed meat [*tushenka*]. It was so tasty that I have liked it for the rest of my life.[55]

Gennadii's father was soon drafted and dispatched to the front. He managed to evacuate his family to Voroshilovgrad[56] shortly before Bryansk was occupied in October 1941:

---

[53] Donald Filtzer, "Standard of Living Versus Quality of Life: Struggling with the Urban Environment in Russia during the Early Years of Post-war Reconstruction," in Juliane Fürst, ed., *Late Stalinist Russia: Society Between Reconstruction and Reinvention* (London and New York: Routledge, 2006), p. 81.

[54] Interview 1 with Rimma Liubovskaia, Chernogolovka, October 2010.

[55] Interview 1 with Gennadii Bogdanov, Chernogolovka, September 2009.

[56] Voroshilovgrad, or present-day Lugansk, is a city in the southeast of Ukraine.

We went on a train, and it was constantly bombed from the air. Every time my father grabbed me in his arms and ran into the field. Once, I remember, we stopped at Liski, which had been raided only a couple hours earlier. As I stepped off the train, I saw a torn child's leg in a sandal on the ground in front of me. It was so terrifying that I cried. This was my first real taste of war.[57]

While Mileiko, Liubovskaia, and Bogdanov witnessed wartime brutality and violence firsthand, most of my interviewees were evacuated to the country's interior, along with 16.5 million other displaced Soviet citizens.[58] Evacuation, however, was not always the lesser of two evils. The journey itself and life in evacuation were fraught with danger, as well as material and psychological difficulties.[59] It took Bogdanov and his mother almost two months to reach Omsk, as a freight train they traveled on had to let other trains carrying troops to the front pass first. During these two months, he recalled, they shared a plank bed with several dozen people.[60] Lev Vashin's family, residing in Kashira near Moscow before the war, set out to evacuate on foot. "There was a massive panic in Moscow on October 16, 1941, caused by the rumors that the Germans were close to the capital. We left Moscow two days later with the trade school where my father worked as a director." After having walked for three days straight, then taking a train, a barge, and a steamboat, the Vashins arrived in Gornoaltaisk, 2,400 miles to the east of Moscow, on December 22, 1941.[61]

Mezhov-Deglin's experiences in evacuation were, perhaps, the most striking. Khar'kov fell on October 24, 1941, several days after Leonid's family boarded the last train that broke out of the German encirclement. The train set out to Magnitogork in the Urals. "I was only three and a half years old, but I vividly remember the heated freight car in which we travelled. It was bright red inside, and bound with iron on the outside. I think the latter saved our lives: the train was constantly bombed from the air." The Deglins arrived in Magnitogorsk in November 1941. The family of eight was allocated one room in a barrack that had neither bathroom nor kitchen. "The barrack was full of children and we spent most days running around and screaming, while grown-ups were at work," Mezhov-Deglin recalled. There was a concentration camp one hundred meters away from the barrack, and every morning the children could see prisoners marching in and out. To save the family from starvation, Mezhov-Deglin's mother took a job as an engineer at the Magnitogorsk Metallurgical Complex. She was responsible for inspecting

---

[57] Interview 1 with Gennadii Bogdanov, Chernogolovka, September 2009.

[58] Rebecca Manley, *To the Tashkent Station: Evacuation and Survival in the Soviet Union at War* (Ithaca: Cornell University Press, 2009), p. 1.

[59] On the hardship of survival in evacuation, see Manley, *To the Tashkent Station*, Chapters 5 and 6.

[60] Interview 1 with Gennadii Bogdanov, Chernogolovka, September 2009.

[61] Interview 1 with Lev Vashin, Chernogolovka, March 2010.

gas inside a working blast furnace. "It was an extremely difficult job, which required much physical strength and courage. However, it was well paid, and with two children and parents to take care of she had no other choice." Leonid, his brother, and their two cousins were left to themselves. When he grew a bit older, Mezhov-Deglin was enrolled in a kindergarten, located half a kilometer away from his barrack. He walked there and back alone almost every day.[62]

Vladimir Enman and his family resided in Moscow before the war. Despite the panic in October 1941, they did not even consider evacuation, as they had nowhere to go and no one to ask for help. "My childhood was totally overshadowed by the war: how to find something to eat, how to survive ... Every day we listened intensely to reports coming from the front." Acute food shortages – and sometimes its complete absence – were some of the biggest ordeals Vladimir had to endure. Like many Soviet people during the war, the Enmans survived thanks to ration cards.[63] To be eligible for them, Vladimir had to leave school and start working at the age of fifteen:

I finished the fifth grade right before the war, but then in 1941–1942 all schools stopped functioning. When I went to the sixth grade in 1942, it was so cold inside our school building that we had to study in our winter clothes. And all we could think about was the little bread rolls that our teachers distributed for lunch every day.

In the fall of 1943, Vladimir dropped out of school and went to work at an auto-repair factory. In January 1944, he transferred to the factory next to his house to work as a locksmith's apprentice.[64]

Hunger tormented many Soviet children during the war. Oleg Efimov's family left Moscow for Ural'sk, a city in northwest Kazakhstan, in late July 1941. There they suffered so badly from poverty and malnutrition that they decided to come back to Moscow as soon as it became possible. Upon their arrival in 1943, Efimov and his family discovered that their apartment had already been occupied by another family. "We had some relatives in Moscow, and they let us stay with them. We lived somewhere in the basement, in terrible conditions. There was nothing to eat, except potato peels, which we grinded to make pancakes."[65] Rustem Liubovskii, whose parents had settled in the Caucasus shortly before the war, spent his childhood in Gagra, a city on the Black sea. Even though the Nazis never captured Gagra, they came very close and their proximity caused terrible hunger in the city. "We only survived thanks to fruit that grew in the south: figs and grapes. Also our house was located next to a road, and sometimes people on passing trucks threw sunflower cake

[62] Interview 1 with Leonid Mezhov-Deglin, Chernogolovka, March 2010.
[63] By 1945, the rationing system incorporated 80.6 million people, i.e. almost half of the postwar Soviet population. See Zubkova, *Russia After the War*, p. 41.
[64] Interview 1 with Vladimir Enman, Chernogolovka, August 2009.
[65] Interview 1 with Oleg Efimov, Chernogolovka, March 2011.

[*zhmykh ot podsolnechnika*] at us children, and we were very grateful."[66] Gennadii Bogdanov recollected how he once lost his ration cards during the war, and what a great tragedy it was for the family. "Rations cards were the main means to survive. But I was only ten years old and did not fully understand what this meant to my family."[67]

Aleksandr Shilov, Nina Konovalova, and Georgii Manelis, who came from an academic background and whose families lived far from the front line, also went hungry, but they did not face starvation. Konovalova remembered that there were always vegetables, including potatoes, in Tashkent, and that every day school children received a piece of rye bread and a small candy for extra nutrition.[68] Shilov's father had a professor's ration (*professorskii paek*) even during the war, which allowed the family to avoid starvation. Still, when his parents bought home grapes one day, it was "an outstanding event" for him.[69] Manelis's family hosted numerous relatives, who had evacuated from the western parts of the Soviet Union, at their apartment in Tashkent. Georgii, who was twelve years old at the time, recollected that in the fifth grade he and his classmates had to start working in the field, picking cotton, which the army needed. "Many children of my age began working. It was natural for us: the war was under way, and everyone lived like this."[70]

In May 1945, after four years of violence, hunger, and enormous human and material losses, the Great Patriotic War was over. The Soviet victory provoked mixed feelings. On the one hand, "the people's war" gave rise to massive patriotic sentiments and made Soviet citizens feel proud of their achievements.[71] "It seems to me that after the war we began to treat our country differently, with more affection," Konovalova remembered.[72] "We were the children of that war," Manelis agreed. "We grew up with the slogan 'Everything for the war! Everything for Victory!' and we took this very much to heart." "Can you imagine what the year 1945 meant to us? After all these hardships – Victory! We were enormously proud of it. This pride and the realization that 'we could do it' were very important to our generation."[73] Soviet victory made some Chernogolovka scientists into committed Stalinists, too, since they believed – in part due to official propaganda – that Stalin's

[66] Interview 1 with Rustem Liubovskii, Chernogolovka, December 2009; Interview 2 with Rustem Liubovskii, Chernogolovka, February 2011.
[67] Interview 1 with Gennadii Bogdanov, Chernogolovka, September 2009.
[68] Interview with Nina Konovalova, Chernogolovka, March 2011.
[69] Interview 1 with Aleksandr Shilov, Chernogolovka, March 2010.
[70] Interview 1 with Georgii Manelis, Chernogolovka, December 2009.
[71] Zubkova, *Russia After the War*, p. 32; Zubok, *Zhivago's Children*, p. 33; Fürst, *Stalin's Last Generation*, pp. 32–33; Merridale, *Night of Stone*, pp. 212–219; Jenks, *The Cosmonaut Who Couldn't Stop Smiling*, p. 38.
[72] Interview with Nina Konovalova, Chernogolovka, March 2011.
[73] Interview 1 with Geogrii Manelis, Chernogolovka, December 2009.

leadership played a crucial role in winning the war and saving the USSR from the Nazi invasion.[74]

On the other hand, the Soviet victory did not bring any immediate relief to the people exhausted by wartime poverty, deprivation, and suffering.[75] "These were rather dreary years, the years of 1945–1948," Ernest Suvorov recalled. "We still managed to survive only thanks to ration cards." Escaping postwar hunger, in 1947 Suvorov, his mother, and grandmother moved from Buzuluk in the Orenburg region to Tashkent. Tashkent struck Suvorov as an abundant city in comparison to poverty-stricken Buzuluk. Yet, the ten-year-old Ernest usually had to stand in lines to buy bread and other produce.[76] "A bread store opened only in the morning, but people queued up the night before. I remember they used an indelible ink to put a number on my hand, and I had to wait outside of the store all night in order to buy bread in the morning. My grandmother and my mother alternated with me."[77] People returning from evacuation often found their housing destroyed or occupied by strangers.[78] Oleg Efimov's experiences, unfortunately, were far from unique. After his family found their apartment in Moscow occupied, Efimov's mother had to work extremely hard to provide shelter and food for her two sons and mother.[79] Lana Ukrainka's family returned from evacuation in 1944 to find that their home village near Novomoskovsk in Ukraine had been demolished.[80] "When we came back," she recollected, "all that was left from our house was a tiny room and a hallway. The rest of the house had been burned down. My mother, brother and I moved into this remaining room. Postwar Ukraine was a hungry, cold and dangerous place."[81]

For some Chernogolovka scientists, the postwar period presented even more severe challenges than the war itself. Rimma Liubovskaia, who had survived the German occupation and had nearly been executed at the age of five, remembered the years 1946–1947 as "the most difficult and hungriest time." In 1946, a severe drought broke out in much of the European part of the Soviet

---

[74] Zubkova, *Russia After the War*, p. 28.

[75] Zubkova, *Russia After the War*, pp. 20–21; Lovell, *The Shadow of War*, p. 3; Fürst, *Stalin's Last Generation*, pp. 41–43; Filtzer, "Standard of Living Versus Quality of Life," pp. 81–82; Ann Livschiz, "Children's Lives After Zoia's Death: Order, Emotions and Heroism in Children's Lives and Literature in the Post-war Soviet Union," in Fürst, ed., *Late Stalinist Russia*, p. 193.

[76] One line could consist of eight hundred people or more. See Zubkova, *Russia After the War*, p. 50.

[77] Interview 1 with Ernest Suvorov, Chernogolovka, August 2010.

[78] Manley, *To the Tashkent Station*, pp. 255–261; Filtzer, "Standard of Living Versus Quality of Life," pp. 84–85.

[79] Interview 1 with Oleg Efimov, Chernogolovka, March 2011.

[80] See, for example, Karel Berkhoff, *Harvest of Despair: Life and Death in Ukraine Under Nazi Rule* (Cambridge: The Belknap Press of Harvard University Press, 2004).

[81] Interview 1 with Lana Ukrainka, Chernogolovka, September 2010.

Union, causing a bad harvest failure.[82] As a result, the 1946 grain crop was only 39.6 million tons, in comparison to 47.3 million tons in 1945.[83] Despite this, the Soviet regime went ahead with the mandatory state procurements of grain, leaving the rural areas and the cities on the verge of starvation. In the Stavropol' region, where Liubovskaia's family resided, more than 50 percent of the crop was extracted for the state grain reserve.[84] "We had absolutely nothing to eat," Liubovskaia recollected. "At some point my brother and I went to school completely starving. I do not know if all families suffered that much, but we lived awfully. Then a foot-and-mouth disease broke out, and we lost our only cow, our only provider [kormilitsa]." In 1947, Liubovskaia's mother decided to leave the Stavropol' region for Quvasoy, a city in the Uzbek SSR, where her brothers' families lived. The trip to Quvasoy took almost a month, during which the family traveled in a day coach (obshchii vagon) with no beds or benches. All this time, they barely had anything to eat. "But I guess my mother was getting ready for the road," Liubovskaia continued, "because when we boarded the train she opened a bag with little pierogies with kidney beans inside. Sixty years have passed, maybe even more, but I still remember the smell of these pierogies." Liubovskaia and her family suffered even worse in Central Asia. "No one really helped us, but this was no one's fault. People there struggled themselves."[85]

The Great Patriotic War and the immediate postwar years provided Chernogolovka scientists with their first, and exceptionally powerful, collective memory. The war turned this generation from an age cohort into a collective bound together by shared memories and values.[86] Regardless of their social backgrounds, essentially all children suffered during the war. Growing up, many perceived hunger, poverty, and material deprivation as normal and even natural. As Manelis put it, "we all lived in penury, ate poorly and had no housing, but we did not think it was something extraordinary. Everyone lived like this."[87] The war also made the first generation of Chernogolovka scientists into citizens of the Soviet Union. Children of war, they felt proud of the Soviet victory, which had taken such a heavy toll on their lives and the lives of their families. Like Sergei Mileiko, many thought that the most important mission of their generation was to prevent another war and "not let this happen again." This was one of the reasons why many young men and

[82] On the origins of the 1946–1947 Soviet famine, see V.F. Zima, Golod v SSSR 1946–1947 godov: proiskhozhdenie i posledstviia (Moskva: Institut Rossiiskoi Istorii RAN, 1996) and Michael Ellman, "The 1947 Soviet Famine and the Entitlement Approach to Famines," Cambridge Journal of Economics 24.5 (2000), pp. 603–630.

[83] Zima, Golod v SSSR, p. 20; Ellman, "The 1947 Soviet Famine," p. 605.

[84] Zima, Golod v SSSR, p. 29.

[85] Interview 1 with Rimma Liubovskaia, Chernogolovka, October 2010.

[86] Fürst, Stalin's Last Generation, p. 62.

[87] Interview 1 with Georgii Manelis, Chernogolovka, December 2009.

women born in the 1930s chose to go to technical institutions of higher education and pursue careers in science and engineering. Incredible opportunities that a career in sciences opened up during the early days of the Cold War made the profession even more attractive for ambitious Soviet youth.

Becoming a Soviet Scientist

Alexei Abrikosov's mother, a pathologist at the Kremlin hospital, did not want her son to become a physicist. "What kind of career can you make as a physicist, except for being a gymnasium teacher?" she reasoned. Her husband, Alexei Abrikosov, a full member of the Soviet Academy of Sciences and a famous Soviet pathologist who directed Vladimir Lenin's dissection in 1924, agreed with her judgment. "My parents belonged to the older generation, and did not think of physics as a valid science," Abrikosov explained. "My mother, in fact, hoped I would become an engineer, which she considered to be a serious and respected occupation."[88] Following his parents' advice, in 1943 the future Nobel Prize winner enrolled in the Moscow Power Engineering Institute. As soon as the war was over, however, he transferred to the Physics Department at Moscow State University. "The Physics Department was recruiting students to train for the recently launched nuclear program, and I decided to join this group without much hesitation." Abrikosov graduated from MGU in 1948; yet, he refused to go to one of the secret towns of the emerging Soviet nuclear archipelago, using his father's connections to avoid the assignment. Captivated with fundamental research, instead, Abrikosov received admission to a highly competitive graduate program at the Kapitsa Institute of Physical Problems in Moscow, working under the direction of a world-renowned theoretical physicist, Lev Landau.

Few of Abrikosov's future colleagues in Chernogolovka could boast of such a fine path into the scientific profession. Many could not even dream of a career in sciences while growing up; some never heard of such an occupation at all. For most of my interviewees, receiving a higher education was, first and foremost, the most appealing and effective way to escape the miserable circumstances of their youth and rise up in Soviet society.[89] As Benjamin

[88] Interview 1 with Alexei Abrikosov, Lemont (Illinois), July 2010. Alexei Abrikosov was awarded a Nobel Prize in Physics in 2003 (jointly with Vitaly L. Ginzburg and Anthony J. Leggett) "for pioneering contributions to the theory of superconductors and superfluids." On the rapid growth of the engineering profession in the 1920s and 1930s, see Bailes, *Technology and Society Under Lenin and Stalin.*

[89] Boris Grushin demonstrates that getting a higher education was the main priority for the vast majority of Soviet youth under Khrushchev. B.A. Grushin, *Chetyre zhizni Rossii v zerkale oprosov obshchestvennogo mneniia. Ocherki massovogo soznaniia rossiian vremen Khrushcheva, Brezhneva, Gorbacheva i El'tsina. Zhizn' 1-a: Epokha Khrushcheva* (Moskva: Progress-Traditsiia, 2001), p. 205.

Tromly put it, higher education provided a scarred younger generation with a sense of normalcy after the devastating war. It gave postwar students a sense of vitality and social belonging that many so passionately desired.[90]

The number of students enrolled in Soviet higher education institutions rose sharply during the first postwar decade: from 730,200 students in 1945 to 1,867,000 in 1955.[91] This figure continuously increased throughout the Khrushchev era, reaching 2,396,100 students in 1960 and 3,608,400 by the end of his rule.[92] The appeal of higher education to postwar Soviet youth was obvious. The openness of universities to young people who came from diverse social backgrounds and geographic locations remained impressive.[93] The extensive educational and professional opportunities that students in Moscow, Leningrad, and other Soviet cities enjoyed were equally important. Last but not least, the university environment allowed many ambitious young men and women to join the ranks of the Soviet intelligentsia, becoming agents in Communism's core agenda of creating a modern social order, enlightening the masses, and overcoming Russia's "backwardness."[94] In short, receiving a higher education presented Chernogolovka scientists with an exceptional opportunity to fit into the Soviet project.

In the late 1940s and early 1950s, when most of my interviewees were coming of age, scientific and technical higher education became tremendously popular. The scorching memory of the recent war and the determination to "not let this happen again" were some of the major reasons why so many young people fled to study the sciences. The astounding growth of the prestige and state funding of science during World War II and the early Cold War years provided another powerful incentive. The US explosion of the first nuclear bombs in August 1945 convinced Stalin that the development of science had to become a strategic priority. Anxious to restore the balance of power as quickly as possible, the aging dictator took a number of immediate steps to set the Soviet nuclear project on a new footing.[95] Rigorous training of highly skilled scientists and engineers, who would enable the Soviet Union to compete with the West in the Cold War, was one of these steps. Overnight, physicists and chemists became the most wanted professionals. To meet the growing demand,

---

[90] Tromly, *Making the Soviet Intelligentsia*, p. 26.
[91] *Narodnoe obrazovanie, nauka i kul'tura v SSSR: Statisticheskii sbornik*, ed. by G.M. Kharat'ian (Moskva: Izdatel'stvo "Statistika," 1971), p. 151.
[92] S.V. Volkov, *Intellektual'nyi sloi v sovetskom obshchestve* (Sankt-Peterburg: Fond "Razvitie," 1999), pp. 127–128.
[93] Zubok, *Zhivago's Children*, pp. 35–36.
[94] Tromly, *Making the Soviet Intelligentsia*, p. 5. Interestingly, L.G. Churchward argues that in the 1960s the Soviet intelligentsia represented the most rapidly growing sector of Soviet society. See L.G. Churchward, *The Soviet Intelligentsia: An Essay on the Social Structure and Roles of Soviet Intellectuals During the 1960s* (London: Routledge & Kegan Paul, 1973), p. 9.
[95] Holloway, *Stalin and the Bomb*, pp. 129–133.

Stalin worked to raise the prestige of the profession. On March 7, 1946, *Pravda* published a decree, issued by the Council of People's Commissars,[96] establishing high salaries for scientific workers and providing scientists with priority access to housing, food, and goods.[97] In the following year, the government issued a number of unpublicized decrees raising the privileges and status of leading scientists and high-level scientific administrators to the same level as those of the highest state officials.[98] At the same time, new ground-breaking institutions of higher education were established. The Moscow Physical-Technical Institute founded in 1951 became the most prominent among them. Fiztech was launched originally as the Physical-Technical Department at Moscow State University in 1947, following the initiative of leading Soviet scientists, including Nikolai Semenov and Petr Kapitsa. It trained specialists in nuclear physics, chemical physics, radio engineering, aerodynamics, and other critically important sciences, some of them previously unheard of in the Soviet Union.[99]

The cult of science, as Paul Josephson aptly named it, reached unprecedented proportions after Stalin's death, as the new Soviet leadership began to view technology as a panacea for social and economic problems.[100] Under Khrushchev, top party officials, scientists, and ordinary people alike shared the naïve belief that science, and especially atomic energy, would play a central role in building Communism in the USSR.[101] It was against this background that many Chernogolovka scientists decided to join the ranks of the scientific profession. Some, like Abrikosov, enrolled in their studies in the mid- to late 1940s. Others became students a decade later, in the heyday of Khrushchev's Thaw. While the older cohort was initially expected to contribute to the Soviet military–industrial complex, the younger scientists were allowed to focus on fundamental research early on in their professional careers. In the late 1950s and early 1960s, both categories benefited immensely from the expansion of fundamental research, a key component of Khrushchev's new science policy, as well as from the ideological relaxation of the Thaw.

The openness of universities to students of various social backgrounds is well documented.[102] The road to higher education, however, was not always straightforward. For those Chernogolovka scientists who came from the new Soviet intelligentsia milieu, receiving a higher education was a self-evident

---

[96] The Council of People's Commissars was the highest governmental agency in the USSR. It was renamed the Council of Ministers in 1946.

[97] *Pravda*, March 7, 1946.   [98] Krementsov, *Stalinist Science*, pp. 99–100.

[99] N.V. Karlov, *Povest' drevnikh vremen, ili predystoriia Fiztekha* (Moskva: Tsentr gumanitar-nogo obrazovaniia MFTI "Petr Velikii," 2004); A.A. Shchuka, *Fiztekh i fiztekhi*. Izd. 3-e (Moskva: Fiztekh-poligraf, 2010).

[100] Josephson, "Rockets, Reactors, and Soviet Culture," pp. 169–170.

[101] Josephson, "Atomic-Powered Communism," pp. 297–324; Zubok, *Zhivago's Children*, p. 122.

[102] Zubok, *Zhivago's Children*, pp. 34–35; Tromly, *Making the Soviet Intelligentsia*, p. 54.

path to take, as their parents encouraged them to continue their studies and join the ranks of the professional elite.[103] Manelis, for example, was part of the Tashkent intelligentsia. During the war, his parents associated with famous Soviet poets and writers, such as Anna Akhmatova, Kornei Chukovskii, and Aleksei Tolstoi, who had been evacuated to Tashkent. At the age of eighteen, Georgii was admitted to the Department of Chemistry of Central Asian State University, graduating with distinction in 1953. "When I began my education, only three years after the war, few people in the Soviet Union could predict what professions and in what quantity would be in demand in the 1950s," Manelis recollected. "As a result, a gap formed between the growing need for scientists and the insufficient amount of graduates with scientific degrees."[104] In September 1953, Manelis was admitted to a graduate program at the ICP in Moscow. It was only there that he realized that he was cut for a scientific career.

Konovalova and Shilov had no difficulty entering the Soviet educational system either. Konovalova recalled her parents' contributing to her education from early on, signing her up for an elite library and taking her to various theatrical performances in Tashkent. "I remember my father buying the complete collections of Charles Dickens, Aleksandr Pushkin, and Nikolai Gogol. I read avidly at the time."[105] In 1954, Konovalova graduated from the Tashkent Medical Institute. Three years later she became a junior research fellow at the laboratory of experimental chemotherapy at the ICP, where her husband was employed. Shilov studied at the Department of Chemistry of Kiev State University. In 1947, his father was elected a Corresponding Member of the Ukrainian Academy of Sciences, relocating his family to Kiev. Five years later, Shilov's father would introduce the twenty-two-year-old Aleksandr to Nikolai Semenov, thus launching his career at the ICP.[106]

For students of Jewish background, college admissions were much more challenging. The growth of anti-Semitism during World War II, followed by Stalin's anticosmopolitan campaign in the late 1940s, led to further restrictions on education and hiring practices for Jewish youth.[107] Veniamin Shekhtman came from a family of the technical intelligentsia. A Muscovite by birth, he applied to the Department of Physics at MGU in 1946, but failed to achieve a passing score, having received a "B" for his literary composition. The seventeen-year-old Veniamin went to study at the less prestigious

[103] On the elitism of the postwar Soviet intelligentsia, see Tromly, *Making the Soviet Intelligentsia*, p. 54; Volkov, *Intellektual'nyi sloi v sovetskom obshchestve*, pp. 49–50.
[104] Interview 4 with Georgii Manelis, Chernogolovka, February 2011.
[105] Interview with Nina Konovalova, Chernogolovka, March 2011.
[106] "Khimiia i zhizn' akademika Shilova," in *Chernogolovskaia gazeta*, January 14, 2010.
[107] On the anti-Semitic campaigns in Soviet universities, see Tromly, *Making the Soviet Intelligentsia*, pp. 84–88.

Moscow Institute of Steel and Alloys, graduating in June 1952, several months before the notorious Doctors' Plot gathered pace. Despite Shekhtman's excellent academic record, the institute administration denied him a job assignment (*raspredelenie*), a common practice in the USSR. "I stayed unemployed for six months with my scientific diploma," he recollected. "I applied for different jobs, but no organization risked hiring me because of my Jewish origin." Finally, in late 1952 Shekhtman was employed as a laboratory assistant at the Moscow Evening Metallurgical Institute. To his day, he feels grateful to the director of the institute, Pavel Bidulia, who made the decision. "It was people like him, outstanding, terrific people, who tried to prevent the repressive machine from moving ahead." Yet, it was not until the beginning of the Thaw that Shekhtman dared to apply for a graduate program at the Institute of Metallurgy.[108]

Vsevolod Gantmakher was also well aware that his admission to Fiztech in the summer of 1953 was something "absolutely unconventional." Even though his father, Feliks Gantmakher, was one of the founders of Fiztech and was a member of the faculty there, Vsevolod knew that he had to get straight "A" grades on his entrance exams because he was a Soviet Jew. "When the anti-Semitic campaign began I was still in high school. It was generally easy to get into a good college back then. There was not much competition, and many of my classmates had leisurely lives and had fun. But I was studying from early morning till late night, as I knew that it would not be easy for me."[109] The fact that Gantmakher's father worked at Fiztech helped, of course, since it ensured that Vsevolod would receive fair grades for his exams. In his fourth year, Gantmakher was admitted as an intern to the IPP under Kapitsa's direction. He defended his "candidate of sciences" dissertation there in 1964.

The majority of Chernogolovka scientists, however, had little parental guidance in choosing their professional paths. For some, a higher education diploma was a ticket to a professional career and an escape from manual labor.[110] For others, it was the only feasible way of securing better lives for themselves and their families and getting ahead in Soviet society. "No one in my family ever talked to me about becoming a scientist," Bogdanov recalled. "I did not even know that a profession like this existed. But my father often told me that I should strive to get into a university, as this would allow me to avoid manual labor at a factory."[111] Bogdanov finished school with distinction in 1953 and left Bryansk for Moscow. His excellent academic record, as well as his working-class background, allowed him to enter the Department of

---

[108] Interview 1 with Veniamin Shekhtman, Chernogolovka, March 2010; Interview 2 with Veniamin Shekhtman, Chernogolovka, March 2010.
[109] Interview with Vsevolod Gantmakher, Chernogolovka, March 2010.
[110] Tromly, *Making the Soviet Intelligentsia*, p. 55.
[111] Interview 3 with Gennadii Bogdanov, Chernogolovka, August 2010.

Chemistry at MGU without taking any entrance exams. Life in the capital, Bogdanov remembered, opened up a completely new world to him. The young chemist was equally fascinated by the outstanding lecturers at MGU and by his first encounter with high culture in Moscow. As an MGU student, he could buy cheap tickets for symphony orchestras, art galleries, and theatrical performances. "An ordinary boy from Bryansk, I was completely blown away!" After living most of his childhood and adolescent years in a dreary barrack, Bogdanov particularly enjoyed modern dormitories of the recently built MGU building on the Leninskii Hills.[112]

Lana Ukrainka and Rimma Liubovskaia were also captivated by the tremendous opportunities that universities offered. Both came from extremely poor backgrounds. Ukrainka's mother remarried after the war to support her children, and the environment at home was stressful. Lana remembered reading an article about a new MGU building at the age of fifteen. "I did not know yet that I would become a scientist, but I dreamt of leaving home and going to study at the University." As a high school student, she would buy books and brochures on nuclear physics. Ukrainka was admitted to the Physics Department of MGU in 1957. For Rimma Liubovskaia, her enrollment in the Mendeleev Institute of Chemical Technology was also a true blessing. She recalled her adolescence in Kizyl-Kiya, a small mining town lost among the mountains in the Kyrgyz Republic, with good humor but dismay: "The town where we lived was extremely criminal, populated by formerly deported people, who engaged in massacres from time to time. My school was located six kilometers away from this mining town, a distance I walked almost every day by myself for years." Despite this frightful atmosphere, Liubovskia was an exemplary student at school, participating in regional academic contests (*olimpiady*) and extracurricular activities. When, at the age of seventeen, she was admitted to the Mendeleev Institute, Rimma could not have felt happier. Although Liubovskaia arrived in Moscow with nothing but several books, a pillow, and a jacket in her shabby suitcase, she recognized that studying in the capital opened up exceptional opportunities to her.[113]

The resurgence of popular interest in science and technology during late Stalinism and the Thaw had an immediate impact on postwar Soviet youth, Chernogolovka scientists among them. In the 1950s, popular science journals and science fiction flooded the market, while the Soviet media focused much of its attention on atomic power and jet aviation as harbingers of new technologies for a glorious Communist future.[114] Some of my interviewees shared memories

[112] Interview 1 with Gennadii Bogdanov, Chernogolovka, September 2009.
[113] Interview 1 with Rimma Liubovskaia, Chernogolovka, October 2010.
[114] Asif A. Siddiqi, *The Red Rockets' Glare: Spaceflight and the Soviet Imagination, 1857–1957* (New York: Cambridge University Press, 2010), pp. 301–304. On the emergence of popular science in the first post-Revolutionary decade, see Andrews, *Science for the Masses*.

of this mass enthusiasm and faith in the positive role that science could play in improving life in the USSR.[115] Ernest Suvorov, for example, recollected reading a popular book on nuclear physics by Moisei Korsunskii, called *Atomic Nucleus*, at the age of twelve. "I read this book at night, gulping information about atomic energy and the nuclear bomb. It made such a strong impression on me that I decided that I would certainly become a physicist."[116] Suvorov enrolled in the Physical and Mathematical Department of Tashkent State University[117] in 1955, graduating cum laude five years later. In 1964, he was recruited by a deputy dean of the MGU Physics Department to continue his graduate studies in Moscow. Oleg Efimov also developed his interest in science at a young age. "I began reading popular science books when I was in the sixth grade and had my first scientific publication come out at the age of sixteen," he remembered. In 1948, the twelve-year-old Oleg joined the Moscow Planetarium, where he attended public lectures and was able to carry out his first research projects. Efimov's interest in astronomy was gradually replaced by his fascination with nuclear physics and atomic energy. As he was finishing high school in 1954, his friend's uncle, a dean at the Mendeleev Institute, convinced Efimov to apply to the Physical and Chemical Department there, as it would allow him to work on "a big nuclear bomb." Although Efimov's research never dealt with nuclear technologies (at the ICP Branch he worked on electrocatalysis and the synthesis of conductive polymers instead), he never regretted this decision.[118]

The timing of one's college enrollment was crucial, too. What seemed impossible during late Stalinism became feasible under Khrushchev. No one was more aware of this than "children of enemies of the people." The stories of Vladimir Enman and Leonid Mezhov-Deglin illustrate the striking difference between the two eras. Born in 1928, Enman was supposed to enter college in the mid-1940s. Because of his father's persecution, however, he did not dare even think about going to college in Moscow. Still, he was determined to get a higher education. In 1945, Enman took a freight train to Baku in the Azerbaijan SSR, intending to enroll in the Preparatory Naval and Military School (*Podgotovitel'noe voenno-morskoe uchilishche*) there. "It took me nine days to reach Baku. I saw many destroyed villages and towns on my way; the entire country lay in ruins," Enman remembered. When he finally arrived in Baku, Enman found out that there might be a credentials committee present at the entrance exams and decided against applying. "I was afraid that if

[115] For popular responses to the Soviet space exploration, see Andrews and Siddiqi, eds., *Into the Cosmos*. See also Donald J. Raleigh, *Russia's Sputnik Generation: Soviet Baby Boomers Talk about Their Lives* (Bloomington: Indiana University Press, 2006).
[116] Interview 1 with Ernest Suvorov, Chernogolovka, August 2010.
[117] In 1960, Central Asian State University was renamed Tashkent State University.
[118] Interview 1 with Oleg Efimov, Chernogolovka, March 2011.

they learned about my father, they would arrest me, too. How could I know?" A year later, Enman attempted to enter college again. This time he applied to Riga River College in the Latvian SSR and was successfully admitted. To this day, Enman considers himself extremely fortunate to have been able to enter the Soviet educational system.

Leonid Mezhov-Deglin, by contrast, came of age in the mid-1950s, during the short-lived ideological relaxation of the Thaw. The new political atmosphere allowed him not only to receive a higher education, but also to enroll in the Moscow Physical-Technical Institute, a closed elite institution, access to which had previously been restricted for children of the repressed. "In 1955–56, the Soviet regime was taken aback and lost its grip on society for a while," Mezhov-Deglin explained. "By the time it recovered [from the shocks of de-Stalinization], I was already a student at Fiztech." In his fourth year, Leonid was fortunate to get an internship at Kapitsa's institute, working under the direction of Aleksandr Shal'nikov. In 1963, as he was finishing his studies, Mezhov-Deglin was recruited by Yuri Osipyan, a deputy director of the ISSP, to work in Chernogolovka. "At the time, I had neither work nor registration in Moscow, nor permanent housing." Accepting Osipyan's invitation allowed Mezhov-Deglin to break out of this vicious circle and move to Chernogolovka.[119]

Most of the town's first residents went to graduate school either at Kapitsa's IPP or Semenov's ICP. This fact was hardly an accident. The two scientists had been close friends since their work at the Leningrad Physico-Technical Institute in the 1920s. Both underwent persecution under Stalin, and now saw Khrushchev's Thaw as an opportunity to reorient national science policy toward increased support of fundamental research and "pure science." Like their mentor Abram Ioffe in the first post-Revolutionary decade, Semenov and Kapitsa relied on the young generation of Soviet scientists to carry out their scientific vision of building modern scientific centers across the USSR. To use Semenov's metaphor from his 1922 letter to Kapitsa, Chernogolovka scientists were to become that next generation "that would create true science in Russia, a living science with plenty of discoveries and inventions."

Having survived the Great Patriotic War and the immediate postwar years, the first generation of Chernogolovka scientists believed that the worst was behind them and looked to the future with enthusiastic optimism. As Zubok pointed out, "a huge gap separated these young people, numerous, optimistic, and fresh, from their predecessors, who had been decimated by the war and Stalin's terror."[120] Although the war put an end to the "happy childhoods" of many of

[119] Interview 3 with Leonid Mezhov-Deglin, Chernogolovka, March 2011.
[120] Zubok, *Zhivago's Children*, p. 124.

my interviewees, depriving them of their fathers and homes, it did not make them into "cynics who played the system carefully."[121] By contrast, many emerged out of the experience of total war passionately patriotic and deeply committed to the Soviet state and its socialist ideals. The majority of wartime children felt grateful to the Soviet regime that constantly reminded its citizens of the leading role it played in defeating Nazi Germany.[122] Many were eager to prove their worth to the older generation and contribute to the Soviet project.[123]

The unprecedented growth of the prestige and state funding of science during the first Cold War decade opened up myriad professional opportunities to this idealistic youth. From 1940 to 1960, the number of scientists in the USSR increased drastically, reaching 354,158 people in 1960, compared to 98,315 before the war. This number doubled again by the end of the Khrushchev era. There were 927,709 scientists in the USSR by 1970, according to Soviet statistics.[124] Remarkably, the growth of scientific personnel was accompanied by further expansion of research institutes. If in 1950 only 43 percent of Soviet scientists worked at research institutes, while 53 percent were employed at higher education institutions, by 1960 this ratio had shifted to 56 percent and 41 percent respectively.[125] Many of these newly established research facilities were located in "secret cities" of the Soviet military–industrial complex or the scientific centers of the Soviet Academy of Sciences. Both provided their residents with outstanding job opportunities and privileged material conditions.

The Cold War, though, was only partially responsible for Chernogolovka's initial success. The first generation of Chernogolovka scientists were also the products of the Khrushchev era, with its idealism and romanticism, its attempts to promote independent initiatives on the ground, and its belief in the transformative power of science and technology. Despite its modest appearance, Chernogolovka embodied the best of what Khrushchev's Thaw had to offer. The unusual conditions under which the town came into being allowed its residents to participate in transforming the testing ground into a center for fundamental research. How local scientists organized their daily lives in Chernogolovka in the 1960s and 1970s is the subject of the following chapter.

---

[121] Fürst, *Stalin's Last Generation*, p. 24.

[122] On the cult of World War II in Russia, see Nina Tumarkin, *The Living and the Dead: The Rise and Fall of the Cult of World War II in Russia* (New York: Basic Books, 1994). See also Amir Weiner, *Making Sense of War: The Second World War and the Fate of the Bolshevik Revolution* (Princeton: Princeton University Press, 2001).

[123] Remarkably, in his memoirs Andrei Sakharov writes: "I was not recruited as a soldier during the war – but I felt that I was a soldier of another war, the scientific-technical war." Sakharov, *Vospominaniia*, T. 1, p. 221.

[124] *Narodnoe obrazovanie, nauka i kul'tura v SSSR*, p. 247.

[125] Volkov, *Intellektual'nyi sloi v sovetskom obshchestve*, p. 216.

3   "We Were Building a Town for Ourselves": Everyday Life in Chernogolovka in the 1960s and 1970s

> "What is Communism, dear friends? Communism is abundance. It is when we can completely satisfy each person's needs."
>
> Nikita Khrushchev, *Dva tsveta vremeni*, 1962

Gennadii Bogdanov accepted a job at the Branch of the ICP in Chernogolovka in 1962. Despite the town's good location, Bogdanov was apprehensive about going. Established originally as a testing ground for new powerful explosives, by the early 1960s Chernogolovka still lacked basic material comforts. The town had no grocery stores, health care, or education facilities. For the first few years, there was not even a direct road connecting the settlement to Moscow, and residents often had to walk several miles in mud and sludge to get to the nearest highway. The twenty-six-year-old Bogdanov soon discovered, however, that the nascent town abounded in outstanding professional and personal opportunities. His new employer provided modern housing for him and his family within a year of their arrival – an unattainable dream for most Soviet citizens. In 1964, a large grocery store opened in Chernogolovka, improving food supplies in the town. After Bogdanov defended his "candidate of sciences" dissertation in 1967, he was promoted to senior research fellow with a salary of 250 rubles, which was three times higher than the average monthly pay in the USSR. In an interview recorded in 2009, Bogdanov remembered: "I found myself living in a unique community of equals. Back then, we felt that it all belonged to us, and that we owned everything together."[1]

Chernogolovka grew at an incredible pace in the 1960s. From 1958 to 1972, the town's population increased from 129 people to almost 8,000.[2] New residents came from all over the Soviet Union: Kiev, Bryansk, Rostov-on-Don, Gor'kii (Nizhnii Novgorod), Tashkent, and the Far East. They needed permanent housing, grocery stores, health care, and schools, as well as recreational facilities, movie theaters, and other entertainment. While for the first decade Chernogolovka's population was young and relatively healthy, the lack of health care did not pose a serious problem. Yet, most scientists had small

---

[1] Interview 2 with Gennadii Bogdanov, Chernogolovka, December 2009.
[2] TsAOPIM, f. 8099, op. 1, d. 107, l. 29.

children who had to be educated. All these concerns became one of the primary responsibilities of the ICP Branch and Nikolai Semenov's associate, Fedor Dubovitskii (1907–1999).

Organizing the social and cultural life of the town would have been much easier had Chernogolovka belonged to the Soviet military–industrial complex. In the past, the Stalinist command-administrative system proved exceedingly capable of mobilizing limited industrial resources and channeling them into top-priority projects. The construction of secret nuclear cities in the late 1940s demonstrated this convincingly. The inhabitants of Sarov (Arzamas-16), the epicenter of the Soviet nuclear program, enjoyed privileged material conditions at a time when the rest of the country lay in ruins.[3] Ozersk (Cheliabinsk-40) and Zheleznogorsk (Krasnoiarsk-26), engaged in the production of weapon-grade plutonium, were planned as "socialist cities," in which the state took care of all basic social and cultural needs of those who worked there.[4] After the shift in Soviet science policy under Khrushchev, the government also provided extra funds to scientific towns dedicated to fundamental research and technological innovation. In Akademgorodok, for example, Lavrentiev relied on Khrushchev's personal support to secure special provisions for building housing, parks, gardens, shops, dining halls, schools, and kindergartens. Zelenograd residents had access to superior supplies of food and consumer goods, as well as newly built theaters and other cultural amenities.[5]

Chernogolovka, however, did not receive any extra funds or special provisions, since the town emerged in place of a testing ground. In the late 1950s, Semenov's settlement was not even on the radar of the Soviet government. Despite this, Semenov and Dubovitskii were able to create comfortable living conditions for the town residents. For the first fifteen years, the notorious "housing question" did not exist in Chernogolovka: each newly arriving scientist received a separate one-, two-, or three-room apartment within a year of their arrival. Dubovitskii also worked to ensure the town had sufficient food supplies. Thanks to his personal connections, the first large grocery store opened in 1964. It provided residents with all basic products, including meat and milk – both hard to get in the Soviet Union. In 1967, a cultural center, the House of Scientists (*Dom Uchenykh*), opened. If Chernogolovka was not a top priority for the Soviet government, then how did all this come together?

The unprecedented prestige of science and scientists in the post-Stalin era provided part of the explanation. While Semenov's town did not enjoy the same

---

[3] Holloway, *Stalin and the Bomb*, p. 201; Vladimir Matiushkin, *Povsednevnaia zhizn' Arzamasa-16* (Moskva: Molodaia gvardiia, 2008), pp. 111–112. For a personal account of daily life in Arzamas-16, see Sakharov, *Vospominaniia*, T. 1, pp. 255–263.

[4] Brown, *Plutopia*, pp. 133–140, 215, 257; Glazyrina, "Krasnoiarsk-26: A Closed City of the Defence-Industry Complex," p. 197.

[5] Josephson, *New Atlantis Revisited*, p. 16; Usdin, *Engineering Communism*, pp. 215–216.

material privileges as Akademgorodok or secret cities of the military–industrial complex, it benefited tremendously from the cult of science prevalent in Soviet society. In the late 1950s and 1960s, scientific construction was booming in the USSR. Dozens of towns established during this period were constructed as "islands of developed socialism," whose residents enjoyed higher salaries, better housing, and privileged health care and education.[6] This environment made it easier for Semenov and Dubovitskii to secure the funding needed to expand the residential area of the testing ground. After the Presidium of the Academy of Sciences issued a decree about establishing a multidisciplinary scientific center in Chernogolovka in August 1962, obtaining funds became much more straightforward.

The rapid growth of the Soviet economy also played a crucial role in Chernogolovka's success. Between 1950 and 1965, the economy grew at the impressive rate of 5 to 7 percent annually.[7] Although this was mostly extensive, not intensive, growth, it brought a marked increase in prosperity, improving standards of living and breeding hopes and expectations among the Soviet population. Another key factor in Chernogolovka's success was the major change of priorities in the allocation of resources. In the Stalin period, housing construction, clothing, and agriculture were at the bottom of the priority list, while most resources were allocated to the military sector. Khrushchev shifted priorities in favor of the consumer.[8] From 1953 onward, the Soviet government increased investment in housing, health care, education, and consumer-oriented industries.[9] These measures brought tangible improvements in the material well-being of the Soviet people. Khrushchev's "New Deal" reached its apogee in the Third Program of the Communist Party, adopted in 1961. The Program proclaimed that by 1980 all Soviet people would live under Communism, and pledged "to achieve living standards in the Soviet Union higher than in any capitalist country."[10] As elite members of Soviet society, scientists were among the first to experience the advantages of "life under

---

[6] Zubok, *Zhivago's Children*, p. 126.

[7] Georgi Derluguian, *Bourdieu's Secret Admirer in the Caucasus: A World-System Biography* (Chicago: University of Chicago Press, 2005), p. 90.

[8] Philip Hanson, *The Rise and Fall of the Soviet Economy* (London: Longman, 2003), pp. 6, 31; V.M. Kudrov, *Ekonomika Rossii v mirovom kontekste* (Sankt-Peterburg: Aleteiia, 2007), p. 391; Susan E. Reid, "Who Will Beat Whom? Soviet Popular Reception of the America National Exhibition in Moscow, 1959," *Kritika: Explorations in Russian and Eurasian History* 9.4 (2008), pp. 859–863; N.B. Lebina and A.N. Chistikov, *Obyvatel' i reform: Kartiny povsednev-noi zhivni gorozhan* (S.-Peterburg: Dmitrii Bulanin, 2003), p. 151. In fact, the need to reorient the Soviet economy toward the consumer was recognized by Stalin's heirs even before Khrushchev came to power. See Alec Nove, *An Economic History of the USSR, 1917–1991* (London: Penguin Books, 1992), p. 332; Iurii Aksiutin, *Khrushchevskaia "ottepel'" i obshchestvennye nastroeniia v SSSR v 1953–1964 gg.* (Moskva: ROSSPEN, 2010), pp. 62–73.

[9] Zubok, *Zhivago's Children*, p. 123.

[10] *Programma Kommunisticheskoi Partii Sovetskogo Soiuza* (hereafter Programma KPSS) (Moskva: Izdatel'stvo "Pravda," 1961), pp. 91, 93–94.

Communism." The scientific center in Chernogolovka was a perfect embodiment of these new trends.

Finally, Dubovitskii's exuberant energy and his personal connections, as well as the enthusiasm of the first generation of Chernogolovka scientists, contributed to the town's rapid development. A peasant by birth, Dubovitskii saw Chernogolovka as his fiefdom. He was personally involved in building research facilities and housing, organizing customer services, and landscaping the town. He expected the same commitment from the institutes' young employees, obliging them to participate in building recreational facilities and laying out local parks and alleys. Dubovitskii's approach fit well with the spirit of de-Stalinization and Khrushchev's attempts to mobilize people on the ground to take charge of their everyday needs.[11] Remarkably, decades later scientists argued that their participation made them feel that "they were building a town for themselves and their children" – not for the Soviet state or the Communist Party. The picture that emerges from scientists' oral testimonies and the records of the local party organizations is intriguing. It is quite different from the usual image of the inefficient Soviet state, where everything was managed – often poorly – from above, while people on the ground remained largely indifferent and apathetic. The case of Chernogolovka demonstrates that once the Soviet government allowed room for initiatives and encouraged people to improve their own lives, they met enthusiastic responses on the ground. How scientists organized their social and cultural lives in Chernogolovka is the subject of this chapter.

Housing

When Vladimir Enman accepted an engineering position in Chernogolovka in March 1959, there was nothing there but a two-storied residential building.[12] Two months later, however, the Enmans received two rooms in a communal apartment in a recently finished building on Pervaia [First] Street. In 1960, when their first daughter was born, they moved into their own two-room apartment. The family was upgraded to a three-room apartment after the birth of their second daughter in 1963. Their housing was modern and spacious: it had a 3-meter-high ceiling, wooden floors, hot running water, and its own kitchen and bathroom.[13] To Enman, who had just turned thirty-five, their new

---

[11] The Third Party Program, adopted in 1961, announced that the Soviet state had entered a new period of development, during which the dictatorship of the proletariat would be replaced with a "state of the entire people" or "all-people's state" (*obshchenarodnoe gosudarstvo*). See Evans, *Soviet Marxism-Leninism*, p. 93; Pyzhikov, *Khrushchevskaia "ottepel'*," pp. 115–122.

[12] *Reestry aktov vvoda po godam stroitel'stva, 1961–2001–2005.* Otdel kapital'nogo stroitel'stva Prezidiuma Nauchnogo Tsentra RAN v Chernogolovke.

[13] Interview 3 with Vladimir Enman, Chernogolovka, March 2012.

residence looked like a palace. After his father's arrest in 1938, Vladimir and five other members of his family found themselves squeezed into a single room of a communal apartment (*kommunalka*) in the basement.[14] "It was a small room, cold and dark," Enman recollected. "It had a tiny window and a 1.65-meter-high ceiling. When I grew up I always hit my head against that ceiling." Enman lived in the basement for eight years, until he left for college in 1946. His mother and three sisters stayed there until 1959, when they finally received a separate apartment in Cheremushki, an area on the outskirts of Moscow.[15] Unlike Vladimir's spacious housing in Chernogolovka, his mother's new apartment was small and poorly constructed. Yet, for most Soviet people even this was a dream. Enman was well aware of his outstanding living conditions, which signified his privileged status in Soviet society.

An acute housing shortage existed in the Soviet Union from the early days of the Bolshevik rule. After the 1917 Revolution, the government confiscated private homes and apartments that belonged to the nobility and middle class and redistributed them among workers, peasants, and party functionaries.[16] The state monopoly over housing construction and distribution led to mismanagement and deterioration of many residential buildings. Housing conditions became even worse once Stalin launched large-scale industrialization in the early 1930s. As the urban population increased rapidly, Stalin refused to invest in house-building, neglecting to provide accommodation for the millions of people moving into cities from the countryside. From 1923 to 1940, urban living space per person dropped by 40 percent, from 6.45 square meters to 4.09 square meters – just large enough for a bed, nightstand, and chair.[17] During the Great Patriotic War, the urban housing stock, already inadequate, fell even further, by as much as 87 percent in some cities.[18] In Moscow itself, a family of five people often had to occupy a single room in a communal apartment, sharing a kitchen and bathroom with several other families. In 1947, more than half of all dwellings in the Soviet capital still had neither running water nor sewage.[19] From 1944 to 1950, the Soviet government attempted various policies to improve people's living conditions. The fifth Five-Year Plan

---

[14] On the communal living in Soviet Russia, see Lynne Attwood, *Gender and Housing in Soviet Russia: Private Life in a Public Space* (Manchester: Manchester University Press, 2010), pp. 125–127; Eaton, *Daily Life in the Soviet Union*, pp. 158–159; and Viktoria Semenova, "Equality in Poverty: The Symbolic Meaning of *Kommunalki* in the 1930s–50s," in Daniel Bertaux, Paul Thompson, and Anna Rotkirch, eds., *Living Through the Soviet System* (New Brunswick and London: Transaction Publishers, 2005), pp. 54–67.

[15] Interview 1 with Vladimir Enman, Chernogolovka, August 2009.

[16] Eaton, *Daily Life in the Soviet Union*, p. 153.

[17] Alfred John DiMaio, *Soviet Urban Housing: Problems and Policies* (New York: Praeger Publishers, 1974), pp. 9–15.

[18] Smith, *Property of Communists*, p. 26; Filtzer, "Standard of Living Versus Quality of Life," p. 84.

[19] Filtzer, "Standard of Living Versus Quality of Life," p. 85.

(1951–1955) increased state investments in housing by 100 percent.[20] In the last decade of Stalin's rule, Soviet officials also tried to introduce new housing policies that encouraged the input of individual citizens to tackle the housing crisis. However, most of them remained piecemeal and incoherent.[21]

Khrushchev was the first Soviet leader who attempted to resolve the chronic housing shortage on a massive scale.[22] "Improving the living conditions of the toiling people is one of the most important tasks of our party," he proclaimed at the Twentieth Party Congress in February 1956.[23] On July 31, 1957, the Soviet government launched a massive construction program that pledged to end the housing shortage in the country "in the next ten to twelve years."[24] As a result, by 1960 the overall living space in Soviet cities had doubled: 291 million square meters in comparison to 129 million square meters in the early 1950s. It reached 377 million square meters by 1970.[25] Although the new housing program focused mainly on cities and failed to achieve good-quality housing, it drastically improved the living conditions of millions of Soviet citizens who moved into separate apartments – for the first time in their lives.

This visible success notwithstanding, housing shortages and waiting lists remained a reality of Soviet life. In the 1970s, around a quarter to a third of Soviet people still lived in communal apartments.[26] By contrast, the living conditions in Chernogolovka were exceptional, especially for the first decade. On September 23, 1964, Dubovitskii stated proudly at the party meeting of the ICP Branch that no housing shortage existed in the town. "As for housing, next year we will be able to accommodate 100 percent of the town inhabitants," he said. "Right now we have 442 apartments at our disposal and only 135 people who need housing."[27] If Khrushchev failed to provide a separate apartment for each Soviet family, which he considered to be one of the hallmarks of Communism, how could Dubovitskii solve the problem? After all, when the ICP started the construction of a testing ground in Chernogolovka, there was nothing there but a tiny village made up of a dozen peasant huts, which were part of a local state farm.

Housing was a top priority for Semenov and Dubovitskii from the very beginning. This determined how they distributed funds allocated to the testing ground.[28]

---

[20] DiMaio, *Soviet Urban Housing*, p. 1.   [21] Smith, *Property of Communists*, pp. 32–37.

[22] For recent research on Khrushchev's campaign to resolve the "housing question," see Smith, *Property of Communists*, and Harris, *Communism on Tomorrow Street*.

[23] N.S. Khrushchev, "Otchetnyi doklad TsK KPSS XX s'ezdu Partii," in *XX s'ezd Kommunisticheskoi Partii Sovetskogo Soiuza*, T. 1, p. 90.

[24] Smith, *Property of Communists*, pp. 59–60.

[25] J.A.A. Sillince, ed., *Housing Policies in Eastern Europe and the Soviet Union* (London: Routledge, 1990), p. 242.

[26] Eaton, *Daily Life in the Soviet Union*, p. 158.   [27] TsAOPIM, f. 8099, op. 1, d. 53, l. 50.

[28] Such distribution of funds was, in fact, typical for other scientific centers of the Academy of Sciences that were built from scratch. 60 percent of all investments usually went toward the

Few people knew about Chernogolovka in the late 1950s, but many were willing to take a risk and move to an unknown settlement if there was a chance of getting a separate apartment there. While funding came from the Academy of Sciences, the ICP was put in charge of all housing construction and distribution in the town. Dubovitskii, as its assistant director and, from 1962, the authorized representative of the Academy of Sciences in Chernogolovka, had the authority to select a construction organization, and hire architects, engineers, and designers. In 1958, he used his personal connections in the Soviet Council of Ministers to delegate the construction of the testing ground from Tsentrakademstroi, the main contractor of the Academy of Sciences, to Glavspetsstroi, a powerful organization run by the Soviet military. As a result, by late 1959 the emerging town had three new sixteen-apartment residential buildings and two individual houses (cottages) that could accommodate two to four families. In 1960–1962, Glavspetsstroi constructed eight more large residential buildings, placing 176 apartments at Dubovitskii's disposal. Five new individual cottages were built in the town around the same time.[29]

For the first decade, all housing in Chernogolovka was made of red and white brick and equipped with modern amenities, including electricity, gas, and running water. The average area of a sixteen-apartment building was 600 square meters; it constituted 206 square meters for four-apartment cottages, and eighty-five square meters for two-apartment houses.[30] This allowed for roughly 37 to 50 square meters per family, which was not much space, but in comparison with the rest of Soviet housing it was luxurious. Even more unusual by Soviet standards was the layout of some of these houses. Two-storied cottages had a spacious hallway, kitchen, and living room on the first floor, and a study, bedroom, and nursery on the second floor.[31] All cottages were located separately from apartment buildings, in a picturesque birch grove. Their resemblance to Western townhouses was not an accident. According to Lev Vashin, the idea to build two-storied apartments belonged to Nikolai Semenov, who borrowed it from England. The cottages were distributed among leading scientists of the ICP Branch.[32] For example, Georgii Manelis and Lev Vashin, who moved to Chernogolovka in June 1960 to head new laboratories, each got a two-storied cottage. Prominent scientists of the ISSP and the Landau ITP, who moved to the town in the mid-1960s and early 1970s, enjoyed similar luxury residences.

---

construction of housing and consumer sector, while only 40 percent was spent on building research facilities. See ARAN, f. 2, op. 6, d. 527, l. 49.
[29] *Reestry aktov vvoda po godam stroitel'stva.*   [30] *Reestry aktov vvoda po godam stroitel'stva.*
[31] Interview 2 with Emma Mironova, Chernogolovka, March 2012.
[32] Paul Josephson describes similar luxury housing in Akademgorodok, in Josephson, *New Atlantis Revisited*, p. 17.

Initially, Dubovitskii insisted that only scientists and engineers were eligible for housing in the emerging scientific center, and was reluctant to provide accommodation for people who worked in construction and communal services. This caused resentment and animosity from workers in nearby villages who had to commute to Chernogolovka on a daily basis. To address this concern, in 1963–1964 the institute started building pre-fabricated apartment buildings, popularly known as "khrushchevki." They were not as nice as the original brick houses distributed among scientists, but they allowed Dubovitskii to solve the housing problem, at least for the time being. In the second half of the 1960s, the residential area of the town continued to grow at full speed (see Figures 3.1 and 3.2). The construction of twelve nine-story apartment buildings in 1965–1971 gave Chernogolovka a new, modern look. At the same time, the ICP Branch built another half-dozen individual cottages that were distributed among the scientific elite of the town.[33]

At the end of the day, the question of who got what, when, and why is well worth investigating, as it sheds light not only on the institute's housing policy, but also on the social hierarchy that existed in Chernogolovka in the 1960s and 1970s. For the first decade, all housing in the town was distributed almost exclusively by Dubovitskii, who prioritized scientists and engineers over workers. Scientists in charge of new laboratories usually received luxury housing

Figure 3.1: Chernogolovka under construction, 1964

[33] *Reestry aktov vvoda po godam stroitel'stva.*

Figure 3.2: First Street (*Pervaia ulitsa*) in the mid-1960s

shortly upon their arrival, while the rest of the junior research fellows had to put their names on the institute's waiting list. Most of my interviewees stated that they received separate apartments within a year of starting work in Chernogolovka. Not nearly as nice as the two-storied individual houses, their accommodation was still superior to the housing of the vast majority of Soviet citizens. Rustem Liubovskii, for example, started working at the ICP Branch in September 1963, right after his graduation from Fiztech. Several months later, he moved into a new one-room apartment. "It was truly incredible. Most of my former classmates refused to believe it," he remembered.[34] Liubovskii's future wife, Rimma Stepanova, came to Chernogolovka in 1965. In 1967, after the couple got married and had their first child, they received a three-room apartment from the institute.[35]

In the late 1960s, once the construction of the ISSP and the Landau ITP was complete, the distribution of housing was delegated to the housing committees and trade unions that existed at every research institute. Still, Dubovitskii retained the final say. According to the 1970–1971 report of the ISSP trade union, scientists and engineers continued to enjoy privileged

---

[34] Interview 2 with Rustem Liubovskii, Chernogolovka, February 2011.
[35] Interview 2 with Rimma Liubovskaia, Chernogolovka, February 2011.

access to housing. "Over the previous year, we distributed 70 new apart-ments," the report stated. "We were able to satisfy the housing needs of all employees who had worked at the ISSP for at least two years."[36] The size of one's family was another consideration in distributing new housing: single employees were only eligible for one-room apartments, while families with one or two children could put their names on the waiting list for two- or three-room accommodation.

The years 1971–1972 saw a substantial decline in residential construction in Chernogolovka, as the bulk of resources were redirected toward building the Experimental Factory of Scientific Instrumentation. On January 19, 1971, the ICP Branch's party bureau identified housing for new employees as one of the biggest problems the institute was facing. Newly arriving scientists were assigned rooms at a local dormitory, which was built in 1967, housing 600 young specialists and their families.[37] The housing situation continued to deteriorate throughout the 1970s, as the Soviet government cut down funding for scientific towns, partly as a result of the continuous slowdown of the national economy. In 1979, there were more than 250 employees at the ISSP alone who desperately needed accommodation.[38] The next generation of scientists, who arrived in Chernogolovka in the late Brezhnev era, witnessed no "housing paradise" whatsoever. Khrushchev's lofty goal to provide every Soviet family with modern, free accommodation by 1980 – the year when the Soviet Union was supposed to finish construction of the first stage of Communism – proved unsustainable even within a small, privileged community.

Yet, the fact that the first generation of Chernogolovka scientists enjoyed privileged housing conditions at such a young age was significant. Most of them grew up in communal apartments and barracks. When scientists compared their living conditions to those of their parents, they could not help feeling fortunate. "My father was a famous Soviet mathematician, one of the founders of Fiztech," Vsevolod Gantmakher recollected, "but not even one single day did he live in his own apartment. Our family had two rooms in a communal apartment, with no kitchen, bathtub, or sewage. As soon as cooperative housing became available, my father signed up for it; but he died six months before it was finished."[39] Rimma Shibaeva, who spent her childhood and student years in communal apartments and dormitories, remembered what it felt like to enter her new home in Chernogolovka. "I walked in and thought: 'Goodness, and all this is mine!' I could read as long as I wanted at night and I did not have to share a bathroom with anyone.

---

[36] Archive of the Institute of Solid State Physics, f. 1, op. 1, d. 1, l. 19, "Report of the ISSP Trade Union from October 1970 to October 1971."
[37] TsAOPIM, f. 8099, op. 1, d. 99, l. 111.   [38] Archive of the ISSP, f. 1, op. 1, d. 382, l. 57.
[39] Interview with Vsevolod Gantmakher, Chernogolovka, March 2010.

It felt like complete freedom."[40] Oleg Efimov, one of the few scientists in Chernogolovka who had friends among Soviet dissidents, still supported the Soviet regime because "it took good care of its scientists." "Housing was extremely scarce in the Soviet Union, and the fact that people who came to work in Chernogolovka received their own accommodation showed that the state prioritized science."[41]

For many of my interviewees, receiving a separate apartment, after years of communal living, was not just about securing private space.[42] It was exceptionally strong proof that the Soviet Union was moving in the right direction, and that building a socialist society, where everyone would have equal access to material security, was not merely a utopian dream. It strengthened scientists' commitment to the Soviet project. Most of them never questioned the cost that the rest of society had to pay to support the privileged living conditions in closed scientific towns. Ironically, scientists usually accepted their outstanding housing situation as a norm, a standard that could be achieved across the country.

Food Supplies

On September 24, 1964, the ICP Branch held a reception to celebrate the opening of a large grocery store – "Gastronom" – in Chernogolovka. The store was built on the right side of Pervaia Street, in the heart of the growing town. Its construction, which was part of the 1962 general plan, began in 1963, and was finished in less than two years. Dubovitskii made sure that everything went well. The institute's assembly shop was put in charge of installing refrigerators for meat and other produce storage in the basement. Dubovitskii himself visited various trade authorities in and around Moscow, such as Mosobltorg and Noginsk Torg, to arrange for the best food supplies possible. He even invited the head of Mosobltorg to Chernogolovka, and organized festivities and a reception in his honor.[43]

Dubovitskii's initiative made a lot of sense in a country where permanent shortages of food and other consumer goods were the order of the day. After the destruction of the private sector during Stalin's industrialization, the material well-being of Soviet people declined dramatically. In the early 1930s, being unable to provision the entire country, the regime gave priority to supplying the political elite and those closest to industrial production, neglecting the rest of

---

[40] Interview 1 with Rimma Shibaeva, Chernogolovka, October 2010.
[41] Interview 2 with Oleg Efimov, Chernogolovka, March 2011.
[42] On the relationship between public and private space in Soviet Russia, see Attwood, *Gender and Housing in Soviet Russia*.
[43] Interview 2 with Vladimir Enman, Chernogolovka, October 2010.

the population.[44] Only by the mid-1930s did ordinary Soviet consumers begin to see foodstuffs, clothes, and household items available for sale, as the Soviet government and the Party struggled to fulfill Stalin's slogan, "life has become more joyous, comrades."[45] Per capita private consumption again fell sharply during the Great Patriotic War. It remained extremely low in the immediate postwar years.[46]

The economic growth of the late 1940s and early 1950s led to the limited normalization of the consumer sector and an improvement in living standards.[47] Yet, it was not until Stalin's death that consumption, and living standards more generally, came to the forefront of party rhetoric and state policy. Under Khrushchev, catching up with the United States in per capita consumption became an important factor of the Soviet "peaceful competition" in the Cold War. It also became an issue on which the regime staked its legitimacy at home.[48] The Third Party Program of 1961 promised that within the next decade all Soviet people would have plenty high-quality food on their tables, including meat, dairy products, fruit, and vegetables.[49] From 1953 to 1964, per capita consumption in the Soviet Union indeed increased, by almost 45 percent.[50] Still, food and consumer goods remained in scarce supply across the country. They were often distributed according to the status of certain professional groups in the social hierarchy of Soviet society.

While industrial workers and the technical intelligentsia constituted the two main privileged categories during the industrialization drive of the 1930s, by the late 1950s the scientific intelligentsia largely took their place. Under Khrushchev, and then Brezhnev, select scientists enjoyed privileges similar to those of high-ranking party officials. Some were able to shop in closed retail establishments that carried many products unavailable to ordinary Soviet consumers. This was especially true in scientific towns. In 1962–1964, for example, while there was rationing of bread and other foodstuffs in virtually all Soviet cities, residents of Krasnoiarsk-26, a closed city engaged in the

---

[44] Elena Osokina, *Our Daily Bread: Socialist Distribution and the Art of Survival in Stalin's Russia, 1927–1941*, ed. and transl. by Kate Transchel (New York: M.E. Sharpe, 2001), pp. xiii–xv.

[45] On the emergence of Soviet consumer culture and the "new Soviet middle class" in the 1930s, see Jukka Gronow, *Caviar with Champagne: Common Luxury and the Ideals of Good Life in Stalin's Russia* (Oxford: Berg, 2003). Consider also Amy E. Randall, *The Soviet Dream World of Retail Trade and Consumption in the 1930s* (London: Palgrave Macmillan, 2008).

[46] Philip Hanson, *The Consumer in the Soviet Economy* (Evanston: Northwestern University Press, 1968), p. 31.

[47] Julie Hessler, *A Social History of Soviet Trade: Trade Policy, Retail Practices, and Consumption, 1917–1953* (Princeton: Princeton University Press, 2004), pp. 296–297.

[48] Reid, "Cold War in the Kitchen," p. 212. Consider also Taubman, *Khrushchev*, pp. 507–512.

[49] *XXII s'ezd Kommunisticheskoi Partii Sovetskogo Soiuza*, T. 3, p. 297. See also Taubman, *Khrushchev*, pp. 507–512; Khrushchev, *Reformator*, pp. 755–760.

[50] Hanson, *The Rise and Fall of the Soviet Economy*, p. 65.

separation of plutonium, enjoyed supplies three times greater than the level of the regional center.[51] This was also the case in Ozersk, whose residents grew increasingly affluent throughout the 1960s and 1970s.[52] In Akademgorodok, the state built shops such as "Meat," "Milk," "Bakery," and "Vegetables and Fruits," and maintained provisions rather well.[53] Did Chernogolovka scientists enjoy the same privileged food supplies?

From 1958 to the late 1970s, the town went through three different stages. During the first one, which lasted from 1958 to 1964, its residents survived thanks to the settlement's proximity to Moscow and Dubovitskii's private initiatives.[54] One such initiative was the organization of a small grocery store in a research facility of the ICP Branch. Many of the institute's employees remember it as a short period of relative prosperity during which the scientific center enjoyed certain material privileges. Then, in September 1964, a large grocery store – "Gastronom" – opened, which managed to maintain relatively high levels of food supplies for the first several years. The last stage coincided with the second half of Brezhnev's rule, and was characterized by constant shortages and empty shelves in local grocery and department stores. In the mid- to late 1970s, scientists usually had to travel to Moscow and forage for food there.

Since Chernogolovka was not planned as an academic town, the 1956 decree did not mention building a grocery store there. This meant that for the first six years Dubovitskii had to figure out on his own how to provide his employees with food. A gifted administrator and an energetic man, he turned to various trade organizations and closed retail establishments located in and around Moscow. Emphasizing the institute's work on classified state assignments, he managed to negotiate a deal through which Chernogolovka would enjoy some privileged access to these supplies.[55] But even Dubovitskii's exuberant energy was not always enough to provide the town with sufficient food, even in the first half of the 1960s when the population was still small.

From 1958, when the first residents arrived in Chernogolovka, until 1962, there were no grocery stores at the testing ground. "Each time we needed groceries," Vladimir Enman recollected, "we had to travel to Moscow. The present-day road to Moscow had not been built yet, and often times we had to walk five kilometers

[51] Glazyrina, "Krasnoiarsk-26: A Closed City of the Defence-Industry Complex," p. 197.

[52] Brown, *Plutopia*, pp. 255–267. See also Kate Brown, "Utopia Gone Terribly Right: Plutonium's 'Gated Communities' in the Soviet Union and United States," in Paulina Bren and Mary Neuburger, eds., *Communism Unwrapped: Consumption in Cold War Eastern Europe* (Oxford: Oxford University Press, 2012), pp. 52–53.

[53] Josephson, *New Atlantis Revisited*, p. 16.

[54] Interestingly, Elena Osokina argues that individual initiatives played a crucial role in the re-emergence of elements of the market in the Soviet Union in the 1930s: "With scanty and preferential state provisioning, people had no other choice but to look after themselves." See Osokina, *Our Daily Bread*, p. xiii.

[55] Interview 2 with Vladimir Enman, Chernogolovka, October 2010; Interview 2 with Gennadii Bogdanov, Chernogolovka, December 2009.

Figure 3.3: Vladimir Enman (right) at his garden plot, 1960

to get to the nearest highway."[56] "There was absolutely nothing here in the first several years," Georgii Manelis confirmed. "We had to bring everything from Moscow. There was a small canteen for soldiers, who were building Chernogolovka, and sometimes we could buy bread, green peas and canned crabs there, but that was it."[57] Dubovitskii was well aware of the situation, and initially tried to resolve it by granting each new employee a plot of land, across from the residential area (see Figure 3.3). "There was a large wasteland in front of our house, and the institute employees were encouraged to plant some basic vegetables there," one of the first residents recalled.[58] "We grew potatoes, carrots, cucumbers, tomatoes, and apple trees. As we found out later, residents of local villages[59] planted only potatoes, but following our example began to grow other vegetables, too. Sometimes they came to us to buy extra vegetables we had left."[60] In 1963 and 1964, however, the land was reassigned for the construction of new housing, which put an end to the scientists' gardening.

[56] Enman, "Pro to, kak zhili my, druz'ia," in *Chernogolovskaia gazeta*, June 22, 2006.
[57] Interview 2 with Georgii Manelis, Chernogolovka, December 2009.
[58] Dubovitskii, *Nauchnyi Tsentr*, p. 55.
[59] There was a large state farm next to the scientific center, called the Chapaev State Farm (*Sovkhoz imeni Chapaeva*), which included the villages of Chernogolovka, Iamkino, Iakimovo, Botovo, and several others.
[60] Interview 3 with Vladimir Enman, Chernogolovka, March 2012.

Another source of supplies during the first few years was a system of rationed food parcels (*systema zakazov*), which scientists organized themselves around 1960.[61] Once a week, a volunteer made a list of required foodstuffs and went to Moscow to place an order either at GUM, the State Department Store, located on Red Square, or at "Dieta," a department store on Leninskii Prospect next to the Soviet Academy of Sciences. A general food parcel included 1 kg of cheese, 1 kg of butter, and 2 kg of meat.[62] Additionally, in summer and early fall most employees supplemented their rations with mushrooms and berries which they gathered in local forests.

It soon became obvious, however, that neither local gardening nor the food parcel system was enough. In 1962, Dubovitskii decided that the only solution was to organize the institute's own grocery store, and allocated the shorter side of the Polymer building for this purpose. Oleg Efimov, who moved to Chernogolovka in 1962 to work at the Department of Kinetics and Catalysis, remembered how he would pass by the store each morning and stop to see what was available. It was mostly basic foodstuffs such as bread and milk, and occasionally meat and butter.[63] For the first two years, Dubovitskii was able to maintain a relatively high level of food supplies in the store.[64] According to one scientist, "he carried his powerful explosives proudly in front of him, and, in return, many closed distributors opened their doors to him."[65] Every week a special bus would set off to a closed retail establishment in Moscow, and come back loaded with food. Many scientists remember how one time, in late 1963, the bus brought back a large barrel of red caviar.[66] The barrel was put in the center of the store, and anyone could take as much caviar as he wanted. "It cost 5 rubles per kilogram, and we could easily afford it: a salary of a junior research assistant was 120 rubles at that time. We did not complain."[67] On several occasions, Dubovitskii managed to provide the store with whole beef carcasses (*tushi*). When this happened, the institute's employees put a thick log in the middle of the store, and scientists themselves had to chop the carcass into smaller pieces.[68] It seems that caviar and meat were rare: both made such strong impression on customers that fifty years later they still remember and recount this episode as proof of their privileged status.

---

[61] The system of rationed food parcels was common in the USSR; see Eaton, *Daily Life in the Soviet Union*, p. 121.
[62] Interview 1 with Emma Mironova, Chernogolovka, March 2012.
[63] Interview 2 with Oleg Efimov, Chernogolovka, Mach 2011.
[64] Interview 2 with Georgii Manelis, Chernogolovka, December 2009.
[65] Interview 2 with Gennadii Bogdanov, Chernogolovka, December 2009.
[66] Interview 2 with Gennadii Bogdanov, Chernogolovka, December 2009; Interview 2 with Oleg Efimov, Chernogolovka, March 2011; Interview 2 with Vladimir Enman, Chernogolovka, October 2010; Interview 2 with Rustem Liubovskii, Chernogolovka, February 2011.
[67] Interview 1 with Gennadii Bogdanov, Chernogolovka, September 2009.
[68] Interview 1 with Gennadii Bogdanov, Chernogolovka, September 2009.

These bright memories, however, are not entirely supported by evidence from the archives. Proceedings of the local party organization present a different picture. For example, on March 4, 1964, the party bureau of the ICP Branch held an extended meeting to discuss consumer services in Chernogolovka. A committee of public supervision (*komitet obschestvennogo kontrolia*), formed by the institute's employees, reported the results of its two-week-long investigation. They identified the institute's grocery store as the most troublesome issue: "Every morning, before the store opens, almost one hundred people gather by its entrance, among them soldiers, janitors, and employees of the chemical kinetics building. By noon, there is barely anyone in the store, but there is no food there either," one member of the committee complained. "When scientists arrive, there is absolutely nothing for them to buy, except stale black bread." The person delivering the report suggested that the institute's administration solve the problem by prohibiting the sale of bread to soldiers, whom he blamed for buying fifteen loaves of bread at a time.[69] Another committee member pointed out that the stock of meat and butter at the store was so small that the institute should probably introduce ration cards to sell these "goods in short supply."[70]

Another challenge was to provide the institute's employees with vegetables, which in the Soviet context usually meant potatoes and cabbage. "This fall," Leonid Eremenko, the head of the laboratory of organic synthesis, reported at the same meeting on March 4, 1964, "our employees helped the local state farm gather and store potatoes. If we had sold potatoes to the institute's employees right away, each person would have preserved them for winter. Instead, the potatoes were stored on the premises, which were not suitable for this, and they began to rot. In addition, the pipe in the building broke, and all our hard work turned out to be in vain."[71] Eremenko put all the blame for this misfortune on the committee of public control.[72] To improve the poor food supplies, he offered to reintroduce a system of rationed food parcels. When the director of the store, present at the meeting, complained that she did not have enough staff to do this,[73] Eremenko pointed out that "the general public" (i.e., scientists, engineers, workers) could help her go to Moscow to get food, and then package it.[74] If scientists in Chernogolovka wanted to have food on their tables, they would have to participate in getting this food and bringing it to the town.

No wonder most employees felt relief when, in fall 1964, a large grocery store opened in Chernogolovka. Emma Mironova, who worked as a designer at GIPRONII, remembered her first visit to "Gastronom": "We walked in, and it was like a fairy tale: there was a confectionery department, a dairy department,

---

[69] TsAOPIM, f. 8099, op. 1, d. 53, ll. 74–79.   [70] TsAOPIM, f. 8099, op. 1, d. 53, l. 73.
[71] TsAOPIM, f. 8099, op. 1, d. 53, l. 74.   [72] TsAOPIM, f. 8099, op. 1, d. 53, l. 74.
[73] TsAOPIM, f. 8099, op. 1, d. 53, l. 79.   [74] TsAOPIM, f. 8099, op. 1, d. 53, l. 74.

and a meat department; there were clean counters and friendly shop assistants. It was a real store, like the ones they had in big cities."[75] Dubovitskii did his best to maintain food supplies to "Gastronom" at a high level: using Semenov's name and authority, he called various trade organizations and negotiated for better provisions. His efforts, however, were impeded by population growth, which skyrocketed in the second half of the 1960s.

Although "Gastronom" opened its doors in 1964, no interviewees indicated that their food supplies improved significantly as a result. On the contrary, they recollected that the new store was half-empty most of the time. Salt and basic cereals were available, but to get milk, for example, scientists needed to stand in line.[76] The milk was bottled right at the store, and a person could only get one bottle of milk at a time, which often meant that, if a young couple had any children, both spouses would have to stand in line. Everyone knew they had to be at the store during their lunch time to get milk: by 2 pm, there was usually no milk left. None of the institute's employees enjoyed any privileged distribution: a head of a laboratory had to stand in line like everyone else.

Around the same time, Dubovitskii had a small farmer's market built behind "Gastronom," which he hoped would improve the fruit and vegetables supplies. Emma Mironova, who designed the market place, remembered that one could buy basic vegetables there, sold by the villagers of the local sovkhoz. On certain days, there was also milk and other dairy products. "This little market helped us out quite a lot, though one always had to stand in line to buy milk."[77]

On December 14, 1965, Georgii Manelis addressed the food shortages at the local party meeting. He criticized the scarce assortment of goods and pointed out that while the quality of food supplies to the town was not worse than in the local villages, a scientific center had to strive for more. In comparison with Akademgorodok, which, according to Manelis, enjoyed "excellent provisions," Chernogolovka had "a very poor range of goods." "We need to find ways to improve our provisions. In Novosibirsk people travel from the city to the scientific center to buy food there."[78] Most Chernogolovka scientists had to travel to Moscow to buy meat, butter, and buckwheat. Sometimes they combined shopping with attending mandatory party organization meetings in Moscow. This "irresponsible behavior" was discussed at the local party organization meeting on January 26, 1968. "We send comrades to Moscow party meetings and give them a half day off," one indignant Communist Party

[75] Interview 2 with Emma Mironova, Chernogolovka, March 2012.
[76] Interview 1 with Ernest Suvorov, Chernogolovka, August 2010; Interview 1 with Nina Konovalova, Chernogolovka, March 2011; Interview 1 with Ernest Suvorov, Chernogolovka, August 2010; Interview 2 with Rustem Liubovskii, Chernogolovka, February 2011.
[77] Interview 2 with Emma Mironova, Chernogolovka, March 2012.
[78] TsAOPIM, f. 8099, op. 1, d. 59, l. 192.

member complained, "but instead they simply go shopping there. Some people come to the meetings late, others do not come at all – we only see them at the end of the day, on the bus back to Chernogolovka."[79]

In the second half of the 1960s, the situation got even worse, as new research institutes began hiring personnel and more people moved to Chernogolovka. The newcomers could not remember any "prosperity." They admitted hearing legendary stories about the first few years, when scientists could buy caviar from a barrel, but said it was a short period that ended quickly.[80] In the 1970s, the town population survived thanks to the food rationing system and Chernogolovka's proximity to Moscow. "We could not buy anything in the town in the 1970s," Ernest Suvorov remembered. "Every Saturday I had to get up at 5 am, take a large backpack and all kinds of bags, and go to Moscow. I did not know exactly where to go and what to look for, so I wandered from one store to another, hoping to come across something that I could buy."[81]

In this respect, Chernogolovka was no different from an average Soviet town. Unlike the vast majority of academic towns, built from above and supplied centrally by the Soviet state, Chernogolovka did not enjoy privileged food supplies. The only exception was a short period from 1962 to 1964, but it ended too soon for most scientists to have experienced it. Remarkably, most Chernogolovka residents did not even think to complain about poor food supplies. Many survived hunger and starvation during the Great Patriotic War, and were used to having potatoes and scarce meat and dairy products as part of their diets. What upset them more was the amount of time they were expected to spend away from their labs working at the local state farm or participating in various public committees in charge of the food parcel system. But again, many scientists perceived both merely as part of daily life in the USSR.

Landscaping the Town

Most people who came to live and work in Chernogolovka in the late 1950s and 1960s remembered it as a special time, when everyone "felt part of one large family" whose members helped and supported each other, and shared the same cultural and moral values. For the first six or seven years, from 1958 to 1964, there was no theft or crime in the town. Many residents kept their apartments unlocked or left keys under the doormat. Pervaia Street was full of bikes and

---

[79] TsAOPIM, f. 8099, op. 1, d. 76, l. 9.

[80] Interview 1 with Ernest Suvorov, Chernogolovka, August 2010; Interview 1 with Vera Sedykh, Chernogolovka, March 2010; Interview 2 with Veniamin Shekhtman, Chernogolovka, March 2010.

[81] Interview 1 with Ernest Suvorov, Chernogolovka, August 2010.

strollers, which people left unlocked throughout the night.[82] Gennadii Bogdanov recalled how he and his small daughters would go for a walk in the forest next to their house and take plastic bags with them to collect garbage that someone left behind.[83]

This sentiment is quite common, and can be found in many other interviews. Here, I will examine why the town residents were eager to participate in landscaping the town: building recreational facilities, planting trees, and laying out a local park, all in their free time. Was the first generation of Chernogolovka scientists a successful example of a "highly organized society of free and conscientious toilers"? Did they become, as the Third Party Program promised, well-rounded individuals for whom "work for the good of society became a matter of vital necessity for everyone"?[84] Or should we merely attribute the sentiment to scientists' nostalgia for their youth and a time long gone? First, let us see what scientists contributed to landscaping the town and how they remembered it.

Many of my male interviewees identified the construction of the recreational facilities in the northern part of the town as their most significant contribution to Chernogolovka's appearance. A sports complex was part of the 1962 general plan. But while the ICP Branch's administration allocated a certain amount of money for building sports facilities and provided materials and equipment, scientists themselves had to carry out the actual construction.[85] It was mostly a matter of necessity: since the town emerged out of a testing ground, residents had to take the initiative to improve their living space. This approach, conveniently, corresponded to the spirit of the time, as the Khrushchev regime hoped to solve some of the urgent social problems by encouraging people on the ground to take charge of organizing their daily lives.[86]

Most of the recreational facilities were built in 1963 and 1964. They included a soccer field and basketball, volleyball, and tennis courts. The construction usually took place on weekends, in the form of *subbotnik*, or community work day. No one got paid for the work, but it probably never occurred to anyone to even ask for money. Bogdanov, who was not able to take part in the construction, could observe his friends building the soccer field:

There was a dense forest where the soccer field would be, and I could see how scientists cut down trees and uprooted stumps, which left large lumps of soil on the ground.

[82] Interview 1 with Vera Sedykh, Chernogolovka, March 2010; Interview 1 with Gennadii Bogdanov, Chernogolovka, September 2009.

[83] Interview 2 with Gennadii Bogdanov, Chernogolovka, December 2009.

[84] *Programma KPSS*, p 62.

[85] Interview 2 with Vladimir Enman, Chernogolovka, October 2010; Interview 4 with Georgii Manelis, Chernogolovka, February 2010.

[86] For more on this, see Brown, *Plutopia*, pp. 213, 216–218.

I remember thinking back then: "Good God, what can they make out of it? How can they make it all even? But they did, with their bare hands."[87]

According to Bogdanov, the institute's employees had minimal equipment at their disposal. Instead, they took a long, thick wooden plank, tied the ropes to its ends, then twenty people grabbed the ropes and dragged the plank across the field, with fifteen more people pushing it from behind. Dubovitskii directed the whole process, running from one lump of soil to another, making sure they were all even.[88] It appears that Dubovitskii was present at many public construction events, at least in the early 1960s, which inspired the young scientists and other institute's employees. A peasant by birth, Dubovitskii was familiar with manual labor: at the age of thirteen he knew how to cut hay, reap the harvest, and put a harness on a horse.[89] Chernogolovka scientists often saw him working among them, with a shovel in his hands.

The soccer field was only part of the planned recreational facilities. Around the same time, the institute's employees built two basketball courts and a volleyball court. Enman, an eager volleyball player, directed the construction of the latter. "It was all built thanks to our enthusiasm," Manelis remembered fifty years later. "We realized that if we did not do this, no one else would."[90] Manelis also recollected how, in August 1962, several days before the opening of a new school, he and his colleagues helped get the school ready for September 1, the first day of class. "It was natural to do this: after all, we were building a town for ourselves."[91] At approximately the same time, Manelis and other scientists started planting trees alongside Pervaia Street.

Rustem Liubovskii, in turn, recalled how he directed building a recreational park in the mid-1970s. Since 1969, he had organized *shabashki* trips, or unofficial seasonal work trips, usually well paid, for the town employees. "Dubovitskii scolded me for this," Liubovskii remembered. "He thought we should invest all our energy in Chernogolovka. So he called me to his office one day and said that he wanted me to organize the construction of a park on April 21, which was Lenin's subbotnik."[92] It snowed that day, but Liubovskii decided to proceed anyways, breaking up institute's employees into groups to cut down trees and dig ditches for electric cables. "By noon we found out that the institute's party organization had a meeting in the morning and decided to cancel the subbotnik due to inclement weather. Yet the work was

[87] Interview 1 with Gennadii Bogdanov, Chernogolovka, September 2009.
[88] Interview 1 with Gennadii Bogdanov, Chernogolovka, September 2009.
[89] F.I. Dubovitskii, *O proshlom (Avtobiograficheskii ocherk)* (Chernogolovka: Tipografiia IKhFCh RAN, 1994), pp. 5–8.
[90] Interview 4 with Georgii Manelis, Chernogolovka, February 2010.
[91] Interview 4 with Georgii Manelis, Chernogolovka, February 2010.   [92] Lenin's birthday.

already under way, and Dubovitskii had no choice but to order hot tea and meat pie be brought to the construction site."[93]

How accurate are all these memories? Were scientists indeed as enthusiastic about helping landscape the town as they remember it today? To answer this question, let us turn to the limited written sources at our disposal: the proceedings of the ICP Branch's party organization. First, it looks like Dubovitskii was the one who initiated the construction of the sports complex. On March 21, 1962, he complained at the ICP's party bureau in Moscow: "We have more than 800 young people at the Branch of the Institute in Chernogolovka now, but no sports facilities or sports center. We have to pay more attention to sports and taking care of these young people. It is a serious problem."[94] Second, the party documents suggest that the town residents were not always eager to spend their weekends or evenings planting trees and building sports grounds. On February 20, 1963, Leonid Eremenko addressed this problem at the meeting of the institute's party organization. "In 1962, more than 800 young people came to work at the ICP Branch," he stated. "We tried to engage them in public activity, but failed so far. They have high expectations, but no one wants to do anything."[95] On December 9, 1964, after the construction of the sports complex was mostly finished, Dubovitskii noted at the newly established party bureau of the ICP Branch that "while the town residents refuse to work at the sports complex, they are happy to play soccer there."[96]

Another official record of the ICP Branch's party organization indicates that Dubovitskii was oftentimes behind many "grassroots initiatives." For instance, on July 13, 1965, the sports committee of the ICP Branch held an extended meeting with local party activists to discuss the construction of the sports complex. Checherin, the head of the sports committee, reported that in 1965 almost nothing had been done to finish the sports facilities. "At the present time we have no tools: no rakes, shovels, or wheelbarrows. We have no people, either."[97] "Last year Dubovitskii was forcing people to work on building the sports complex over the weekends, and the construction went fast," another committee member continued. "He no longer forces anyone, and everything has come to a standstill."[98] Another party member noted: "The real problem is the complete apathy and sluggishness of our employees. Their hearts do not ache for it (*dusha ne bolit*). Basketball and volleyball players take care of their courts, but tennis players do not. We do not have any professional coaches on the staff. That is why we must do all work ourselves, on a voluntary basis."[99] "I am upset that there are no good organizers among our youth," Dubovitskii

[93] Interview 2 with Rustem Liubovskii, Chernogolovka, February 2011.
[94] TsAOPIM, f. 8099, op.1, d. 44, l. 42.   [95] TsAOPIM, f. 8099, op. 1, d. 46, ll. 59–60.
[96] TsAOPIM, f. 8099, op. 1, d. 53, l. 63.   [97] TsAOPIM, f. 8099, op. 1, d. 59, l. 129.
[98] TsAOPIM, f. 8099, op. 1, d. 59, l. 130.   [99] TsAOPIM, f. 8099, op. 1, d. 59, l. 129.

concluded the discussion.[100] The committee agreed that while the local Komsomol organization was mostly at fault for failing to organize and inspire the youth, the institute's employees themselves had to contribute to finishing the construction and maintaining order at the sports complex. "We need to educate our young people in how to use the facilities and to organize their free time."[101] The meeting adopted a resolution stating that the construction of the sports complex had to be completed by August 1, 1965. It pointed out that Komsomol members were responsible for organizing the last stage of construction and the work of the local sports groups (*sektsii*).

Which testimony should we trust? Did Chernogolovka scientists willingly participate in "building a town for themselves," as they remember during interviews, or did Dubovitskii, a strong-willed man, force them to work for the good of the community in their free time, as most party records indicate? The answer to this question lies somewhere in the middle. In most cases, Dubovitskii took the lead. According to many scientists, he considered Chernogolovka to be his "child" (*detishche*), and its construction to be the most important achievement of his life. He wanted the town to be modern and comfortable for living. He spared no energy or time to try to achieve this goal. Dubovitskii expected the same commitment from young residents of the town.

At the same time, Dubovitskii's approach appealed to the collective identity of the Soviet people in general, and Chernogolovka scientists in particular. "We were all together, and it was very joyful for us," Manelis remembered.[102] "There was no differentiation between people back then," Bogdanov agreed. "It was all ours, and everyone was happy to devote himself to building a new life here, establishing a new research institute, and carrying out important state assignments."[103] In the late 1950s and 1960s, Chernogolovka indeed looked like a "community of equals." The social origins of the first residents were typically secondary to their educational backgrounds and, most importantly, their scientific achievements.

"Everyone knew each other personally, and felt a part of one big family," Enman testified in his interview to the local newspaper in 2006.[104] "There was some kind of euphoria in the town, especially when we had just moved here," Vsevolod Gantmakher, who came to Chernogolovka in 1968, agreed. There was "an impression that you had a lot of friends and they all lived nearby. I remember I would go out for a walk in the evening, notice that someone had their light on, and go visit them" (see Figure 3.4).[105] "If the light was on," another scientist recalled, "you could come in at any time, even at midnight or

[100] TsAOPIM, f. 8099, op. 1, d. 59, l. 131.   [101] TsAOPIM, f. 8099, op. 1, d. 59, l. 131.
[102] Interview 1 with Georgii Manelis, Chernogolovka, December 2009.
[103] Interview 2 with Gennadii Bogdanov, Chernogolovka, December 2009.
[104] *Chernogolovskaia gazeta*, June 22, 2006.
[105] Interview 1 with Vsevolod Gantmakher, Chernogolovka, March 2010.

Figure 3.4: Vsevolod Gantmakher (second from the right), Chernogolovka ca. 1964

at 2 am. No one could ever imagine that he would not be welcome. Our doors were always open for each other."[106] This sense of belonging is crucial to understanding why the scientists not only helped Dubovitskii landscape the town, but also why they have fond memories about it decades later.

The House of Scientists and Informal Cultural Life in the Town

Not everyone from the first generation of Chernogolovka scientists was happy to start their life from scratch in the new place. Nina Konovalova, who moved to the testing ground permanently in 1962 to join her husband, Georgii Manelis, was at first terrified by what she saw there. "I have always been an avid theater-goer, and when we lived in Moscow we often went to various concerts and performances. After we came here, however, we found out that there was absolutely nothing in Chernogolovka but a tiny village." For the first five years, according to Konovalova, "life at the settlement was rather dreary."[107]

Konovalova's recollections were quite accurate. While Dubovitskii relied on his personal network and Semenov's authority to build the residential area, he could hardly convince the Council of Ministers to allocate funds for the entertainment of the testing ground's employees. This meant that, for the first five years, the scientists were left to their own resources and imagination.

---

[106] Interview 1 with Vera Sedykh, Chernogolovka, March 2010.
[107] Interview 1 with Nina Konovalova, Chernogolovka, March 2011.

The result was impressive. By the late 1960s, Chernogolovka had an exciting and eventful cultural life, with its own House of Scientists (*Dom Uchenykh*), a cinema club, a theater studio, and a poetry association. Both well-known actors such as Mikhail Kozakov and semi-official artists such as Vladimir Vysotskii and Bulat Okudzhava gave performances there. Some of the movies that were played at "Kaleidoscope," a cinema club established in 1969, were hard to find even in the most liberal Moscow theaters. How did all this come together?

Three main factors seem to have been at play here. First, Chernogolovka scientists, their tastes and values, as well as their enthusiasm, had a tremendous impact on shaping local cultural life. Second, the decision to expand the testing ground into a scientific center was crucial: the 1962 general plan specified that a future academic town should have a cultural club, *Dom Uchenykh*, where scientists could come together to watch movies and attend concerts.[108] Finally, Semenov, Dubovitskii, and Osipyan did their best to protect the scientific center from possible meddling by regional party committees.[109] The combination of these three factors was essential. Even though enthusiastic people came to Chernogolovka early on, they could not radically transform the cultural landscape of the town until 1967, when the House of Scientists was built.

Rustem Liubovskii, for example, arrived in Chernogolovka in fall 1963, after his graduation from the Moscow Physical-Technical Institute. An energetic young man, at Fiztech he organized guest lectures by prominent writers and artists, including Il'ia Erenburg and Mikhail Romm. When Liubovskii attempted to invite lecturers and artists to Chernogolovka, however, he discovered that it was nearly impossible to accomplish, as his guests would need to have special permission to enter the institute.[110] In December 1964, Liubovskii complained at the joint meeting of the party and Komsomol organizations of the ICP Branch:

I have worked here for more than a year, and I believe that we have to take an active part in organizing the cultural life for institute's employees. However, I keep running into myriad obstacles. It turns out that we cannot have any outside people [*postoronnie liudi*] give lectures at the ICP Branch. Neither do we have transportation to bring them here. We tried to organize a cinema club, but the idea fell through.[111]

Until the mid-1960s, the only cinema in town was set up in one of the wooden barracks of Glavspetsstroi in the southern part of the settlement. It played

---

[108] TsAOPIM, f. 8099, op. 1, d. 46, l. 65.
[109] I discuss scientists' relationship with the Communist Party in Chapter 4.
[110] "Sobytiia prokhodiat predo mnoi," in *Chernogolovskaia gazeta*, November 5, 2009.
[111] TsAOPIM, f. 8099, op. 1, d. 53, l. 59.

typical Soviet films for 20 kopeks per session. Yet, the conditions were so bad that many scientists avoided it entirely.[112]

Trying to accommodate the young employees, Dubovitskii allowed them to use an institute's bus to go to Moscow theaters and concert halls. In 1965, he also helped Liubovskii organize a one-time performance at the ICP Branch. The performance, called *A Couple on the Swings* ("*Dvoe na kacheliakh*"), was to take place inside the building located at the first ground (*pervaia ploshchadka*) of the ICP Branch, which was usually closed to the general public. Mikhail Kozakov and Tatiana Lavrentieva, who played leading roles in the performance, came from the cutting-edge Moscow theater "Sovremennik." Liubovskii remembered that several hours prior to the scheduled show, Dubovitskii received a call from above, prohibiting the actors from entering the first ground. Dubovitskii solved the problem by moving the performance to a recently finished building which had a tiny stage but was open to the general public. The play was a success among scientists.[113]

On June 30, 1967, a cinema theater opened its doors next to the barracks of Glavspetsstroi.[114] It was a typical Soviet building, poorly ventilated in summer and hard to heat in winter. Still, it provided scientists with the facilities they needed to invite artists and organize concerts. Georgii Manelis recalled that, around the same time, a group of four scientists, including himself, formed an "initiative group" (*initsiativnaia gruppa*) that appealed to Dubovitskii, asking him to expand the cinema theater into a cultural club: a House of Scientists. The group also included Lev Gor'kov, employed at the Landau ITP, and Vladimir Broude from the ISSP. Both were prominent Soviet scientists and laureates of the prestigious Lenin Prize.[115] Dubovitskii, as an authorized representative of the scientific center, agreed to help. A House of Scientists was a common institution within the Soviet Academy of Sciences, and Dubovitskii's request was not unusual.[116] As a result, on October 23, 1967, the Presidium of the Academy of Sciences issued a decree, according to which the Academy had to establish a House of Scientists at the Noginsk Scientific Center. The organization was funded by the Academy of Sciences. Yet, the House of Scientists had the right to gather membership fees and revenues from cultural events, to rent out its facilities, and to use the money to cover its expenses.[117] In December 1967, the Presidium appointed Valentina

---

[112] Interview 2 with Vladimir Enman, Chernogolovka, October 2010; Interview with Nina Konovalova, Chernogolovka, March 2011.

[113] Rustem Liubovskii, "Dvoe na kacheliakh," in *Chernogolovskaia gazeta*, November 12, 2009.

[114] *Reestry aktov vvoda po godam stroitel'stva.*

[115] Interview 5 with Georgii Manelis, Chernogolovka, February 2011. This oral testimony is supported by archival evidence: see TsAOPIM, f. 8099, op. 1, d. 68, l. 72.

[116] Interview with Valentina Chernozemova, Chernogolovka, February 2011.

[117] Archive of the House of Scientists at the Scientific Center in Chernogolovka, Decree №37–1442 of the Presidium of the Academy of Sciences of the USSR, October 23, 1967.

Chernozemova as the acting director of the House of Scientists.[118] A graduate of the Institute of Marxism and Leninism, she had previously worked as a secretary of the Komsomol organization at a large research institute in Moscow and had experience dealing with various party officials.

Any scientist with a doctorate degree who worked at one of Chernogolovka's research institutes could become a member of the House of Scientists. All members had to pay fees and, in return, were eligible to attend any events organized at the club. Once every three to five years, members held elections for a Board of Directors. The board consisted of eleven people, and met four times a year (once per quarter) to discuss an operating plan and schedule of events for the House of Scientists. It also approved proposals from its members. In 1967, Georgii Manelis was unanimously elected chairman of the board. Besides Manelis, various other scholars served on the board at different times, including Lev Vashin, Vsevolod Gantmakher, and Veniamin Shekhtman.

The House of Scientists had its own staff, but it could not afford to hire a full-time plumber, electrician, or chauffeur who would bring artists to Chernogolovka. Chernozemova constantly had to ask Dubovitskii and Osipyan to help out with technical personnel. At the time, each research institute in Chernogolovka was in charge of one or more social institutions in town – a school, a hospital, or a library. The ISSP became the patron of the House of Scientists. Apart from helping out with the maintenance of the building, the ISSP's party organization had to supervise the ideological work of the party cell of the cultural club.

What kind of work did the House of Scientists carry out? The Statute of the organization (*Ustav Doma Uchenykh*) specified three major goals: first, "to develop a creative atmosphere at the scientific center in Chernogolovka, which is so necessary for any efficient research work"; second, "to fulfill the cultural needs of the institutes' employees"; and, finally, "to provide scientists with the opportunity to meaningfully spend their leisure in order to increase their productivity at work."[119] In practice, this meant that many initiatives of the local scientific community would be supported by the House of Scientists and the institutes' administration. For example, in 1968 a theater studio was created in Chernogolovka. It was directed by Stal' Ledogorova, the wife of prominent Soviet actor Igor' Ledogorov. Many scientists took part in it. Bogdanov recalled attending most of their plays and even participating in one called *The Town at Dawn*

---

[118] Archive of the House of Scientists, Decree №32–1652 of the Presidium of the Academy of Sciences of the USSR, December 12, 1967. Interview with Valentina Chernozemova, Chernogolovka, February 2011.

[119] The Archive of the House of Scientists, "Ustav Doma Uchenykh nauchnogo tsentra RAN v Chernogolovke," l. 1.

("*Gorod na zare*").[120] Vera Sedykh, who moved to Chernogolovka in the late 1960s to join her husband Ernest Suvorov, became a permanent member of the studio. She recollected that all of the actors were members of the scientific community, employed at one of the research institutes in the town.[121] Later, in 1983, Sedykh organized a poetry association, called "Litob'edinenie," which allowed scientists to get together to study poetry and share their own poems with each other.

The House of Scientists certainly had to comply with the ideological require-ments received from Moscow. For example, all official events for the year 1970 revolved around celebrating the 100th anniversary of Vladimir Lenin's birth. Scientists were invited to watch films about Lenin's life and attend a series of lectures on "Lenin's theoretical legacy," as well as an exhibition by young artists, dedicated to Lenin's anniversary.[122] At the same time, the schedule of events included a concert by Zara Dolukhanova, a famous Soviet singer, and David Oistrakh, a world-renowned Soviet violinist, as well as a recital with the participation of Galina Vishnevskaia and Rudolf Barshai.[123] At different times, the House of Scientists had various hobby groups (*kruzhki*) and clubs within its structure: a chess club, an art studio, a German language club, a mountain skiing club, and many others. Yet the most remarkable phenomenon was the informal cinema club, "Kaleidoscope."

The cinema club was established by scientists in December 1969. It was a grassroots organization which "united people who liked cinema and shared the same intellectual views and values." In its heyday, the organization had almost 600 members, all of them candidates and doctors of sciences.[124] Each member had to pay an entrance fee of 2 rubles, and a monthly fee of 1 ruble. This money covered the expenses of the club, which was a self-sustaining organization.[125] The major goal of "Kaleidoscope," according to its Statute, was "to promote the best Soviet and foreign films in order to improve the cultural level and aesthetic education of movie-goers" ("*povyshenie kul'tur-nogo urovnia i esteticheskogo vospitaniia kinozritelei*"). In practice, the people who organized the cinema club wanted to have an opportunity to see foreign films that were not shown either on widescreen or on TV, as well as Soviet films that were not accessible to the general public.

The initiative to organize "Kaleidoscope" came from three scientists employed at the ISSP and the ICP Branch: Al'bert Timirbaev, Gennadii Babkin, and Iurii Poliakov. Timirbaev graduated from the Geology Department of MGU. "I was always interested in cinema," he remembered.

[120] Interview 2 with Gennadii Bogdanov, Chernogolovka, December 2009.
[121] Interview 1 with Vera Sedykh, Chernogolovka, March 2010.
[122] TsAOPIM, f. 1288, op. 1, d. 5, l. 165.   [123] TsAOPIM, f. 1288, op. 1, d. 5, l. 165.
[124] Archive of the House of Scientists, "Spravka ot 4 ianvaria 1987 goda."
[125] Archive of the House of Scientists, "Ustav Kinokluba 'Kaleidoskop.'"

"As I was finishing my studies at the university, I found out about the MGU cinema club. I went to several meetings, where I established connections with students from VGIK (the Russian State Institute of Cinematography). When I moved to Chernogolovka, I wanted to do something similar here."[126] Timirbaev's initiative became a subject of discussion at the meeting of the ISSP's trade union committee on November 27, 1969.[127] "Kaleidoscope" was created two weeks later.

For the first few years, Timirbaev, Babkin, and Poliakov traveled to Moscow film festivals and cinema clubs in order to rent films and bring them to Chernogolovka. One of them had connections at the Polish Embassy, which allowed "Kaleidoscope" to obtain films by well-known Polish directors. "We managed to see almost all of Andrzej Wajda's films at a time when no one else in the Soviet Union could see them," Timirbaev recalled. "The Poles would tell us that we could have a film for one night and bring it back to the embassy the next day. So we would take a car that belonged to the House of Scientists or a bus and go get it."[128] Needless to say, all the work was done on a voluntary basis.

Connections with film directors and artists were crucial for the success of the enterprise. For example, Chernogolovka scientists were among the few Soviet citizens who saw the uncensored version of *Andrei Rublev*, directed by Andrei Tarkovskii. Set against the background of fifteenth-century Russia, the film deals with the life of a famous Russian monk and icon painter, Andrei Rublev. Although Tarkovskii completed his masterpiece in 1966, it was not officially released in the Soviet Union until December 1971, when a censored version of the film came out in cinema theaters. The film was shelved for almost five years, except for the two premiers for the film industry at *Dom Kino* in Moscow in late 1966 and in 1969.[129]

In spite of this, in early 1970 the House of Scientists in Chernogolovka showed the uncensored version of *Andrei Rublev* to its members. Moreover, after the screening Tarkovskii appeared in front of the audience in person to answer questions and discuss the film.[130] Timirbaev managed to get in touch with Tarkovskii through Maria Chugunova, a young film director and

[126] Interview with Al'bert Timirbaev, Chernogolovka, March 2012.
[127] Archive of the ISSP, f. 1, op. 1, d. 93, l. 47, "Proceedings of the ISSP's Trade Union Committee (November 27, 1969)."
[128] Interview with Al'bert Timirbaev, Chernogolovka, March 2012.
[129] On the production history of *Andrei Rublev*, see Maia Turovskaya, *7 ½ ili Fil'my Andreia Tarkovskogo* (Moskva: Izdatel'stvo "Iskusstvo," 1991), pp. 65, 69–70; Vidad T. Johnson and Graham Petrie, *The Films of Andrei Tarkovskii: A Visual Figure* (Bloomington: Indiana University Press, 1994), pp. 79–85; and Sean Martin, *Andrei Tarkovsky* (Harpenden: Pocket Essentials, 2005), pp. 82–85.
[130] Archive of the ISSP, f. 1, op. 1, d. 97, l. 16, "Proceedings of the Annual Meeting of the ISSP's Trade Union Committee (October 14, 1970)."

Tarkovskii's stage manager at the time. It was Chugunova who arranged for Tarkovskii to bring his personal copy of the film to Chernogolovka. "It was an incredibly exciting evening," Timirbaev recalled. "Members of 'Kaleidoscope' would call up their friends in Moscow and tell them that they had to come immediately. It was a controversial film, in my opinion, reflecting on the role of the artist in society. It stunned us. For the whole week after the screening all people could talk about at research institutes was *Andrei Rublev*."[131]

In 1971, "Kaleidoscope" treated its members to another event that they all remembered warmly fifty years later: a concert by Vladimir Vysotskii. Vysotskii was a Soviet actor who worked at the Taganka Theater in Moscow at the time, but was best known to the Soviet intelligentsia as a semi-official singer poet, or *bard*, who indirectly criticized the Soviet system:[132] "We could not invite Vysotskii officially," the director of the House of Scientists, Valentina Chernozemova, recalled. "So all members of 'Kaleidoscope' chipped in to bring him here. The concert hall was packed; some people had to stand in aisles. One of them kept telling me: 'You will lose your party membership because of this concert.' But nothing like that happened."[133]

The annual report of the ISSP's trade union committee, issued in October 1971, mentioned Vysotskii's concert as "a meeting of Chernogolovka scientists with an actor V. Vysotskii."[134] Yet when Timirbaev and his colleagues attempted to invite Vysotskii again the following year, their plan fell through. Several days before the concert, Chernozemova received a call from the October Regional Committee in Moscow. The person on the other end of the line warned her that if she invited Vysotskii one more time, she would lose her job and her party membership.[135] The concert was canceled at the last minute.

Semenov, Dubovitskii, and Osipyan did not take part in organizing any of these events. According to Timirbaev, they could not be involved officially, because then they would have to take responsibility for whatever the cinema club was doing. "Why would they want this unnecessary headache?"[136] At the same time, most scientists testified in their interviews that both Dubovitskii and Osipyan attended "Kaleidoscope" on a regular basis, as the cinema club gave scientists an opportunity to see something new and unique, "something that we could not dream of seeing otherwise."[137] "Dubovitskii went to many events,"

[131] Interview with Al'bert Timirbaev, March 6, 2012, Chernogolovka.
[132] Vladimir Novikov, *Vysotskii: Zhizn' zamechatel'nykh liudei* (Moskva: Molodaia gvardia, 2008), pp. 113–120.
[133] Interview with Valentina Chernozemova, Chernogolovka, February 2011.
[134] Archive of the ISSP, f. 1, op. 1, d. 116, l. 23, "The Annual Report of the ISSP's Trade Union Committee (from October 1970 to October 1971)."
[135] Interview with Valentina Chernozemova, Chernogolovka, February 2011.
[136] Interview with Al'bert Timirbaev, Chernogolovka, March 2012.
[137] Interview with Al'bert Timirbaev, Chernogolovka, March 2012.

Manelis echoed. "We were all together at that time, building a town for ourselves, organizing our life here."[138]

Dubovitskii and Osipyan also assisted scientists in getting access to film repositories. In 1970, they invited Aleksei Romanov, the chairman of the State Committee for Cinematography (*Goskino*), to Chernogolovka, where they held a private meeting at Osipyan's office at the ISSP.[139] The goal of the meeting was to sign an official paper that would allow the organizers of "Kaleidoscope" to borrow movies from Gosfilmofond (the State Film Foundation of the Soviet Union) and the cinema repository at Belye Stolby near Moscow. The first had mostly Soviet films that were not available to the general public; the second owned a collection of foreign films. Timirbaev, who was present at the meeting, testified that, according to the signed agreement, "Kaleidoscope" could borrow one film per month from either Gosfilmofond or Belye Stolby, and no more than ten films per year. All films had to be returned the next day.[140]

Throughout the 1970s, "Kaleidoscope" remained the center of cultural life in Chernogolovka. "If the cinema club organized any cultural event, we knew we had to attend it," Gantmakher remembered.[141] What kind of movies did Chernogolovka's scientists see back then, and who decided which movies to bring to the town? First, there were myriad Soviet movies, mostly unavailable to the general audience. In many cases, movie directors presented their work in person. Andrei Tarkovskii, Rolan Bykov, Aleksandr Mitta, Vasilii Shukshin, Aleksandr Kaidanovskii, and Vadim Abdrashitov all visited Chernogolovka at one point or another. "Many directors enjoyed coming here, because they found discussions with our audience to be rewarding: here they met people who could read between the lines and who understood their work."[142]

"Kaleidoscope" members were also able to see a number of Italian, Polish, German, and other foreign movies, at a time when they were barely accessible to the rest of the Soviet population. They watched the films of such renowned Italian directors as Federico Fellini, Michelangelo Antonioni, and Pier Paolo Pasolini, as well as movies by Polish directors such as Andrzej Wajda, Jerzy Kawalerowicz, and Krzysztof Kieślowski.[143] "For the first time in our lives we saw another kind of cinema, which did not praise the Soviet Union and the Party and which told us about the life we did not know," Bogdanov recalled. "It was something completely different from what we were used to. In a sense,

[138] Interview 5 with Georgii Manelis, Chernogolovka, February 2011.
[139] Aleksei Romanov (1908–1998) was a chairman of the State Committee for Cinematography at the Council of Ministers from 1963 to 1972.
[140] Interview with Al'bert Timirbaev, Chernogolovka, March 2012.
[141] Interview with Vsevolod Gantmakher, Chernogolovka, March 2010.
[142] Interview with Al'bert Timirbaev, Chernogolovka, March 2012.
[143] Interview with Al'bert Timirbaev, Chernogolovka, March 2012.

it was our first encounter with life outside the Soviet Union, a slight opening [*priotkrytie*] of the 'iron curtain.'"[144]

Although "Kaleidoscope" had a formal council that was elected by the club members and consisted of ten to twelve people, it was mostly Timirbaev, Poliakov, and Babkin who decided what films to show, and then went to Gosfilmofond and Belye Stolby to get them. They met at least twice a month to discuss the film schedule. Later, a few other scientists from the ICP Branch and the ISSP joined them. Scientists decided what films and filmmakers to bring to the House of Scientists based on their knowledge of contemporary art and their tastes. In order to protect "Kaleidoscope" from any criticism on the part of the Noginsk City Committee and the October Regional Committee of the CPSU, its organizers invited Vladimir Broude from the ISSP to be chairman of the club's official council. A laureate of the Lenin Prize and a doctor of sciences, Broude was a powerful figure to have on their side. Moreover, he was a member of the Communist Party, which silenced possible discontent from local party officials.

How should we interpret the fact that, in the 1970s, Chernogolovka scientists had more intellectual leeway than the majority of the Soviet population? Does it mean that the town became "an oasis of intellectual freedom," or, even worse, a hotbed of dissent? While some scientists agreed with the former, all of them unanimously rejected the latter. "Even if there was some sort of opposition, it was very insignificant," Gantmakher explained (*"Eto byla fronda dovol'no nizkogo urovnia"*).[145] "Ours was not any kind of explicit dissent," Timirbaev confirmed. "We simply did not think about it in these terms back then. If we had had to violate any official rules, none of us would have done it. Everyone knew too well what the cost of it would be."[146]

Nonetheless, in hindsight, all interviewees agreed that in the 1970s, during Brezhnev's conservative rule, "Kaleidoscope" was like "a taste of freedom" (*"glotok svobody"*). "When I think today about why everyone was so eager to be part of the cinema club, my answer is because it provided an outlet [*otdushina*] for us. More often than not, one could see something there which did not fit into the usual framework, something worthwhile [*chto-to stoiashchee*]."[147] The paradox of the situation was that none of the films shown at "Kaleidoscope" were officially banned in the Soviet Union. While they were not available to the general audience, they could be found in state cinema repositories. With proper personal connections and arrangements, certain groups of the Soviet population could get access to them. Chernogolovka scientists were among the select few who were not only

144 Interview 3 with Gennadii Bogdanov, Chernogolovka, August 2010.
145 Interview with Vsevolod Gantmakher, Chernogolovka, March 2010.
146 Interview with Al'bert Timirbaev, Chernogolovka, March 2012.
147 Interview with Al'bert Timirbaev, Chernogolovka, March 2012.

interested in watching these films, but who also had an opportunity to do so. It is important to note that all movie screenings were in strict compliance with the ISSP party organization's requirements. Moreover, there were state security officials present at screenings, who reported to the Noginsk department of the KGB on a regular basis. One should also add that, at the end of the day, only several hundred people saw films and attended concerts organized by "Kaleidoscope," which constituted a small minority even among Chernogolovka's population.

In her recent study of Ozersk, Kate Brown argued that residents of the pluto-nium city lived in "a socialist paradise." They were among select Soviet citizens who enjoyed affluence and consumer freedom, which were important factors in the Soviet competition with the West during the Cold War. "As plutopia matured," Brown contends, its "residents gave up their civil and biological rights for consumer rights."[148] While "superior purchasing power" might have translated into "feelings of loyalty and belonging" for residents of Ozersk and other secret nuclear communities, this was certainly not the case in Chernogolovka. Since the physical-chemical center was never a priority for the Soviet government, Semenov's town did not receive any special provisions or extra funds. Chernogolovka's residents did not enjoy any privileged consumer rights, either. During Brezhnev's rule they had to travel to Moscow to buy food and basic consumer goods, just like millions of other Soviet citizens. Yet, most of my interviewees shared the same feelings of loyalty and belonging as residents of Ozersk. Many maintained that they had lived in a privileged community. Why was this the case?

First, there was an overall improvement in the standard of living in the post-Stalin Soviet Union, which was a result of the rapid economic growth and the shift toward the consumer sector in the late 1950s. When Chernogolovka scientists compared their living conditions to those of their parents in the 1930s and 1940s, they clearly saw an improvement. Even though they did not enjoy the material abundance that residents of nuclear towns had, at no point did inhabitants of Chernogolovka have to starve, like they did during the war. Thanks to the town's proximity to Moscow and Dubovitskii's private initiatives, scientists usually had all basic foodstuffs on their tables.

Second, in comparison to the vast majority of Soviet urban settlements, Chernogolovka was still relatively well-off. This was especially obvious when it came to the distribution of housing. While an average Soviet family had to wait for years for a poorly built apartment, Chernogolovka residents typically received modern and comfortable housing within a year of their arrival. Many naively perceived their privileged housing conditions as

---

[148] Brown, *Plutopia*, pp. 5, 256–258.

evidence of the progressive development of Soviet society and the superiority of the socialist model.

Finally, the privileges that the Chernogolovka scientific community enjoyed could only last as long as the Soviet regime saw science and scientific development as the panacea to the country's economic and social problems. As the Soviet economy began to slow down, the state decreased its funding of fundamental sciences. In the context of the state-centralized distribution system, this gradually led to the decline of the quality of living in towns such as Chernogolovka that were never a priority for the military–industrial complex. These changes were especially tangible for the next generation of scientists, who came of age under Brezhnev and who arrived in Chernogolovka in the late 1970s and early 1980s.

4   Scientists, Ideology, and the Communist Party in Chernogolovka

Vladimir Enman refused to join the ranks of the Communist Party of the Soviet Union for personal reasons. After his father's execution in 1938, he tried to avoid any political engagement. "Some inner voice always stopped me. Before 1956, I concealed that my father had been repressed from everyone, including my wife. Even after the rehabilitation I still kept writing in all official documents that my father died a natural death. He died instead when they shot him dead on the day of his trial."[1] As Enman kept climbing up the professional ladder – by 1967 he was in charge of the ICP Branch's Machine Shop, which employed 240 people – the pressure on him to become a CPSU member increased. One day, Dubovitskii invited Vladimir to his office, where the head of the institute's party organization was already waiting. They insisted that Enman not be permitted to occupy such a high-ranking position unless he joined the party. Eventually, Enman acquiesced. He was admitted to the CPSU in February 1968.[2] As a party member, Enman had to regularly attend party meetings and participate in philosophical and ideological seminars. He never challenged the official party resolutions, but he gradually came to think that his membership in the party had certain advantages: after all, it allowed Enman to have a positive impact on the work of the Machine Shop.

The Communist Party penetrated all corners of Soviet society, controlling people's lives from cradle to grave. Every Soviet institution had to have a primary party organization (PPO), which aspired to manage all aspects of its employees' lives. The party organizations were subordinate to regional party committees, which, in turn, received instructions from the Central Committee of the CPSU. The Politburo topped the entire structure. The small scientific community in Chernogolovka was no exception. In the spirit of the Thaw, research institutes in the town were allowed to have their own primary party organizations dominated by scientists. This provided Chernogolovka relative independence in dealing with higher party committees. It also allowed

---

[1] Interview 1 with Vladimir Enman, Chernogolovka, August 2009; Interview 2 with Vladimir Enman, Chernogolovka, October 2010.
[2] TsAOPIM, f. 8099, op. 1, d. 75, l. 44.

scientists to significantly shape the professional, cultural, and social development of the town. Fedor Dubovitskii and Yuri Osipyan worked hard to establish a good relationship with the regional party committee. While geographically Chernogolovka's institutes fell under the jurisdiction of the Noginsk city party committee (*Noginskii gorkom KPSS*), Dubovitskii and Osipyan insisted that their institutes were subordinate to the October regional party committee (*Oktiabr'skii raikom KPSS*) in Moscow. The difference between the two was drastic. Noginskii gorkom was a typical Soviet institution staffed with dogmatic and usually poorly educated people who did not know much about scientific research. Oktiabr'skii raikom, on the contrary, was renowned for its employees' open-mindedness. Located on Leninskii Prospect, right in the heart of Moscow, it was in charge of the Presidium of the Soviet Academy of Sciences, as well as dozens of research institutes. Many of its employees had doctorate degrees and were more tolerant of the critical thinking among the scientific intelligentsia.

This chapter investigates Chernogolovka scientists' relationship with the Communist Party on the ground and the ways in which the inhabitants of the town reconciled their lives with the constant presence of the CPSU. It also explores the formation of scientists' political opinions before they moved to Chernogolovka.[3] I show that many young scientists who came to live and work in the town in the late 1950s and the 1960s were typical representatives of Stalin's last generation, to borrow Juliane Fürst's term, whose "identity was irrevocably linked with the Soviet state."[4] Like millions of their peers, they grew up with a strong faith in socialist values, and readily recognized the supremacy of the collective over the individual. Many believed that in the postwar USSR equal opportunities existed for all members of the collective.[5] As children, these scientists had been educated to devote their lives to labor for the common good, which later translated naturally into their professional lives. They also learned to love Lenin, Stalin, and the Soviet Fatherland. Like millions of their peers, young scientists were expected to preach unquestionable loyalty to the Communist Party, which proclaimed building a classless Communist society in the Soviet Union as its primary goal. Many scientists of the first Cold War generation enthusiastically embraced these values, and continued to cherish them throughout their adult lives, despite the confusion and doubts planted in their hearts and minds by Khrushchev's denunciation of Stalin and the emergence of the dissident movement in the late 1960s.

---

[3] I examine scientists' mature political outlook in Chapter 5, where I discuss the attitudes of the local scientific community to the Soviet state and its critics.

[4] Fürst, *Stalin's Last Generation*, p. 4.

[5] On the Russian intelligentsia's belief in the "Holy Grail of collectivism," see Zubok, *Zhivago's Children*, pp. 33–39, 64–65.

I demonstrate that, while many of my interviewees grew up as devout Communists, Khrushchev's report at the Twentieth Party Congress in February 1956 provoked a wide range of reactions among them. Some Chernogolovka scientists felt betrayed by Khrushchev, convinced that he attacked Stalin in order to strengthen his own position in power. Others embraced the de-Stalinization process, hoping that after Stalin's death the Soviet Union would finally embark on the correct path. There were also scientists who became partially disillusioned with the Communist Party after the Twentieth Congress. In the 1960s and 1970s, some of them would begin their individual "search for truth," reading samizdat and listening to foreign radio broadcasts.

Curiously, scientists' political views oftentimes did not directly translate into their relationship with the Communist Party. Even though after 1956 fewer scientists joined the CPSU for ideological considerations, many found membership of the party to be a necessary and acceptable part of their everyday lives. For one thing, party membership allowed scientists to have a positive impact on the life of their community. Having "their own people" (*svoi liudi*) in local party organizations meant that scientists could participate in defining the directions of scientific research, distributing funding, facilitating travel to foreign conferences, and even inviting semi-official artists to Chernogolovka. Being a party member was also beneficial for one's professional career, as it indicated to the higher-ups that a person was politically reliable, and could therefore be entrusted with supervising a research group or laboratory.

At the same time, scientists in closed scientific towns enjoyed what I call "the privilege of passive participation."[6] The post-Stalin regime needed scientists to participate in the system, by joining the party and publicly displaying their consent. Yet it no longer demanded that scientists denounced each other or actively participated in various ideological campaigns, as was the case during the "scholarly discussions" of the late 1940s and the early 1950s. The residents of Chernogolovka considered their party membership to be acceptable precisely because the state no longer strove to instill ideological purity among the scientific intelligentsia. Scientists were now permitted to hold on to their private opinions, as long as they did not voice their discontent in public. The fact that the state did not openly interfere in scientific affairs, at least in disciplines such as physics and chemistry, was yet another argument for scientists to join the Communist Party.[7]

Chernogolovka scientists' relative independence in dealing with the higher party committee did not come to an end after Khrushchev's ouster in the fall of

[6] I am grateful to Semion Lyandres for helping me develop this term.
[7] On Soviet scientists' reclaiming their professional autonomy, see Josephson, "Soviet Scientists and the State," p. 607; Josephson, *New Atlantis Revisited*, p. 278.

1964. Paul Josephson demonstrated that after 1968 Akademgorodok lost its unique scientist-dominated party organization and academic freedom, as the Brezhnev regime sought to re-establish the supremacy of the central party apparatus and exert greater control over scientific research.[8] The crackdown of the late 1960s did not affect the scientific community in Chernogolovka in the same manner. All research institutes in the town were able to maintain their own primary party organizations, in which scientists occupied leading positions. By 1970, Dubovitskii and Osipyan brought all the PPOs under the jurisdiction of Oktiabr'skii raikom. This gave them more leeway in planning the agendas of party meetings. Chernogolovka was also allowed to have its own party organization that oversaw the work of the institutes' PPOs. In this respect, the fact that the town was never a priority for the Soviet government played into the hands of Semenov and Dubovitskii. While Akademgorodok's special status as a symbol of academic freedom eventually provoked the wrath of the Communist Party officials, Chernogolovka avoided this fate, largely thanks to the cautious and wise policies of the local administration. But let us first look at scientists' attitudes toward the Communist Party and ideology before they even moved to the town.

Coming of Age During Late Stalinism and the Thaw

One day, when Rimma Liubovskaia was in the third grade, a teacher asked her to leave the classroom for a few minutes. She was a straight "A" student and could not think of any previous misbehavior on her part. Puzzled, she went out. Several days later, on December 21 – which was Rimma's birthday – her teacher presented her with a mechanical pen, bought with her classmates' money. "It turned out that I was born on the same day as Stalin, and this supposedly shed some special light on me," Liubovskaia joked in her interview. "It seems comical now, but back then I was proud of it. It was my first pen. I did not even know how to use it."[9]

Like Liubovskaia, the rest of Chernogolovka scientists were products of mature Stalinist society – a fact that had a significant impact on their adult lives. They grew up in a totalitarian dictatorship, where Stalin was "the Great Leader" (*Vozhd'*) and where the powerful repressive and propaganda machines worked to physically eradicate all dissent. While recent scholarship argues that the cracks in the Soviet monolith appeared during late Stalinism, they certainly did not engulf all Soviet citizens, let alone children.[10] Those of my interviewees

---

[8] Josephson, *New Atlantis Revisited*, pp. 263–265, 277.

[9] Interview 1 with Rimma Liubovskaia, Chernogolovka, October 2010.

[10] See, for example, B. M. Firsov, *Raznomyslie v SSSR 1940–1960-e gody: Istoriia, teoriia i praktika* (Sankt-Peterburg: Izdatel'stvo Evropeiskogo Universiteta, 2008) and Zubkova, *Russia After the War*.

who were born during the First Five-Year Plan admired Stalin's industrialization campaign, which, they believed even decades later, wiped out poverty and improved the standards of living in the USSR. Younger and older children embraced the myth of Stalin as "the savior of the Soviet Fatherland from the Nazi invasion." In kindergartens, future scientists sang Soviet songs praising Lenin and Stalin. Some of them remembered planting wheat in long pots, and when the wheat grew up and their teachers cut it, children could read "Glory to Great Stalin!" ("Slava Velikomu Stalinu!"), written inside the pots.[11] Crucially, the overwhelming majority of my interviewees grew up in isolation from the outside world, and simply did not know any alternative way of life. Even at the height of the Great Terror many were convinced that they lived in the best country in the world. Such was the frightening power of the Stalinist propaganda machine.

Becoming a worthy member of the collective and absorbing the Soviet way of life were primary goals of Soviet youth born in the 1930s. A true Communist had to be hardworking and well educated, obedient, and willing to contribute to the common good. He or she had to be passionately patriotic, committed to building a Communist society in the Soviet Union, and grateful to a powerful state for the opportunities that it provided. The Communist Party was there to help educate Soviet youth, indoctrinating children from a very young age. The Octobrist organization, established around 1924, prepared children from seven to nine years old to join the Pioneer movement, which was set up as a junior equivalent of the Komsomol.[12] At fourteen, every student was expected to apply for membership in the Komsomol, or the Communist Youth League, which was the final step before joining the Communist Party and an essential requirement in applying for any higher education institution across the USSR.[13] Chernogolovka scientists participated in all three stages of young Communists' education, usually taking pride in belonging to a higher cause. It was natural for them to be part of a Communist collective. Growing up, many were convinced that individual needs should always be secondary to collective needs. The Great Patriotic War and the Soviet victory in that war only strengthened my interviewees' unquestionable loyalty to the Communist Party. Manelis, who entered the Komsomol in 1944, remembered that all his peers were eager to become a Komsomolets: "No one forced us to join, but the war was under way. How could we stay away from it?"[14] The war also enhanced

---

[11] Interview 1 with Leonid Mezhov-Deglin, Chernogolovka, March 2010.

[12] On the pioneer movement, see Kelly, *Children's World*, pp. 547–555.

[13] For research on the Communist Youth League, see Kitty Weaver, *Russia's Future: The Communist Education of Soviet Youth* (New York: Praeger, 1981); Fürst, *Stalin's Last Generation*; and Matthias Neumann, *The Communist Youth League and the Transformation of the Soviet Union, 1917–1932* (New York: Routledge, 2011).

[14] Interview 1 with Georgii Manelis, Chernogolovka, December 2009.

scientists' trust in Comrade Stalin. Those of them who lost their fathers in the war were educated to see Stalin as their substitute father, whom they were expected to love and respect.[15]

For many Chernogolovka scientists, the notorious Doctors' Plot was their first real encounter with the repressive side of the Stalinist system. In January 1953, *Pravda*, the official newspaper of the Central Committee, published an article that accused a group of prominent Moscow doctors, mostly of Jewish decent, of plotting to assassinate Soviet leaders. Persecutions of Soviet Jews followed: some were dismissed from their jobs; others were arrested and even executed.[16] The anti-Semitic campaign was stopped short by Stalin's death in March 1953. However, it made a strong impression on numerous university students. Abrikosov, whose parents were high-ranking pathologists at the Kremlin hospital, recollected that it was a very disturbing time for his family. "Luckily my parents were not targeted but many of my father's students were arrested."[17] Bogdanov, who was seventeen, identified the Doctors' Plot as an episode which made him "rush around" (*metat'sia tuda suida*) for the first time in his life. "I could not really understand how doctors could have murdered top Soviet officials. I had a difficult time believing the whole story. This episode brought a lot of confusion (*razbrod*) in my head, forcing me to start analyzing the situation on my own."[18] Manelis also admitted that his generation was "alarmed by the Doctors' Plot." "But it was a single episode," he added, "and we interpreted it as some kind of deviation from the official party line."[19]

Not surprisingly, scientists of Jewish origin felt the effects of the Doctors' Plot much more acutely. Gantmakher, also seventeen years old at the time, studied from early morning till late at night to earn top grades for his entrance exams at Fiztech. Even though he passed his exams with flying colors and was admitted to Fiztech, he considered himself to be extremely lucky. After all, one of his friends, a brilliant student with a talent for linguistics, was denied access to Moscow State University because of his Jewish background. He had to enroll in a third-tier college studying physics instead, which eventually ruined his life. The persecution of Gantmakher's father's Jewish colleagues was further proof that the repressive machine was moving full speed ahead.[20] Shekhtman

---

[15] Zubok, *Zhivago's Children*, p. 21.
[16] For a detailed examination of the Stalin anti-Semitic campaign, see Jonathan Brent, *Stalin's Last Crime: The Plot Against the Jewish Doctors* (New York: Perennial, 2004) and Louis Rapoport, *Stalin's War Against the Jews: The Doctors' Plot and the Soviet Solution* (New York: Free Press, 1990).
[17] Interview with Alexei Abrikosov, Lemont (Illinois), July 2010.
[18] Interview 3 with Gennadii Bogdanov, Chernogolovka, August 2010.
[19] Interview 1 with Georgii Manelis, Chernogolovka, December 2009.
[20] Interview with Vsevolod Gantmakher, Chernogolovka, March 2010. On the emergence of anti-Semitism at Soviet universities, see Tromly, *The Making of the Soviet Intelligentsia*, pp. 84–101.

graduated from the Moscow Institute of Steel and Alloys in June 1952. Despite his cum laude diploma and the high demand for scientific and engineering specialists, he was unemployed for almost half a year because he was a Soviet Jew. He was finally hired as a laboratory assistant at the Evening Metallurgical Institute. Even so, he did not dare apply to graduate school until the summer of 1956.[21]

Stalin's death on March 5, 1953, put an end to the anti-Semitic campaign. Few people, however, felt relieved. Millions of Soviet citizens perceived Stalin's death as a personal tragedy and mourned the deceased leader.[22] Huge crowds rushed to the Hall of Columns in the House of the Soviets, located near the Kremlin, where Stalin's body was temporarily displayed. The crowds were so dense that hundreds of people were crushed to death in a human jam that formed as a result of a terrible congestion in the narrow old streets of Moscow. The vast majority of Chernogolovka scientists grieved with the rest of the population, although the individual reactions of scientists varied based on their age and family history.

Gennadii Bogdanov and Lana Ukrainka admitted they started weeping when they heard the news. "I cried and cried relentlessly standing in front of Stalin's portrait with a black ribbon on my arm," Bogdanov recalled. "Back then I thought that only Stalin's steel determination allowed the USSR to defeat Nazi Germany in the Great Patriotic War. How could I not grieve?"[23] Alexei Abrikosov, whose parents nearly perished during the Doctors' Plot, also felt shaken. "We believed that Stalin was our indispensable leader and without him we would all perish." In early March, Abrikosov attempted to reach the Hall of Columns, but fortunately was stopped by the police. This prevented him from getting hurt in the terrible congestion.[24] Shekhtman and Efimov tried to see Stalin's body, too. The former changed his mind after he had heard about the deadly stampede from his older brother.[25] Efimov persevered, confessing in an interview that he was among "those mad boys who tried to reach the Hall of Columns by walking on roofs." It took him several days to get to the place. When he finally did, he was unpleasantly surprised by the sight. "As I walked by Stalin," Efimov remembered, "I saw a dead person: his face was dark and covered in smallpox scars; his huge swollen hand resting on top of his body." When I asked Efimov what made him go there, he shrugged his shoulders and

[21] Interview 1 with Veniamin Shekhtman, Chernogolovka, March 2010. See also Archive of the ISSP, "1986. Kandidaty v chleny-korrespondenty" (folder), "Shekhtman Veniamin Sholomovich. Lichnyi listok po uchetu kadrov" and "Avtobiografiia."

[22] On the popular reactions to Stalin's death, see Aksiutin, *Khrushchevskaia "ottepel'*," pp. 24–32; and Zubok, *Zhivago's Children*, pp. 45–46.

[23] Interview 2 with Gennadii Bogdanov, Chernogolovka, December 2009; Interview 1 with Lana Ukrainka, Chernogolovka, September 2010.

[24] Interview with Alexei Abrikosov, Lemont (Illinois), July 2010.

[25] Interview 1 with Veniamin Shekhtman, Chernogolovka, March 2010.

said "My boyish curiosity."[26] Even Enman, who felt resentful after his father's arrest, joined his coworkers on a train trip from Leningrad to Moscow to say goodbye to Stalin. "Why did I go? Well, how can I explain this to you? Our brains were cluttered up (*nam zasorili mozgi*): every day we heard how great and irreplaceable Stalin was. So when he died, we all thought that everything would fall apart without him. This is the way we were raised."[27]

Younger scientists appear to have been less affected by Stalin's death. Many recollected not their own experiences, but the reactions of their teachers and parents instead. Rimma Liubovskaia was still a high school student at the time. "I remember our school director came to our drawing class and announced that Stalin died. People around me started sobbing, but I was most shocked by our teacher's reaction who simply said: 'Well, he was an old man, so he died.'"[28] Mileiko remembered running into his physics teacher the day after Stalin's death. "Aleksandr Pavlovich, what are we going to do now?" he asked. "Do you know what he said to me? My teacher said: 'So what?' Our school director, a war veteran, was sobbing like a child, and my physics teacher could not care less. I could never forget his reaction."[29] Suvorov recalled joining a large mourning crowd in front of Stalin's statue in Tashkent. But when he came home, his grandmother, who had lost almost all her relatives in 1937, told him: "Remember this day, grandson. The beast has died (*zver' sdokh*)." Suvorov admitted that at the moment he did not really understand her words. "Yet I remembered them, and it all became clear later."[30]

Why did Chernogolovka scientists mourn the death of the dictator? It was partially a result of the psychosis that swept across Soviet society in early March 1953. For more than two decades, Soviet people lived under a regime that revolved around Stalin. Although it suppressed all types of dissent and brutally punished the opposition, when the dictator died only a small minority did not give in to the hysteria.[31] Stalin was also the only Soviet leader that the postwar Soviet youth really knew: when they were born, between 1928 and 1939, Stalin was already in power. All their childhood and adolescence, these scientists were immersed in propaganda that eulogized Stalin and his rule. In 1953, they simply did not know any alternative.

Chernogolovka scientists' youthful delusions about Stalin ended rather abruptly. On February 25, 1956, Nikita Khrushchev walked up to the Central Committee podium at the Twentieth Party Congress to deliver a four-hour-long speech. At the heart of his speech was a devastating attack on Stalin. The report

[26] Interview 1 with Oleg Efimov, Chernogolovka, March 2011.
[27] Interview 1 with Vladimir Enman, Chernogolovka, August 2009.
[28] Interview 1 with Rimma Liubovskaia, Chernogolovka, October 2010.
[29] Interview 1 with Sergei Mileiko, Chernogolovka, August 2010.
[30] Interview 1 with Ernest Suvorov, Chernogolovka, August 2010.
[31] Aksiutin, *Khrushchevskaia "ottepel'*," p. 31.

accused Stalin of creating a "cult of personality," accumulating all power in his hands and grossly violating the principles of "party democracy."[32] It indicted Stalin for the destruction of party elites in the 1930s, for incompetent wartime leadership, for the deportations of entire nationalities, and for instigating the Doctors' Plot, among other things.[33] At the same time, Khrushchev aspired to separate Stalin's crimes from the Communist Party and ideology, insisting that Stalin had betrayed Lenin.[34] "We are fully confident," the First Secretary ended his speech, "that our party, guided by the historical decisions of the Twentieth Congress, will lead the Soviet people down the Leninist path to new successes and new victories."[35]

Khrushchev's report was quickly named the "secret speech." Yet, as Vladislav Zubok maintains, it became "anything but secret for tens of millions in the Soviet Union and hundreds of millions around the world." Even though Khrushchev's indictment was incomplete, the report produced a profound shock among idealistic, educated Russians who had grown up as Communist believers, but were now forced to admit the criminal nature of the leader whom they had been raised to love and admire.[36] Confusion and resentment were widespread among Chernogolovka scientists, especially during the first several months. Bogdanov admitted that he felt betrayed and resentful when he heard the speech. Remaining a naïve Stalinist, he was convinced that Khrushchev attacked Stalin in order to improve his own stakes in the political power struggle. "Much later I was able to give up my delusions and uproot my naïve Stalinism, but I still could not forgive Khrushchev for the betrayal."[37] Vashin was not as open during his interviews, but he also testified that he did not see any positive implications of the speech. "Some people say that Khrushchev's denunciation of the cult of personality was his major accomplishment. But what good could come out of it? Did it make anyone's life easier?"[38] Vashin found out about the speech from his father, a loyal party member. He claimed that he and his father "did not lose their heads over it," but that both perceived the speech as an extraordinary event. "When you find out that the leader of your party was a traitor who had engaged in anti-party activity, it is natural to be shocked."[39]

[32] *Doklad Pervogo sekretaria TsK KPSS tov. Khrushcheva "O kul'te lichnosti i ego posledst-viiakh,"* pp. 5–6.

[33] *Doklad Pervogo sekretaria TsK KPSS tov. Khrushcheva*, pp. 46, 52.

[34] Taubman, *Khrushchev*, p. 272.

[35] *Doklad Pervogo sekretaria TsK KPSS tov. Khrushcheva*, p. 71.

[36] For an excellent discussion of the impact of the secret speech on the educated Soviet youth, see Zubok, *Zhivago's Children*, pp. 60–70. Consider also Susanne Schattenberg, "'Democracy' or 'Despotism'? How the Secret Speech was Translated into Everyday Life," in Jones, ed., *The Dilemmas of De-Stalinization*, pp. 64–79; Aksiutin, *Khrushchevskaia "ottepel',"* pp. 212–228; and Jones, *Myth, Memory, Trauma*, pp. 28–43.

[37] Interview 2 with Gennadii Bogdanov, Chernogolovka, December 2009.

[38] Interview 2 with Lev Vashin, Chernogolovka, April 2010.

[39] Interview 1 with Lev Vashin, Chernogolovka, March 2010.

Other scientists were also confused, but many perceived the report positively. Shilov was pleased by Khrushchev's revelations. "The revolution had stirred up a lot different people," he explained, "but Khrushchev owned up to the past errors and pledged to correct them in the future. I thought that the party would now take the right course."[40] Shekhtman welcomed the report, too. In February 1956, he was elected secretary of the Komsomol organization at his institute, a position that obliged him to read the secret speech at the closed Komsomol meeting. He found the content to be shocking, but was attracted by the report's candor, which made Khrushchev look like a more humane ruler.[41] Abrikosov also thought the fact that Khrushchev spoke about Stalin's crimes openly, from the podium of the Central Committee, was his greatest accomplishment. "I do not think that Khrushchev was a great ruler, but what he did was tremendous. Things like this could not happen again after he named them openly."[42] "After Khrushchev's speech, it became clear that some drastic positive changes were under way," Manelis confirmed. "We welcomed them, but we did not really know how to proceed down the road."[43]

Finally, a significant minority of my interviewees admitted that the secret speech undermined their trust in the Communist Party, although not their commitment to the socialist cause. Gantmakher, for example, was an active Komsomol member in his high school and at Fiztech. Yet, when he learned about Khrushchev's revelations, he lost all interest in public activity. "For me that was it [*mne kak otrezalo*]. The report made me rethink and re-evaluate my previous beliefs and get rid of some of the stereotypes I grew up with. For example, I could no longer read Soviet newspapers without questioning their content."[44] Despite this, Gantmakher maintained that he stayed a socialist in his political beliefs. Efimov's reaction was more dramatic:

Once I heard about the speech, I realized that there existed no such thing as an ideal ruler. If people in power had lied to me all this time, I could not believe them any longer. I did not think that Khrushchev was any better than them. He claimed he was too afraid to speak up before Stalin died. But what kind of a Communist are you, if you put your own life above the common good?[45]

While the secret speech provoked different reactions among Chernogolovka scientists, it did not prompt them to act. None of my interviewees recounted participating in any political, social, or literary debates that took place at Soviet universities. Nor did they join any student organizations that aspired to

---

[40] Interview 3 with Aleksandr Shilov, Chernogolovka, March 2010.
[41] Interview 2 with Veniamin Shekhtman, Chernogolovka, March 2010.
[42] Interview 1 with Alexei Abrikosov, Lemont (Illinois), July 2010.
[43] Interview 3 with Georgii Manelis, Chernogolovka, December 2009.
[44] Interview 1 with Vsevolod Gantmakher, Chernogolovka, March 2010.
[45] Interview 2 with Oleg Efimov, Chernogolovka, March 2011.

contribute to the de-Stalinization process.[46] As Zubok noted, ideological unrest was marginal among students of physics, chemistry, geology, and biology.[47] Remarkably, young Chernogolovka scientists did not feel alienated from the Soviet state either. Many welcomed the cultural awakening and the first Soviet attempts to come to terms with the Stalinist past. But they saw the real opportunities of the Thaw in the more trustworthy relationship between scientists and the state, which led to the relaxation of party controls over scientific enterprises and increased autonomy for Soviet scientists.

Scientists and the Communist Party in Chernogolovka

At the ICP, Nikolai Semenov welcomed de-Stalinization and the outcome of the Twentieth Party Congress. In September 1956, the ICP dissolved the Political Department, a highly politicized organization in charge of propaganda and agitation, which was subordinate to the Ministry of Medium Machine-Building and which had replaced an elected party organization. The functioning of the regular party organization resumed. On September 26, 1956, in his address to the ICP party committee, Semenov expressed his institute's enthusiastic support of Khrushchev's speech. He especially commended the Communist Party's struggle against the personality cult and its return to the principles of collective leadership.[48] In the spirit of the Thaw, in October 1956 the ICP party bureau voted in favor of the rehabilitation of a scientist who had been unfairly persecuted in the late 1940s.[49]

After the Hungarian Uprising, however, the tone of the ICP party meetings became much more rigid. On February 20, 1957, the secretary of the ICP party organization delivered a report at a closed party meeting, in which he characterized the Hungarian Uprising as "the renewed attack of imperialists, led by the United States, on the socialist camp and the working class."[50] After the failed coup against Khrushchev in June 1957, the institute's party organization condemned the actions of Malenkov, Kaganovich, and Molotov. It also praised the positive economic, political, and cultural changes that had taken place across the USSR since 1953.[51] At the meeting, Dubovitskii took the floor to applaud the party and its courageous "defense of the Leninist ideals which would lead us to the splendid victories in our struggle for Communism."[52]

Dubovitskii's bombastic rhetoric notwithstanding, the defeat of the anti-party group was certainly not the first thing on his mind in the summer of 1957. The construction of the testing ground in Chernogolovka had begun in late 1956. As the first research facilities and residential housing were built,

---

[46] See, for example, Tromly, *Making the Soviet Intelligentsia*, pp. 141–147.
[47] Zubok, *Zhivago's Children*, p. 66.   [48] TsAOPIM, f. 8099, op. 1, d. 24, ll. 16–18.
[49] TsAOPIM, f. 8099, op. 1, d. 25, ll. 16–19.   [50] TsAOPIM, f. 8099, op. 1, d. 26, l. 41.
[51] TsAOPIM, f. 8099, op. 1, d. 27, ll. 3–5.   [52] TsAOPIM, f. 8099, op. 1, d. 27, l. 4.

Dubovitskii and other members of the ICP administration faced a number of organizational issues. The recruitment of scientific personnel capable of carrying out independent research was the most urgent among them. So was managing scientific work and daily life at the testing ground. The establishment of a primary party organization was another necessity, although for the first five years Dubovitskii insisted that all work in Chernogolovka was coordinated through the party organization of the ICP in Moscow. It was not until 1963 that the Branch of the ICP set up its own primary party organization. By then there were half a dozen philosophical and ideological seminars functioning in Chernogolovka. Out of 800 employees, 73 were members of the Communist Party, though scientists still constituted a minority among party members.[53]

In establishing the PPO of the ICP Branch, Dubovitskii initially relied on young scientists who had joined the party while still working at Semenov's institute in Moscow. Lev Vashin, for example, became a party member in 1954, when he had barely turned twenty-five years old. No one forced him to join, Vashin testified in one of his interviews: "I was simply following in my father's footsteps."[54] Vashin's father came from a large and poor peasant family, and benefited tremendously from the October Revolution, which allowed him to become a school teacher, and then a director. He joined the party in 1927, and remained a loyal member until his death. By 1959, Lev Vashin not only had an excellent reputation at the ICP party organization, he was also in charge of seventeen party members employed at the Department of Condensed Systems Combustion.[55] When asked, decades later, if he had recognized the disadvantages of living in a one-party dictatorship, Vashin protested: "What do you mean by a one-party dictatorship? My father came from a peasant milieu, and his party organization consisted of people just like him. What kind of dictatorship is it – do we dictate to ourselves? Ordinary Communists never felt superior to non-party members. If anything, we had to set an example for them."[56] Aleksandr Shilov, who transferred to Chernogolovka in 1962, was known as a devout Communist, too. In 1957, several months after the Hungarian Uprising, he criticized members of the ICP Komsomol organization for being apolitical and listening to American jazz music: "Some young people are simply confused and fail to understand what they should struggle for right now. But it is obvious that a serious struggle lies ahead of us, and it is yet unclear if it will take place in the context of peaceful coexistence, as we want, or something else."[57] These militant remarks were not intended merely to please the higher party committee. Years later, Shilov admitted that he was,

[53] TsAOPIM, f. 8099, op. 1, d. 46, l. 59.
[54] Interview 1 with Lev Vashin, Chernogolovka, March 2010.
[55] TsAOPIM, f. 8099, op. 1, d. 35, l. 27.
[56] Interview 1 with Lev Vashin, Chernogolovka, March 2010.
[57] TsAOPIM, f. 8099, op. 1, d. 26, l. 126.

indeed, a true believer at the time.[58] For Dubovitskii, people like Vashin and Shilov were indispensable as he worked to set up the local PPO in Chernogolovka. At the end of the day, they helped him maintain the image of the institute as a loyal and trustworthy organization in the eyes of the regional party committee. This, in turn, allowed Dubovitskii to create a good working environment at the institute.

In 1964, the PPO of the ICP Branch began keeping its own minutes, which signaled its growing independence from its Moscow headquarters. From January to December 1964, it held six general party meetings and twenty-one meetings of the party bureau.[59] The number of CPSU members at the institute continued to grow, too: from 156 people in 1965 to 233 in 1972.[60] One of Dubovitskii's concerns was that while Vashin and Shilov actively participated in the work of the PPO, other leading scientists such as Manelis, Merzhanov, and Dremin declined to join the ranks of the party.[61] Their decision was not necessarily political. According to scientists' complaints, administrative and public work took up a lot of their time, which many would rather have spent in their laboratories. Prioritizing scientific research over political and public engagement, Dubovitskii left them alone. Manelis did not join the CPSU until 1972.[62] Merzhanov became a party member only in the late 1980s, when he founded the Institute of Structural Macrokinetics and Materials Science in Chernogolovka.

To make sure that the scientific intelligentsia participated in the decision-making process and that scientists occupied leading positions at the institute's PPO, Dubovitskii focused on recruiting rank-and-file scientists into the ICP Branch's party organization. Bogdanov became a party member in September 1964, two years after he moved to Chernogolovka.[63] Konovalova joined the party in May 1968.[64] Neither of them was enthusiastic about their new roles. However, they saw no alternative. Both young scientists were part of the biological group at the ICP Branch run by Nikolai Emanuel, a prominent Soviet chemist and Semenov's former student. Bogdanov recollected that one day Emanuel' gathered his young employees in Chernogolovka, explaining that if they wanted their group to grow into a laboratory they had to establish a party cell. "No one really protested. Everyone knew that this was how things worked back in the day."[65] Konovalova admitted that by 1968 she had grown skeptical about certain decisions of the Communist Party. But as head of a new laboratory, she felt obliged to comply with Emanuel's request.[66]

[58] Interview 3 with Aleskandr Shilov, Chernogolovka, March 2010.
[59] TsAOPIM, f. 8099, op. 1, d. 53.   [60] TsAOPIM, f. 8099, op. 1, d. 59, l. 44.
[61] TsAOPIM, f. 8099, op. 1, d. 53, ll. 15–18.   [62] TsAOPIM, f. 8099, op. 1, d. 107, l. 12.
[63] TsAOPIM, f. 8099, op. 1, d.53, ll. 19–20; "Partiinyi bilet," Bogdanov's family archive.
[64] TsAOPIM, f. 8099, op. 1, d. 75, l. 117.
[65] Interview 1 with Gennadii Bogdanov, Chernogolovka, September 2009.
[66] Interview with Nina Konovalova, Chernogolovka, March 2011.

Other scientists became party members for different reasons. Rustem Liubovskii, for example, applied for a CPSU membership without any encouragement from above. A romantic idealist, he believed that his participation in the system was necessary to reform the party from within.[67] Liubovskii was not alone in his delusion: a number of other young scientists joined the party in early 1968, including Vladimir Martemianov and Vladimir Petinov.[68] Liubovskii and Martemianov were among the few scientists in Chernogolovka who voiced concerns about the Soviet invasion of Czechoslovakia, an incident that I examine in detail in Chapter 5. Overall, however, the number of Chernogolovka scientists who believed that their participation in the party would help build "socialism with a human face" was rather small.

Unlike the ICP Branch, which was originally part of Semenov's institute in Moscow, the ISSP had its own PPO from the moment of its foundation. The institute was established in February 1963, and so was the party organization. For the first six years, the ISSP's party organization fell under the jurisdiction of the Pervomaisk regional committee in Moscow. However, in January 1969 Osipyan had it transferred to Oktiabr'skii raikom.[69] Scientists who had to deal with Oktiabr'skii raikom on a regular basis remembered it fondly. "Oktiabr'skii raikom was a thorn in the side of the Moscow city party committee," Suvorov recollected. "People who worked there usually had higher education. They recognized the significance of Soviet scientific development, and tried to protect scientists from unnecessary meddling from the Central Committee."[70] At the time, Suvorov was a head of the general party organization that supervised the entire town. "Many of my colleagues at Oktiabr'skii raikom were also employed at the Academy of Sciences," he remembered, "and they were intelligent and sensible people. For example, Iurii Karabasov, the secretary of Oktiabr'skii raikom, had a doctorate degree and was a good specialist in materials science."[71] Shekthman also emphasized the significance of Chernogolovka's affiliation with the October regional committee:

If our party organization had been subordinate to Noginskii gorkom, it would have suffered from constant and vigorous check-ups of various party commissions, typical for provincial regional committees. Oktiabr'skii raikom was too busy to engage in this nonsense. They sent commissions here from time to time, but their goal was never to try and find ideological flaws. Their focus was on scientific research at the institute.[72]

[67] Interview 3 with Rustem Liubovskii, Chernogolovka, February 2011.
[68] TsAOPIM, f. 8099, op. 1, d. 76, ll. 1–5.
[69] TsAOPIM, f. 1281, op. 1, d. 3; TsAOPIM, f. 1281, op. 1, d. 4.
[70] Interview 1 with Ernest Suvorov, Chernogolovka, August 2010.
[71] Interview 1 with Ernest Suvorov, Chernogolovka, August 2010.
[72] Interview 1 with Veniamin Shekhtman, Chernogolovka, March 2010.

Being part of the October regional committee had a geographical advantage, too. While Noginskii gorkom was only half an hour away by bus, Oktiabr'skii raikom was part of the Moscow city party committee (*Moskovskii gorkom*). The latter was in charge of various regional committees in and around Moscow and sometimes was simply short of resources. Besides, the fact that the ICP Branch initially carried out research on classified state assignments also implied that party officials did not interfere in the institute's affairs as often as they did elsewhere. This certainly did not mean that Chernogolovka's PPOs could get away with neglecting directives and resolutions coming from Moskovskii gorkom, or the Central Committee: all resolutions were subject to discussion and approval at party organizations' meetings. It did mean, however, that their focus shifted from rigid ideological debates toward more practical discussions of scientific research and its applications.

Since scientists were allowed to focus more on research and less on ideological indoctrination, many found the party membership and the participation in meetings of the institute's party organization to be less objectionable. For one thing, joining the party made one's professional life much easier: being a CPSU member in a one-party Soviet state was similar to having a preliminary "seal of approval" for one's scientific endeavors. For another, party membership allowed scientists to participate in the decision-making process at their respective institutes.

The size of the ISSP's party organization continued to grow along with the institute. In 1963, when the ISSP was just emerging, seven out of twenty-one of the institute's employees were Communists, i.e., one-third of its personnel. By 1973, the institute had 983 employees, 150 of whom were Communists.[73] Scientists constituted a minority among the ISSP party members, although their number increased gradually. For example, in 1968 the institute had 363 employees, 64 of whom were members of the CPSU.[74] Of these sixty-four, only ten were scientists, while the rest were engineers, workers, laboratory assistants, and staff.[75] By November 1972, the number of Communists at the ISSP rose to 126 people. Scientists constituted 15.6 percent of the total number, or 20 people.[76]

Such a low number was partially a result of the official policy of the CPSU, which prioritized members of the working class while reserving a much lower quota for the scientific intelligentsia. It was also due to the fact that some scientists with good professional credentials simply refused to apply for party membership. Gantmakher, for example, recognized that becoming a party member would make traveling abroad much easier for him, but he declined to join the

---

[73] Archive of the ISSP, Newsletter "Partiinye, profsoiuznye, komsomol'skie lidery" ("The Party, Trade Union and Komsomol Leaders").

[74] Archive of the ISSP, Newsletter "Partiinye, profsoiuznye, komsomol'skie lidery."

[75] TsAOPIM, f. 1281, op. 1, d. 3, l. 41.   [76] TsAOPIM, f. 1281, op. 1, d. 10, l. 88.

ranks of the party, struggling to overcome his youthful disillusionment with the CPSU.[77] Efimov also was invited to join the ranks of the party on multiple occasions, but he always refused. "After the Twentieth Congress, we broke down [*my raskololis'*]," he explained in one of his interviews, "our ideology broke down. I knew that I had to search for my own 'truth' now." Efimov's distrust of the official party line made it difficult for him to even consider becoming a party member.[78] Other scientists, such as Merzhanov and Dremin, did not apply, hoping to avoid additional party and public work (*partiinaia i obshchestvennaia rabota*) responsibilities. There were also scientists at the ISSP who declined to join the Communist Party due to political considerations. One of them, Mezhov-Deglin, consciously stayed away from politics:

I never thought about entering the party or trying to change it from within, like some of my friends and colleagues did. I knew too well what they could say to people like me: "Sit quietly and do not stick your neck out [*ne vysovyvaisia*]. You are a son of an enemy of the people. Yet we gave you access to education and other benefits of a socialist society. What else do you want?"[79]

While the majority of the ICP Branch's and the ISSP's party organizations were workers and staff, Dubovitskii and Osipyan put a lot of effort into recruiting scientists and engineers to occupy the leading positions. Perhaps they realized that their own work of building an academic town and developing new directions of scientific research would go much faster and be more efficient if they had educated and agreeable people in these positions. This was especially true for the party bureau, which was an elected ruling body at primary party organizations across the Soviet Union. Most Chernogolovka scientists who were members of the CPSU served on their institute's party bureau at some point of their professional careers. Some served as secretaries of the party bureau or party organization. Bogdanov, for example, became a head of the ICP Branch's party organization in 1966 and stayed in this position for four years.[80] Shekhtman worked as a secretary of the ISSP's party bureau from 1963 to 1965, and then again from 1966 to 1968.[81] Mileiko, who joined the party in 1960 "to improve it from within," served as a secretary of the ISSP's party bureau in 1965 and 1966.[82] Poniatovskii, who had been persuaded to become a CPSU member, despite his father's persecution in the late 1930s, worked as a secretary of the ISSP's party bureau from 1968 to 1973. Even non-party members, such as Efimov

[77] Interview with Vsevolod Gantmakher, Chernogolovka, March 2010.
[78] Interview 2 with Oleg Efimov, Chernogolovka, March 2011.
[79] Interview 3 with Leonid Mezhov-Deglin, Chernogolovka, March, 2011.
[80] Interview 3 with Gennadii Bogdanov, Chernogolovka, August 2010.
[81] Archive of the ISSP, Newsletter "Partiinye, profsoiuznye, komsomol'skie lidery."
[82] Archive of the ISSP, Newsletter "Partiinye, profsoiuznye, komsomol'skie lidery."

and Mezhov-Deglin, had to participate in select commissions of party control and political seminars (see Figure 4.1).[83]

The active participation of the scientific intelligentsia in the work of the Communist Party on the ground was one of the reasons why the rest of Chernogolovka scientists had a benevolent, even positive view, of the party. Moreover, many perceived the party organizations in the town as friendly, not hostile, institutions. As Efimov put it in one of his interviews, "all these public organizations – party bureaus and trade unions – were staffed with our own people [*svoi liudi*]. We knew each of them personally, communicated with them on a daily basis. They were good, decent people. There were mostly no scoundrels among them."[84] Even scientists who were skeptical of the politics of the Soviet government tended to believe that their local party organizations were staffed with "decent people" whose loyalty lay with their research institutes first, and the Communist Party only second. "People who occupied these high positions, like a secretary of the party organization, had a lot of power in their hands," Gantmakher recalled. "They could destroy an institute instantaneously, because they had direct access to the Central Committee and the KGB. That is why it was important to find honest and amiable people for these positions." According to Gantmakher, the scientific success of the ISSP was largely due to the fact that Osipyan managed to recruit the right people.[85] The rest of my interviewees from the ISSP generally agreed with this assessment.

If scientists perceived members of the local party organizations as "their own people," who protected the town and its research institutes from the excesses of the Central Committee, then logic dictated that scientists would have these people's back in return. In retrospect, some of them called it "playing by the rules of the game,"[86] which had two major components. First, "playing by the rules" implied that both party and non-party members of the Chernogolovka scientific community had to participate in the everyday functioning of primary party organizations. The former had to attend monthly meetings of party committees and party bureaus. They also had to display their consent with the official party line by voting in favor of various party resolutions. Non-party members were strongly encouraged to participate in philosophical and

---

[83] Interview 1 with Oleg Efimov, Chernogolovka, March 2011; Interview 3 with Leonid Mezhov-Deglin, Chernogolovka, March 2011.

[84] Interview 2 with Oleg Efimov, Chernogolovka, March 2011.

[85] Interview with Vsevolod Gantmakher, Chernogolovka, March 2010.

[86] Philip Boobbyer explores the "rules of the game" concept in Philip Boobbyer, "Truth-telling, Conscience and Dissent in Late Soviet Russia: Evidence from Oral Histories," *European History Quarterly* 30.4 (2000), pp. 568–571. Robert Hornsby also refers to the "rules of the game" in his recent monograph, arguing that the post-Stalin regime "no longer repressed those who had done nothing at all" and that "this new clarity in the 'rules of the game' felt like liberalization for those who experienced it." See Hornsby, *Protest, Reform and Repression*, pp. 54, 72.

Figure 4.1: Evgenii Poniatovskii, Yuri Osipyan, and Veniamin Shekhtman (left to right) at the Presidium of the Soviet Academy of Sciences, 1971

ideological seminars. These seminars often served the purposes of the official Soviet propaganda, indoctrinating scientists, inter alia, about the aggressive foreign politics of various "imperialist countries" or "the solidarity of the world Communist movement." Yet, sometimes philosophical seminars could turn into discussions of scientific methods or ways to increase scientists' productivity, instead of ideological indoctrination, depending on who was in charge.

The second component of "playing by the rules of the game" implied that scientists had to avoid any provocative actions that would force a secretary of the local party organization or the party bureau to report about it to the higher-ups. For example, the overwhelming majority of Chernogolovka scientists voted to approve the resolution on the Soviet invasion of Czechoslovakia in 1968.[87] Their failure to vote in favor of the invasion would have raised alarm at

---

[87] For a detailed discussion of Chernogolovka scientists' responses to the Soviet invasion of Czechoslovakia, see Chapter 5.

the October regional committee. In this case, scientists "played by the rules" and officially supported the invasion, even though many disagreed that the Soviet military interference was justified. These restrictions applied not only to meetings of primary party organizations, but also to other spheres where scientists had a chance to voice their views in public. For example, film screenings at the cinema club "Kaleidoscope" were usually followed by discussions. Yet, scientists were often apprehensive to say out loud what they thought, as everyone knew that there was a KGB officer present at every screening. Gantmakher described it in the following way:

Osipyan, the director of our institute, was constantly under the surveillance of the regional party organization and the KGB. He knew about it and tried to establish a good personal relationship with people who watched him. He found decent people to serve as a head of the human resources department and secretaries of the institute's party organization and party bureau. But then the rest of us had to play by the rules and not let these people down.[88]

I heard similar testimonies from other Chernogolovka scientists. What Gantmakher and his colleagues referred to, then, was yet another privilege that the scientific intelligentsia enjoyed: "the privilege of passive participation." This privilege – as it was not available to many other professional groups – meant that scientists were now permitted to hold on to their private beliefs, but only as long as they avoided voicing their potentially critical views in public. This privilege allowed the local community to find their niche in Soviet society and to work comfortably within the system (see Figure 4.2). Unlike many members of the cultural intelligentsia (writers, poets, artists), the scientific intelligentsia was able to participate in the Soviet system without compromising their professional and personal integrity, largely thanks to the more objective nature of their work.[89] While Chernogolovka scientists often acquiesced to pressure to join the Communist Party, they usually had an opportunity to avoid politicized discussions and public denunciations of their colleagues. Many felt that, in the Soviet context, "behaving decently" was an important accomplishment already.[90] Living in a closed town, ironically, secured its residents better opportunities to do so, since rank-and-file party functionaries were usually apprehensive to challenge decisions of scientists involved, even indirectly, in the military–industrial complex.

What questions did the local PPOs deal with on a daily basis? The issues that scientists discussed during meetings of party organizations and party bureaus

---

[88] Interview with Vsevolod Gantmakher, Chernogolovka, March 2010.

[89] For more on this, see Pollock, *Stalin and the Soviet Science Wars*, pp. 217–222.

[90] For an in-depth discussion of intellectuals' striving to preserve their moral dignity in the late Soviet Union, see Boobbyer, "Truth-telling, Conscience and Dissent in Late Soviet Russia," pp. 553–585.

Figure 4.2: Chernogolovka scientists at the November 7th Demonstration, 1986

focused on administrative, scientific, and ideological matters. For the first ten years, administrative problems took up a significant amount of time at party meetings. They involved, but were not limited to, the construction of new research facilities, as well as building up the residential area of the town, including housing, grocery stores, a hospital, schools, and kindergartens. Scientific issues were also regularly on the agenda. The PPOs often outlined how the institutes' scientific results corresponded with the goals set at most recent plenums of the CPSU. They also discussed directions of scientific research and academic accomplishments of individual laboratories. Industrial application of fundamental research carried out at Chernogolovka's institutes was another common topic.

The questions on the agenda also included the admission of new party members, approval of employees' characteristics for traveling abroad, elections of party bureaus, and annual reports on the work of the institutes' party organizations. The PPOs also had to discuss and approve resolutions of the CPSU plenums and conferences, the Central Committee's closed letters, and Soviet foreign policy. While participants were usually encouraged to voice their concerns regarding administrative and scientific issues, they were never allowed to disagree on political and ideological matters. All resolutions of the

Central Committee of the CPSU invariably met with full and consistent approval of all party members. In rare cases when a scientist publicly questioned the actions of the Soviet government, the rest of the party organization put him or her in their place, since that person violated the commonly accepted "rules of the game." He or she would immediately become an object of criticism on the part of the rest of the party organization, which usually put an end to this scientist's "dissent."

What did Chernogolovka scientists think about their participation in party meetings and ideological seminars? This is a challenging question, since there are few written records at our disposal that can shed light on this deeply personal matter. For the most part we have to rely on scientists' collective memory, which is not always accurate. Yet, treated carefully, the interviews can offer some valuable insights into the thinking of the scientific intelligentsia. Both party and non-party members saw the work of the local party organizations as an integral part of life in the Soviet Union. As Mezhov-Deglin ironically put it in one of his interviews, "if you had a group of five people back then, you had to have a party cell; this is just the way it was."[91] In hindsight, many scientists who were party members or who worked in party organizations felt the need to justify their participation. They claimed that although the CPSU was a political organization, their role in it was limited to taking care of public work (*obshchestvennaia rabota*). "My activity as a party member was not tarnished by any indecent behavior," Bogdanov stated in his interview. "As a secretary of the ICP Branch's party organization, for example, I was responsible for many daily life issues, such as distributing housing in Chernogolovka, supplying local grocery stores with food, and allocating the institute's funding among other things. I had a lot of pressing issues to take care of."[92] Suvorov also remembered that housing distribution was one of the main questions he had to deal with as a secretary of Chernogolovka's party organization in the late 1970s. "The distribution of housing was always a source of tension in the town. We received endless letters from people complaining that someone got housing ahead of them. So we came up with a solution: we developed a code of housing distribution, and started following this document. The process became much more transparent and less stressful."[93] Some scientists maintained that their membership of the party allowed them to preserve a good working environment at their institute. Others admitted that it had a positive impact on their own professional development.

[91] Interview 3 with Leonid Mezhov-Deglin, Chernogolovka, March 2011.
[92] Interview 3 with Gennadii Bogdanov, Chernogolovka, August 2010.
[93] Interview 1 with Ernest Suvorov, Chernogolovka, August 2010.

As a rule, many of my interviewees tried to avoid discussing their silent approval of various party resolutions on Soviet domestic and foreign policy. As I show in Chapter 5, by the 1960s there existed a wide spectrum of political opinions among Chernogolovka scientists, ranging from passive dissidents to Communist believers. Only in exceptional cases, however, did the local scientific intelligentsia feel the need to challenge the decisions of the party directly. The vast majority learned to reconcile their lives with the constant presence of the CPSU. Many agreed to "play by the rules," recognizing the privileged status of their community in comparison to the rest of the country. At the end of the day, most of my interviewees were grateful to Dubovitskii and Osipyan for creating "a healthy working environment" in the town.

Unlike Akademgorodok, Chernogolovka was never really an "oasis of academic freedom." At no point did scientists who came to live and work there during the Thaw cherish hopes for greater individual rights. Everyone seemed to understand the special status of Chernogolovka among other scientific towns, and was content to "play by the rules of the game" set by the local administration and the post-Stalin regime: scientists would mind their own business and avoid political "provocations" in return for a higher degree of professional autonomy.

Curiously, scientists' membership in the Communist Party did not always correspond either to their political views or to their attitudes toward the Soviet state. For example, a scientist who claimed that his faith in the CPSU was shattered by the Twentieth Party Congress and who refused to apply for party membership, even at the cost of his own professional advancement, could still be an ardent supporter of the Soviet regime, because the latter invested in science. By contrast, a scientist who approved of the domestic and foreign policies of the Soviet government could refuse to join the ranks of the CPSU, often in order to avoid unnecessary distractions from his or her research. Finally, scientists who served as secretaries of party organizations, and thus implemented CPSU resolutions on the ground, were not always Communist believers, but held a wide range of political opinions.

At the end of the day, residents of Chernogolovka considered their work in the local party organizations as an integral part of their daily lives. Both party and non-party members attended regular ideological and philosophical seminars, which were largely nothing short of ideological indoctrination. Party members participated in meetings of the institutes' party organizations and party bureaus, where they had to approve various resolutions of the Central Committee, as well as discuss practical administrative and scientific issues. Overall, Chernogolovka scientists believed they could come to an agreement with the CPSU on the ground, since both were more interested in promoting scientific research and development than in achieving ideological purity among the institutes' employees. I discuss the scientists' mature political outlooks and their attitudes toward the Soviet state and its critics in the next chapter.

5 Chernogolovka Scientists between Loyalty and Dissent: The Soviet Invasion of Czechoslovakia and the Liubarskii Affair

On August 29, 1973, *Pravda* published a letter denouncing Andrei Sakharov. The letter was signed by leading Soviet scientists, who criticized the father of the Soviet hydrogen bomb and, since the late 1960s, a key figure in the human rights movement, for abandoning his research and attacking the Soviet political system. The signatories condemned Sakharov's dissent as "completely alien to Soviet scientists."[1] This notorious episode, which involved Nikolai Semenov and many other prominent scholars, sheds light on the ambiguous status of the scientific intelligentsia in late Soviet society. Scientists were among the most highly educated and critically minded individuals in the late USSR. Yet, the state demanded their complete political loyalty. The post-Stalin regime considered scientists' participation in the Soviet project essential to its success and, in return for their loyalty, granted scientists unprecedented privileges, including a higher degree of professional autonomy. Did the scientific community form the foundation of social stability in the late Soviet era, as the letter in *Pravda* suggests? Or did it constitute "an embryonic civil society,"[2] striving to expand its professional autonomy into the political sphere and prepared to challenge the legitimacy of the regime one day? In the following chapter, I argue that we should not assume that all Soviet scientists fell into one or the other camp, as either tacit dissidents or eager supporters of the regime. In fact, there existed a wide spectrum of political opinions among the late Soviet scientific intelligentsia, which included people who consented and dissented[3] in part.

During the Cold War, scholars in the West portrayed Soviet scientists as behind-the-scenes supporters of the dissident movement. Kendall Bailes maintained that it was scientists who most actively protested the violation of human

---

[1] *Pravda*, August 29, 1973.   [2] Holloway, *Stalin and the Bomb*, p. 367.
[3] Here, I accept Robert Hornsby's definition of "dissent." He distinguishes between "active dissent" and "passive dissent," explaining that "in the Soviet context, a dissenter does more than simply disagree and think differently; he openly proclaims his dissent and demonstrates it in one way or another to his compatriots and the state." According to this definition, listening to foreign radio broadcasts or criticizing the authorities in conversations with friends constituted "passive dissent." Robert Hornsby, *Protest, Reform and Repression*, pp. 12–13. For a broader definition of dissent see Philipp Boobbyer, *Conscience, Dissent and Reform*, p. 2.

rights in the wake of the 1966 trial of Siniavskii and Daniel.[4] Abraham Rothberg, Peter Reddaway, and Marshall Shatz argued that scientists and writers constituted the two main pillars of dissent in the USSR and that the vast majority of the scientific intelligentsia shared dissidents' values, but many lacked the courage to make their views public.[5] The collapse of the Soviet Union and the opening of the archives allowed historians to contest this prevalent assumption and to highlight instead the intimate relationship between scientists and the state. Loren Graham argued that, by the 1950s, engineers had been integrated into the Soviet military–industrial complex.[6] Douglas Weiner maintained that environmental scientists wanted to participate in the Leviathan-state, hoping to promote their own professional aims by working through the system.[7] Slava Gerovitch came to a similar conclusion in his article on elite rocket engineers during the Khrushchev era, showing that there were no dissidents among them.[8] Most recently, studies on "secret cities" of the military–industrial complex confirmed the image of the technical intelligentsia as loyal supporters of the regime. Kate Brown suggested, for example, that nuclear families in Ozersk, one of ten secret nuclear cities in the USSR, became the foundation of social stability in the late Soviet era.[9]

At the same time, the image of scientists as loyal supporters of the regime was partially challenged by those historians who argued, correctly, that during the last years of Stalin's rule, and especially after his death, the academic community used science's growing prestige to loosen rigid ideological constraints and to reclaim control of the scientific enterprise.[10] In some cases, this increased professional autonomy translated into demands for more political liberties.[11] The inevitable result was a clash between liberal-minded scientists and the Soviet regime. Sakharov's transformation from a nuclear scientist into a dissident seemed to substantiate this claim.[12] Paul Josephson's study of

---

[4] Bailes, *Technology and Society Under Lenin and Stalin*, p. 7.
[5] Abraham Rothberg, *The Heirs of Stalin: Dissidence and the Soviet Regime, 1953–1970* (Ithaca: Cornell University Press, 1972), pp. 315, 326–327; Peter Reddaway, ed. and transl., *Uncensored Russia: Protest and Dissent in the Soviet Union* (New York: American Heritage Press, 1972), p. 28; Marshall S. Shatz, *Soviet Dissent in Historical Perspective* (New York: Cambridge University Press, 1980), p. 140. See also Liudmila Alexeyeva, *Istoriia inakomysliia v SSSR: Noveishii period* (Vil'nius-Moskva: Vest', 1992), p. 228.
[6] Graham, *The Ghost of the Executed Engineer*, p. 77.
[7] Weiner, *A Little Corner of Freedom*, pp. 10, 19, 30.
[8] Gerovitch, "Stalin's Rocket Designers' Leap into Space," p. 208.
[9] Brown, *Plutopia*, pp. 4–5, 265–267.
[10] Josephson, "Soviet Scientists and the State," p. 607; Holloway, *Stalin and the Bomb*, p. 366; and Pollock, *Stalin and the Soviet Science Wars*, p. 218.
[11] Josephson, *New Atlantis Revisited*, p. xxii; Holloway, *Stalin and the Bomb*, p. 367; and Pollock, *Stalin and the Soviet Science Wars*, p. 222.
[12] For Sakharov's most recent biographies, see Jay Bergman, *Meeting the Demands of Reason: The Life and Thought of Andrei Sakharov* (Ithaca: Cornell University Press, 2009) and Richard Lourie, *Sakharov: A Biography* (Hanover: Brandeis University Press, 2002).

Akademgorodok, a city of science in Siberia, also maintained that residents of the "New Atlantis" more readily engaged in political discussions, hoping to expand the atmosphere of openness from the academic into the political sphere.[13]

This chapter examines the case study of Chernogolovka to draw a more nuanced portrait of the scientific intelligentsia during the early Brezhnev years. I argue that there existed a wide spectrum of political opinions among the local scientific community. This spectrum ranged from die-hard Communist believers to active dissidents, although the latter category was almost non-existent in Chernogolovka.[14] Between these two opposite poles, various patterns of conformity and dissent existed. Some scientists identified with the regime's goals, but were wary of its repressive features. Others were "passive dissidents," to use Robert Hornsby's definition – that is, people who searched for alternative sources of information, but did not engage in overt challenges to the state.[15] Yet others aspired to ignore political matters altogether, claiming that science was above politics. There were also myriad *Weltanschauungen* that fell in-between these broad categories. Remarkably, their political views notwithstanding, all categories of scientists (except active dissidents) were thoroughly integrated into the post-Stalin system. Many believed in the development of Soviet society on a scientific basis and saw their work for the Party-state as a necessary part of that effort. Having entered the profession in the mid-1950s, the first generation of Chernogolovka scientists enthusiastically identified with the idealism and social optimism of the Khrushchev regime that claimed science would play a crucial role in the construction of Communism. They happily embraced their new elite status in society, as well as the privileges that came with it.

The case study of Chernogolovka also demonstrates that scientists' increased professional autonomy did not necessarily translate into demands for further political liberties. According to the unspoken compromise reached between scientists and the state after Stalin's death, Soviet leaders no longer directly interfered in scientific affairs. In return, scientists agreed to preserve the status quo, avoiding demands for greater individual rights and political freedom. Many scientists found this compromise to be acceptable, especially since the process of re-Stalinization, against which many dissidents and members of the cultural intelligentsia protested, did not directly threaten scientists' autonomy. Human, nationalist, and religious rights – three principal fields of protest activity in the Brezhnev era – were not issues that spurred local

---

[13] Josephson, *New Atlantis Revisited*, p. 296.

[14] Conversely, several prominent dissident scientists, including Zhores Medvedev, lived and worked in Obninsk, a scientific town sixty-five miles southwest of Moscow, in the 1960s.

[15] Hornsby, *Protest, Reform and Repression*, pp. 12–13.

scientists to openly challenge the system.[16] Many believed that "playing by the rules of the game"[17] was necessary to preserve a healthy working environment at their research institutes.

This chapter does not deal with prominent dissident scientists such as Yuri Orlov, Zhores Medvedev, Revol't Pimenov, or Aleksandr Esenin-Vol'pin.[18] Instead, it focuses on the non-dissident majority of the scientific intelligentsia, and their attitudes toward the Soviet state and its critics. I use Chernogolovka as a lens to examine the wide spectrum of political opinions among the local scientific intelligentsia, as well as reasons for scientists' tacit compliance with the Party-state. I start by exploring the political outlook of the town's scientific community in the 1960s and early 1970s. I then move on to investigate two politically charged episodes in the life of Chernogolovka's residents. I first study scientists' responses to the Soviet invasion of Czechoslovakia in 1968, an event that had profound international and domestic significance. Second, I analyze the Chernogolovka scientists' reactions to the 1972 KGB persecution of a local dissident scientist, Kronid Liubarskii. Liubarskii had lived in the town since 1967. On January 17, 1972, he was arrested after a search of his apartment, accused of spreading samizdat literature, and sentenced to five years in a labor camp. Both episodes shed further light on the ways in which scientists exercised their privilege of passive participation that I started to explore in the previous chapter.

Spectrum of Conformity and Dissent in Chernogolovka

By the mid-1960s, there existed a diverse spectrum of political opinions among the first generation of Chernogolovka scientists. Here, I identify four categories into which we can place members of the local scientific community, based on their political outlooks. The first category I analyze is Communist believers. These people identified with the political and ideological goals of the Soviet regime and fully accepted all policies of the Communist Party. The second

---

[16] By contrast, environmental and health-related issues seem to have motivated more scientists to dissent, as Douglas Weiner has argued in Weiner, *A Little Corner of Freedom*, p. 9. Another good example of scientists openly challenging the state is the late Lysenko Affair, when in the mid-1960s a number of prominent Soviet scientists, including Nikolai Semenov, spoke out against Trofim Lysenko in defense of modern genetics. For more information on this see, for example, Vucinich, *Empire of Knowledge*, pp. 260–264.

[17] For the discussion of "playing by the rules of the game," see Chapter 4.

[18] For recent research on dissident scientists, see: Benjamin Nathans, "The Dictatorship of Reason: Aleksandr Vol'pin and the Idea of Rights under 'Developed Socialism,'" *Slavic Review* 66.4 (2007), pp. 630–663; Philip Boobbyer, "Vladimir Bukovskii and Soviet Communism," *The Slavonic and East European Review* 87.3 (2009), pp. 452–487; and Benjamin Tromly, "Intelligentsia Self-Fashioning in the Postwar Soviet Union: Revol't Pimenov's Political Struggle, 1949–57," *Kritika: Explorations in Russian and Eurasian History* 13.1 (2012), pp. 151–176.

category consisted of scientists who welcomed Khrushchev's secret speech at the Twentieth Party Congress and believed that the CPSU had embarked on the correct path after 1956; however, they were wary of the repressive side of the Soviet system. Third, there were scientists who qualified as "passive dissidents": people who were critical of the domestic and foreign violence of the Soviet government, but never overtly challenged the Soviet state. The fourth category consisted of scientists who conscientiously avoided political engagement, claiming that a scientist can work under different political regimes, as long as the state supports science. While I acknowledge that these categories do not capture the intricacies of each person's beliefs, I maintain that they serve as helpful markers as we move down the spectrum of scientists' political opinions. I deliberately focus on the non-dissident majority of the Chernogolovka scientific community, leaving out the political views of Kronid Liubarskii, the only active dissident scientist who resided in the town for a brief period of time. Liubarskii's transformation from a scientist into a dissident is representative of the paths traveled by other dissident scientists and, as such, warrants a separate investigation.

Out of the three dozen people I interviewed in Chernogolovka, only two scientists belonged to the first category. They completely internalized the official ideology and resented the dissident movement, considering it to be harmful to Soviet power. Both scientists had joined the Communist Party in the early 1950s and remained staunch Communist believers even after the Soviet collapse. In his interview, Lev Vashin explained that it was natural and desirable for him to live in a one-party state and be a part of the Soviet collective. He believed that socialism suited the needs of ordinary people better than capitalism, and vehemently rejected the individualism and freedom of speech propagated, in his view, by Soviet dissidents.[19] Vashin was convinced that the Soviet people were not ready either for freedom of speech or for making choices of their own. He thought the state was better equipped to make such choices.[20] Aleksandr Shilov also admitted that he never felt any contradictions between the official party promises and the reality of Soviet life.[21] The two scientists had a hard time understanding what Soviet dissidents protested against and criticized their attempts to undermine Soviet power, which, they thought, was generally fair and humane.[22] Vashin and Shilov actively participated in the work of the party organization at the ICP Branch, where they were employed. They often voiced their consent with the official party resolutions, took active roles in recommending other scientists for party membership, and condemned

---

[19] Interview 2 with Lev Vashin, Chernogolovka, April 2010.
[20] Interview 1 with Lev Vashin, Chernogolovka, March 2010.
[21] Interview 3 with Aleskandr Shilov, Chernogolovka, March 2010.
[22] Interview 1 Vashin, March 2010; Interview 2 with Vashin, April 2010; Interview 3 with Shilov, March 2010.

the rare cases of public political discontent. At some point, both served as Dubovitskii's deputy directors at the ICP Branch, which helped him maintain the image of the institute as a loyal and trustworthy organization in the eyes of the October regional committee of the CPSU. At the same time, both Vashin and Shilov were accomplished scientists in their respective fields, and recognized the priority of scientific over ideological considerations.

Further along the spectrum, there were scientists who approved of the official course of the Communist Party, but disagreed with some of its policies. About one-third of my interviewees belonged to this category. Many of its members welcomed Khrushchev's denunciation of Stalin's crimes at the Twentieth Party Congress. Some joined the party shortly after that. They usually sympathized with dissidents' protests against the re-Stalinization of Soviet society, but thought that the dissidents' struggle was futile, since in the Soviet context political change could only come from above. For example, Veniamin Shekhtman, a senior research fellow at the ISSP, joined the Communist Party in 1956, optimistic about Khrushchev's reforms. He maintained his faith in the progressive development of Soviet society throughout the 1960s and 1970s, yet he disapproved of the escalating political repressions under Brezhnev.[23] Evgenii Poniatovskii, also employed at the ISSP, knew that his father had been executed in 1938 because of his Polish background. Khrushchev's revelations helped Poniatovskii overcome his resentment and even join the Communist Party. In the late 1960s and 1970s, he readily identified with "semi-dissident" songs of Bulat Okudzhava and Aleksandr Galich that, in his opinion, helped prevent the return to the practices of high Stalinism. Yet, he was a strong supporter of the Soviet command economy that made possible the rapid and much needed modernization of the Soviet Union.[24] Scientists of this category typically relied on the official Soviet media for information; many remained staunch supporters of the regime until the late 1980s. They often joined the ranks of the CPSU, and took part in meetings of primary party organizations, although they usually remained silent during discussions that involved politics and ideology. Both Shekhtman and Poniatovskii served as secretaries of the ISSP party bureau and party organization at different times of their career.

The third category, "passive dissidents," included another one-third of scientists in Chernogolovka. These people were more critical of the Soviet state, especially its repressive policies against dissidents. They disapproved of the violations of human rights and other restrictions of political freedoms. Many also condemned the Soviet invasion of Czechoslovakia in August 1968 and admired those dissidents who publicly protested against the invasion at Red

---

[23] Interview 2 with Veniamin Shekhtman, Chernogolovka, March 2010.
[24] Interview with Evgenii Poniatovskii, Chernogolovka, March 2010.

Square. However, members of this category never overtly challenged either domestic or foreign policies of the Soviet government. Passive dissidents were more likely to sign letters of protest, or even attend demonstrations. Many searched for alternative sources of information, listening to broadcasts of foreign radio stations such as Voice of America, the BBC, and Radio Liberty. They read samizdat in the privacy of their own home, and could later discuss what they read or heard during conversations with friends and family, striving to form their own opinion on the matter. The vast majority of this group believed that the dissidents' activity was crucial to the awakening of Soviet society, as this activity encouraged ordinary people to start reading and thinking on their own. Many admired Andrei Sakharov's courageous struggle for human rights, while admitting that "not everyone could follow his path."[25] They were naturally critical of those members of the Academy of Sciences who participated in the anti-Sakharov campaign mentioned above.

The degree of scientists' passive dissent varied based on his or her family history and previous experiences with the Soviet regime. Leonid Mezhov-Deglin, for example, lost his father in the Great Terror in 1938. Ironically, he considered himself to be extremely lucky: not only had he been able to receive higher education at Fiztech, but he also managed to find employment in Chernogolovka. He refused to join the Communist Party multiple times, but he also knew "not to stick his neck out." "I began to see lies around me at an early age," he remembered, "but I realized that any time they could tell me: 'You are a son of an enemy of the people. Yet we gave you access to education and other benefits of a socialist society. What else do you want?'"[26] Oleg Efimov and Rustem Liubovskii, on the contrary, grew up as Communist believers but became increasingly disillusioned with the Communist experiment. They reacted painfully to Khrushchev's revelations at the Twentieth Party Congress. Searching for answers, they turned to Kronid Liubarskii, a dissident who moved to Chernogolovka in 1967. Efimov and Liubovskii were the only two scientists among my interviewees who admitted to having borrowed samizdat literature from him.[27] Their "curiosity" eventually got them in trouble: in 1972, they ended up being directly involved in the Liubarskii affair, to which I will turn shortly.

Finally, the fourth category consisted of scientists who conscientiously distanced themselves from the dissident struggle, and from politics more broadly. These people were convinced that political context had little, if any, impact on scientists' lives and work. For example, Alexei Abrikosov, a Nobel

---

[25] Interview 1 with Ernest Suvorov, Chernogolovka, August 2010; Interview with Vsevolod Gantmakher, Chernogolovka, March 2010.
[26] Interview 3 with Leonid Mezhov-Deglin, Chernogolovka, March 2011.
[27] Interview 1 with Rustem Liubovskii, Chernogolovka, December 2009; Interview 1 with Oleg Efimov, Chernogolovka, March 2011.

Prize winner, argued in his interview that scientists could successfully work under different political regimes, as long as they enjoyed consistent state funding, required for the development of fundamental research. Abrikosov respected Sakharov's dissent, but considered it to be a waste of Sakharov's outstanding talents. "Sakharov's heroism did not serve any purpose, since neither he nor other dissidents could change the Soviet system."[28] Aleksandr Merzhanov described himself as an apolitical person. "I never really reflected on the nature of the Soviet system," he admitted in his interview. "I always focused on specific scientific tasks at hand. I believed that if only everyone had excelled at his or her work, we could have had a fine country."[29]

While we should take these oral testimonies with a grain of salt (people tend to justify their past behavior in hindsight), in this particular case they provide us a unique opportunity to explore a topic that would otherwise be inaccessible to researchers. Unlike the cultural intelligentsia, scientists left few written records behind. The vast majority of them did not keep diaries. Those who published memoirs in the 1990s and 2000s focused on their scientific achievements, leaving out their relationship with the Soviet state. Oral history, therefore, might be our only chance to examine Soviet scientists' political views. Crucially, written documents from the party archive largely corroborate scientists' testimonies, as I demonstrate below.

Their political outlooks notwithstanding, scientists all along the spectrum were thoroughly integrated into the post-Stalin system.[30] Members of the Chernogolovka scientific community were convinced that scientific advancement was indispensable for the progressive development of humanity, and believed that the post-Stalin system created exceptional conditions for scientific progress. Skeptics and passive dissidents alike were willing to suppress their doubts and work for the post-Stalin state. Many considered political liberalization and free access to information to be desirable but secondary goals. Summing up the scientists' position in an interview, Efimov explained:

Even when we started having doubts, it did not affect our loyalty to the Soviet state. What mattered to us was that back then the interests of the state coincided with our interests. The state needed professional people, scientists above all. It committed enormous resources to that. And we were proud to be professionals: it was honorable to belong to the Academy of Sciences, to head a laboratory or a scientific department.[31]

In the following two sections, I investigate the reactions of Chernogolovka scientists to the Soviet invasion of Czechoslovakia in 1968 and their response

[28] Interview with Alexei Abrikosov, Lemont (Illinois), July 2010.
[29] Interview with Aleksandr Merzhanov, Chernogolovka, August 2009.
[30] For a detailed discussion of the ways in which Chernogolovka scientists were integrated into the post-Stalin system, see Chapters 1, 3, and 4.
[31] Interview 2 with Oleg Efimov, Chernogolovka, March 2011.

to the persecution of the local dissident, Kronid Liubarskii, to shed further light on the conformity of the scientific intelligentsia in the late Soviet era. The 1968 invasion provoked a heated discussion among Chernogolovka residents. In fact, it was the only occasion – in more than twenty years – when several scientists openly challenged a Central Committee resolution. Yet, even then, scientists' criticism of the Soviet regime was extremely subdued. In this respect, the Chernogolovka community never lived up to the example of Akademgorodok, where their peers more readily engaged in political discussions, including debates on the Soviet invasion of Czechoslovakia.[32]

The 1968 Invasion of Czechoslovakia and the Chernogolovka Scientific Community

In April 1968 the Communist Party of Czechoslovakia, led by Alexander Dubček, published a new party program that set the country on the path to reforms, known as the Prague Spring. The program called for more openness in the party and society as a whole, and for building what later became known as "socialism with a human face." From April to August 1968, Communist leaders across Eastern Europe kept a watchful eye on developments in Czechoslovakia, fearing their potential implications for their own power. Eventually, on the night of August 20–21, the Soviet army, accompanied by contingents from the German Democratic Republic, Poland, Hungary, and Bulgaria, invaded Czechoslovakia, crushing the Prague Spring. The invasion severely damaged the image of the Soviet Union abroad, especially among Communist Parties in Western Europe. It also undermined hopes among the Soviet intelligentsia for future reforms.

The echo of the Czechoslovak events reached the scientific community in Chernogolovka in early September 1968. On September 10, employees of the ICP Branch gathered for a closed meeting of the institute's party organization attended exclusively by Communist Party members. Gennadii Bogdanov opened the meeting by reading out loud a letter of the Central Committee called "Information on Czechoslovakia." The reading was followed by a lively discussion, during which participants approved of the letter, as well as the "help" from fellow socialist states. "The struggle between the socialist and capitalist systems is the foundation of present-day international relations," one member noted. "Czechoslovakia breaking away from the socialist camp would have created a tangible threat of a Third World War." "Our government made the right decision," another participant agreed. "The counterrevolution in Czechoslovakia had prepared itself well this time and would not have given up easily."[33]

---

[32] Josephson, *New Atlantis Revisited*, p. 296.   [33] TsAOPIM, f. 8099, op.1, d. 76, l. 83.

Unexpectedly, Vladimir Martemianov, a junior research fellow at the ICP Branch, took the floor, claiming that he had the right to share his doubts with the party audience. "First, does one socialist state have the right to send its troops to another state without the agreement of that state's government?" he asked. "When Finland wanted to leave [in 1917], Lenin gave this request a fair consideration. It appears to me that our government's actions do not reflect the Marxist approach to the national question ... Second, was the counter-revolution in Czechoslovakia indeed so strong," he continued, "that the Czechoslovak leadership lost all control over the situation?" Finally, according to Martemianov, sending troops to Czechoslovakia alienated the Communist parties in France and Italy from the Soviet Union. "'Proletarians of all countries, unite!' is written on our banner. But did not our government's actions hamper the Communists' work among the masses in these countries?"[34]

Martemianov's references to Lenin and Marxism were no accident. A true Communist believer at the time, he applied to join the ranks of the party in 1967. He was granted membership in January 1968, being described as "an honest and uncompromising man, demanding of himself and other people."[35] Another record of the ICP Branch's party organization praised Martemianov as one of the best instructors of seminars on Soviet domestic and foreign policy.[36] Despite his excellent reputation, the scientist's "honest and uncompromising" questions about the events in Czechoslovakia received a very cold response from his colleagues. Some of them attacked his position vigorously. "Are you against sending our troops there?" they asked. "What radio station have you been listening to?" When Martemianov insisted that he would like to hear well-grounded objections to his questions, he was silenced. "You need to listen to Soviet radio stations, not only to BBC; you need to arrive at correct conclusions," his colleagues told him.[37]

Lev Vashin, who was also present at the meeting, took the floor to condemn Martemianov. "Unfortunately, there are other ignorant scientists and certain members of the intelligentsia who think this way," he said. "We cannot overlook their opinions, but we need to explain to these comrades that their opinions are wrong." Vashin went on to denounce the "counterrevolution" in Czechoslovakia, arguing that its goal was to remove the Czechoslovak Communist Party from power, and that the Soviet Union was defending the national interests of that country.[38] When Bogdanov attempted to give the floor to Rustem Liubovskii, his request was declined. "This is not a debate club," someone said. "If anyone has further doubts, address them to the party bureau and senior comrades." In the end, the party organization passed a resolution

[34] TsAOPIM, f. 8099, op. 1, d. 76, l. 83.   [35] TsAOPIM, f. 8099, op. 1, d. 76, l. 3.
[36] TsAOPIM, f. 8099, op. 1, d. 76, l. 73.   [37] TsAOPIM, f. 8099, op. 1, d. 76, l. 84.
[38] TsAOPIM, f. 8099, op. 1, d. 76, l. 84.

stating its absolute approval of the Central Committee's actions. 134 people voted in favor of the resolution; Martemianov abstained from the vote.[39]

What do we make of this incident? Why did Martemianov end up alone in voicing his concerns, while the rest of his colleagues voted in favor of the invasion? There are several possible explanations here. Some scientists, such as Vashin, genuinely believed that the Soviet intervention was necessary. Remarkably, when I interviewed him forty-two years later, Vashin admitted that he had not changed his position on Czechoslovakia even after more information about the Prague Spring became available in the 1990s. "I believe that if we had not intervened, Czechoslovakia would have followed the same scenario as the Soviet Union did in 1991: reforms that led to the elimination of socialism."[40] Then, there were scientists who had doubts about the invasion, but chose to suppress them, finding justification for Soviet actions in Soviet newspapers. It appears that those who relied on the official sources of information were more inclined to buy into the propaganda and approve of the invasion. Lana Ukrainka acknowledged, for example, that people around her were afraid that the crisis in Czechoslovakia could destabilize the situation in Europe and lead to a large-scale military conflict. "For people of my generation who survived the Great Patriotic War, who lost parents in that war, the fear of war was real," she admitted.[41]

Finally, scientists who listened to the BBC or who had access to foreign newspapers were more critical of the actions of the Soviet government.[42] They usually voiced their concerns to their friends and family. Liubovskii, for instance, remembered discussing it with a small group of colleagues from his laboratory. Very few people, however, spoke out at party meetings. Moreover, those who publicly raised their concerns, such as Martemianov, became a target of immediate criticism. It appears that by openly demonstrating his dissent, Martemianov violated the unspoken "rules of the game" and let the entire research institute down. Many were aware that in Akademgorodok, for example, scientists' discontent over the invasion of Czechoslovakia was one of the reasons for the Communist Party's crackdown on scientists' academic freedom.[43] Could it be different in Chernogolovka? Could it potentially raise questions about scientists' "privilege of passive participation"?

The discussions on Czechoslovakia continued at the ICP Branch throughout September 1968. Another closed party meeting took place

[39] TsAOPIM, f. 8099, op. 1, d. 76, l. 86.
[40] Interview 2 with Lev Vashin, Chernogolovka, April 2010.
[41] Interview 2 with Lana Ukrainka, Chernogolovka, September 2010.
[42] Interview 1 with Rustem Liubovskii, Chernogolovka, December 2009; Interview with Gennadii Bogdanov, Chernogolovka, December 2009; Interview with Vsevolod Gantmakher, Chernogolovka, March 2010; Interview 2 with Sergei Mileiko, Chernogolovka, August 2010.
[43] Josephson, New Atlantis Revisited, p. xv.

on September 26, during which Aleksandr Shilov delivered a report on the ideological work at the institute. The report started out by warning all attendees about the intensification of imperialist propaganda directed against the Soviet regime. "It is well-known that BBC has increased its hours of broadcasting in the USSR. Currently, any time of day and night one can turn on their radio set and listen to Russian-language programs filled with fierce and sometimes extremely clever anti-Soviet propaganda aimed at dividing Soviet people and making them question the policies of our party."[44] Shilov expressed his concern that some employees of the ICP Branch might, in fact, have fallen victim to this propaganda campaign. In addition to Martemianov, he named two other junior scientists who had protested against the events in Czechoslovakia. He commended the institute's party organization for denouncing such "ideological blunders." Following Shilov's report, another party member asked to speak, claiming that two Communists – Rustem Liubovskii and Igor' Shchegolev – had also expressed doubts about Czechoslovakia in private conversations. Both scientists denied having criticized the Soviet government.[45] There was no further investigation of their "imprudent" remarks. However, several years later when Liubovskii applied to travel abroad, he was denied the exit visa needed to leave the USSR.[46]

A close reading of the party records of the ISSP indicates that there was some disagreement with the invasion there as well, but on a much smaller scale. On September 17, 1968, the ISSP party organization held a meeting during which one of the ideological seminar instructors complained that on August 26 a fellow named Kopylov had made some "ill-considered remarks" about Czechoslovakia.[47] The meeting decreed that the party bureau should look further into this matter. Kopylov was summoned to the bureau one week later, on September 24. He defended himself, arguing that he indeed read the information on Czechoslovakia but did not express any doubts about the actions of the Soviet government. "What is your position on this matter now?" the ISSP assistant director asked him. "I have never doubted the correct course of our party and our government," Kopylov responded.[48] His case was closed shortly after that.

The records of the ISSP party organization carry no further evidence of scientists' expressing discontent over the invasion. This is hardly surprising, since most of my respondents from this institute were particularly aware of "playing by the rules." Among them, there were quite a few scientists of Jewish descent, as well as scientists with repressed parents. Both groups were especially vulnerable to potential state persecution. "It was important to maintain

[44] TsAOPIM, f. 8099, op. 1, d. 76, l. 105.   [45] TsAOPIM, f. 8099, op. 1, d. 76, l. 109.
[46] Interview 2 with Rustem Liubovskii, Chernogolovka, February 2011.
[47] TsAOPIM, f. 1281, op. 1, d. 3, l. 18.   [48] TsAOPIM, f. 1281, op. 1, d. 3, l. 114.

order," Shekhtman explained in his interview. In the late 1960s, Shekhtman served as a secretary of the ISSP party organization, a position that obliged him to take a stand on various matters. "For me personally it was a status which allowed me to have a real impact on the outcome of many scientific and administrative questions," Shekhtman said in justification of his behavior. Political and ideological issues were sometimes on the agenda, too, he admitted; however, scientists were not forced to participate in any "ideological struggles."[49] "From time to time, we had to account for our work in front of party regional committees. We held party meetings and organized political seminars in order to preserve a decent working environment at the ISSP. When I think about it now, I realize it was a kind of a game."[50] Like many of his colleagues, Shekhtman used the "game" metaphor to justify his passive participation in the system.

In the late Soviet era, "playing by the rules" went hand in hand with tacit compliance with the state. As long as the scientific intelligentsia considered "the rules of the game" to be fair, it did not mind playing. In return, scientists were allowed to focus on their research, contributing to the advancement of their respective fields, which they found to be extremely exciting and much more important than any political reforms. Many viewed politics with skepticism, even contempt. If maintaining good working conditions required tacit compliance, Chernogolovka scientists thought it was a price clearly worth paying.

The Liubarskii Affair

While the events in Czechoslovakia provoked heated debates across the Soviet Union and abroad, few people outside of Chernogolovka heard about the Liubarskii affair of 1972. Yet, it was the persecution of this particular dissident living next door and teaching astronomy to scientists' children that put their loyalty to the Soviet state to the test. If previously the scientific intelligentsia in Chernogolovka stated that their lives and work were above politics, they found themselves struggling with this claim in January 1972 when the KGB came to town.

Kronid Liubarskii moved to Chernogolovka five years prior to his arrest, in late 1967. He was already a committed dissident, and ended up living in the closed academic town by accident. A professional astronomer and a candidate of physical and mathematical sciences, he could not find a job in Moscow because of his "unreliable" political views. With no permanent job or a place to live, Liubarskii accepted an invitation from his old friend, Isai Braginskii, to

[49] Interview 2 with Veniamin Shekhtman, Chernogolovka, March 2010.
[50] Interview 2 with Veniamin Shekhtman, Chernogolovka, March 2010.

teach astronomy at a local high school. A document in the archive of the ISSP indicates that he had also been employed as senior research fellow at the ISSP, although he never worked there full-time.[51] Liubarskii brought his wife and a seven-year-old daughter to Chernogolovka, receiving a separate apartment shortly upon his arrival.

From the beginning, Liubarskii's status in the town was ambiguous. On the one hand, he was an accomplished astronomer, educated at the prestigious Mechanical and Mathematical Department at MGU, and therefore a member of the scientific intelligentsia. His candidate of sciences degree put him on equal footing with the vast majority of scientists in the town. On the other hand, Liubarskii was an outsider, and was perceived as such by most Chernogolovka residents. Few scientists in the town knew about his academic publications. None of the ISSP employees remembered overlapping with him at work. Some of my interviewees recollected that their children were quite fond of Liubarskii, considering him to be a knowledgeable and passionate teacher. Lev Vashin, for example, admitted that his daughter decided to become an astronomer after taking a class with him.[52] In fact, the vast majority of my interviewees thought of Liubarskii as an astronomy teacher, not a scientist. Few people knew that he had another identity.

Since his studies at MGU in the mid-1950s, Liubarskii saw himself as *vol'nodumets*, or a "freethinker."[53] It was at MGU that he first attracted the attention of the Communist Party and KGB officials. In 1954, Liubarskii became one of the organizers of an open letter in support of Vladimir Pomerantsev's article "On Sincerity in Literature," signed by thirty-nine MGU students. One of the first harbingers of the Thaw, the article attacked the hypocrisy and artificiality of Soviet literature, but was harshly criticized by various members of the Soviet Union of Writers. Two years later, in 1956, Liubarskii and several other students published an informal wall newspaper, the *Literary Bulletin*, which called for further liberalization of the Soviet cultural landscape.[54] Both initiatives infuriated the MGU party organization, as they were pushing the boundaries set by the official Soviet ideology. Yet, in the midst of the Thaw, Liubarskii was allowed to continue his studies. He graduated from MGU in the summer of 1956 and could even find employment

[51] Archive of the ISSP, f. 1, op. 1, d. 73, l. 5, "Proceeding of the Joint Meeting of the ISSP Administration and Trade Union Committee (December 29, 1970)."

[52] Interview 2 with Lev Vashin, Chernogolovka, April 2010.

[53] Archive of the Research Center for East European Studies (Forschungsstelle Osteuropa, or FSO), 01–86 (Raisa Orlova's Interviews), R. Orlova's interview with G. Salova and K. Liubarskii (15.5.1983), l. 16.

[54] For more information on the publication of the *Literary Bulletin*, see Tromly, *The Making of the Soviet Intelligentsia*, pp. 141–146. See also Archive of the Memorial Society (Moscow), f. 156, op. 1, d. 9, "The Literary Bulletin," No. 1-4 (1956).

at a small observatory in southern Turkmenia, not far from Ashkhabad, where he continued to work in meteoric astronomy.[55]

Upon his return to Moscow in 1963, Liubarskii and his wife, Galina Salova, immediately reconnected with their college friends, who introduced them to Petr Iakir, Aleksandr Esenin-Vol'pin, Grigorii Pod'iapol'skii, and other future dissidents.[56] By the time Liubarskii moved to Chernogolovka, he had been actively engaged in a complex clandestine samizdat network, centered in Moscow, which reproduced various social and political texts, including Milovan Djilas's *The New Class*, Anatolii Marchenko's *My Testimony*, and Pavel Litvinov's *The Trial of the Four*.[57] From 1968 until his arrest in 1972, Liubarskii also participated in reproducing and distributing *The Chronicle of Current Events*, the most "criminal" samizdat periodical and the main target of the KGB.[58] Liubarskii's relocation to Chernogolovka did not put an end to his samizdat activities. On the contrary, having an apartment in Chernogolovka allowed him to collect one of the biggest samizdat libraries in the Soviet Union at the time. It was also through samizdat that Liubarskii got to know many future human rights activists in Moscow. Some of them became his close friends, and often visited the Liubarskii family in their apartment in Chernogolovka.

Few residents of the town had known about Liubarskii's engagement in the dissident movement prior to his arrest. Two scientists who became friends with Liubarskii and his family were Oleg Efimov and Rustem Liubovskii. Both worked at the ICP Branch. Efimov had known Kronid and his wife Galina since their days at the Moscow Planetarium in the early 1950s. He lost touch with them afterwards, but readily welcomed the family to Chernogolovka. Efimov also introduced Liubarskii to his friend Rustem Liubovskii, who helped the dissident translate *Chemical Evolution*, a book by a Nobel Prize laureate Melvin Calvin. The two scientists were regular guests at Liubarskii's apartment in Chernogolovka. Among the dozens of scientists I interviewed, they were the only two people who admitted they had been friends with Liubarskii and borrowed samizdat from him.

Efimov and Liubovskii were typical representatives of the *shestidesiatniki*, or men of the 1960s, generation. They grew up under late Stalinism and came of age during the tumultuous Khrushchev era. Efimov remembered that it was Khrushchev's denunciation of Stalin at the Twentieth Party Congress that made him start looking for alternative sources of information. "I left the auditorium

---

[55] FSO 01–42 (K.A. Liubarskii), "Liubarskii's diploma" (dated June 26, 1956).
[56] Interview 1 with Galina Salova, Moscow, November 2010; Interview 2 with Galina Salova, Moscow, March 2011.
[57] FSO 01–86, R. Orlova's interview with G. Salova and K. Liubarskii (15.5.1983), l. 18.
[58] Mark Hopkins, *Russia's Underground Press: The Chronicle of Current Events* (New York: Praeger, 1983), p. 55. For the most recent research on samizdat, see Komaromi, *Uncensored*.

where they read Khrushchev's speech to us Komsomol members with one thought in mind: I have lost everything I believed in, I have lost my ideology."[59] Efimov's friendship with Liubarskii gave him an opportunity to educate himself, to open his mind, and to begin thinking critically about the world around him. He was mostly attracted to samizdat books, which Liubarskii had in great numbers. Efimov borrowed a lot of political, religious, and philosophical samizdat from the dissident.[60] This was how he first read George Orwell's *1984* and Arthur Koestler's *Darkness at Noon*. Efimov was most fascinated, however, by *The Chronicle of Current Events*. He knew that it was the most dangerous samizdat, but he read it nevertheless, since it was the only truthful source of information about political prisoners in the Soviet Union.[61]

Efimov's relationship with Liubarskii was complicated. Although he agreed that samizdat was highly beneficial for Soviet society by forcing people to start thinking on their own, Efimov disagreed with many of the solutions offered by Liubarskii and his dissident friends. "My head was full of science back then," he recollected. "I neither understood Kronid nor shared his views. I used to tell him: 'You and your friends criticize everything, and a lot of your criticism is fair. But you should also have some positive suggestions.' It seemed to me that all they wanted to do was to destroy the existing order of things."[62] Once Efimov and Liubarskii got into a serious argument, at the end of which the dissident got upset with his friend, accusing him of being too "materially minded."

Liubarskii's influence on Liubovskii was more pronounced. This was partially due to the fact that until the Soviet invasion in Czechoslovakia in August 1968, Liubovskii had paid little attention to either the domestic or foreign policy of the Soviet government or dissidents' critique of the regime. His friendship with the dissident was crucial for Liubovskii's political awakening.[63] Their work on the translation of Calvin's *Chemical Evolution* soon developed into a friendship, since Liubarskii, five years older than his "innocent" friend, seemed to have answers to most of the questions with which Liubovskii was now struggling. The dissident showed Liubovskii another, previously unknown, perspective on Soviet reality. He taught him to have less trust in the pompous words of Soviet leaders. He also told Liubovskii about the true dimensions of the Gulag. In the late 1960s and early 1970s, Liubovskii spent many Saturday evenings at Liubarskii's apartment discussing

---

[59] Interview 1 with Oleg Efimov, Chernogolovka, March 2011.
[60] Interview 2 with Oleg Efimov, Chernogolovka, March 2011.
[61] Interview 1 with Oleg Efimov, Chernogolovka, March 2011.
[62] Interview 1 with Oleg Efimov, Chernogolovka, March 2011.
[63] Interview 1 with Rustem Liubovskii, Chernogolovka, December 2009.

politics, current affairs, and samizdat texts he had borrowed, including *The Chronicle of Current Events*.[64]

Both Efimov and Liubovskii sympathized with the dissidents' criticism of the violations of human rights in the Soviet Union, but they found it difficult to identify with Liubarskii's ideas. They agreed that free access to information was important, and they benefited tremendously from reading samizdat. Yet, they also saw many positive changes in the post-Stalin Soviet Union that confirmed the progressive development of Soviet society but that Liubarskii and other dissidents did not fully appreciate, focusing instead on the violations of human rights.

The KGB searched Liubarskii's apartment on January 15, 1972, discovering one of the biggest samizdat libraries in the Soviet Union at the time. The search was one of several dozen searches among dissidents, and part of the KGB campaign to stop the production and dissemination of *The Chronicle of Current Events*, notoriously known as Case 24. Two days later, Liubarskii was arrested. He was accused of "spreading anti-Soviet slanderous fabrications with the purpose of undermining and weakening Soviet power" (article 70 of the Soviet Penal Code). He was put on trial in late October 1972, found guilty and sentenced to five years in a labor camp.[65] Liubarskii's family continued to reside in Chernogolovka until 1977, when he was finally released and the family was forced to emigrate. From 1972 to 1977, Liubarskii's daughter, Veronika, attended the same school where her father had previously been a teacher. Many of her classmates were children of prominent Chernogolovka scientists.[66]

One of the most intriguing aspects of the Liubarskii affair is that it received very little attention from the local scientific community. The arrest was not even mentioned at meetings of the party organizations of the ISSP and the ICP Branch. The only reference to the Liubarskii affair that I found among dozens of party records from 1972 was the proceeding of a closed meeting of the party organization of the ICP Branch.[67] The meeting was held on November 22, 1972, three-and-a-half weeks after the trial, and was attended by 183 party members. Scientists who were not members of the party were not allowed to participate. The Liubarskii affair was not even listed as a separate item on the meeting's agenda, but was discussed under the heading of "The work of the political information network in Chernogolovka."

The brief, two-paragraph entry in the document was vague. It stated that Liubarskii had lived in Chernogolovka since the late 1960s, teaching

---

[64] *Kronid: Izbrannye stat'i Kronida Liubarskogo*, ed. by G.I. Salova (Moskva: RGGU, 2001), p. 44.
[65] Archive of the Memorial Society (Moscow), fond 103 (Biographical Documents of K. Liubarskii), "The Verdict" (*"Prigovor"*), l. 275.
[66] Interview with Veronika Liubarskaia-Hock, Berlin, November 2013.
[67] TsAOPIM, f. 8099, op. 1, d. 107, ll. 75–76.

astronomy at the local school. The entry also mentioned that two bags of samizdat materials were found during the search of his apartment, among them "some anti-Soviet literature published abroad by the union of Russian émigrés." "Liubarskii reproduced these materials on his typewriter and distributed them among his 'fellow comrades' in Leningrad, Khar'kov, and Simferopol'. He was sentenced to five years in prison."[68] The record ended with an explicit warning to other scientists: "Although this type of literature appears to be popular among certain groups, everyone must be aware that reading it is considered a crime."[69] While usually all party announcements were followed by question-and-answer sessions with the participants, no one asked any questions this time. The party organizations of the ISSP and the Landau ITP, the other two main research institutes in Chernogolovka, did not discuss the Liubarskii affair at all.[70] Their silence indicated their administrations' intention to distance their institutes and themselves from the investigation and to limit its impact on the employees.

But why did the Liubarskii affair receive so little attention? Should not the trial over a fellow scientist, whose only crime was promoting free access to information, have provoked a much more heated discussion, maybe an upsurge of discontent? Even though few town residents had heard about the dissident before January 1972, the arrest and the trial cast a shadow over the loyalty of the local academic community. The fact that Liubarskii resided in a closed town but was able to transform his apartment there into a center of what the KGB viewed as "anti-Soviet activity" was highly suspicious. It appeared to call into question the unspoken compromise achieved between scientists and party officials after Stalin's death, thus endangering scientists' privilege of passive participation. After all, scientists could enjoy their professional autonomy only as long as they avoided demands for greater individual rights and political freedom. Liubarskii's engagement in the reproduction and distribution of samizdat seemed to undermine this compromise.

The Liubarskii affair also presented a serious challenge to the administration of Chernogolovka's research institutes. Now that Liubarskii had been arrested, the KGB wanted to know how the dissident had ended up living in a closed scientific town, and if he had any support network there. Fedor Dubovitskii, the assistant director of the ICP Branch and "the authorized representative of the Presidium of the Academy of Sciences in Chernogolovka," decided to handle this precarious situation by emphasizing that Liubarskii was an outsider, a complete stranger, who had not been involved with the local community. Liubarskii had ended up in the town by mistake, he argued; the Liubarskii affair was an anomaly in Chernogolovka's peaceful development. When the trial of

[68] TsAOPIM, f. 8099, op. 1, d. 107, ll. 75–76.   [69] TsAOPIM, f. 8099, op. 1, d. 107, l. 76.
[70] TsAOPIM, f. 1281, op. 1, d. 10; TsAOPIM, f. 4491, op. 1, d. 2.

the dissident began in Noginsk on October 26, 1972, Dubovitskii brought several dozen scientists there by bus. They were all members of the Communist Party and the Komsomol who had proved reliable in the past, Lev Vashin among them. The scientists' presence at the trial was supposed to demonstrate that Liubarskii had no supporters among Chernogolovka's scientific intelligentsia.[71]

At the end of the day, Dubovitskii's strategy worked. The investigation of the Liubarskii affair came to an end shortly after the dissident's trial, and did not spread to the academic community in Chernogolovka. The only two scientists who were summoned to the KGB headquarters on Lubianka Square and at the Lefortovo prison for interrogation were Oleg Efimov and Rustem Liubovskii. The KGB wanted to know if they had received any samizdat from the dissident. Although both scientists had borrowed the literature, they denied having received any, in an attempt to help out their friend and themselves.[72] In the last days of October 1972, they both came to the court where Liubarskii was on trial to see with their own eyes what was going on. They were not allowed to enter the building. Several times the two scientists passed by Andrei Sakharov and other dissidents who were standing outside the courthouse, said hello to them, but then just kept walking. They were too afraid to stop and talk to the dissidents; they knew that everyone was being watched.[73] Coming to the court building that day was already pushing the boundary of what the Soviet state considered acceptable for loyal citizens. Yet, they felt that it was their moral obligation to be there to support their friend. After the trial, both Efimov and Liubovskii were allowed to continue working at the ICP Branch in their existing positions. Liubovskii, who was a member of the Communist Party, even managed to keep his party card. It appears that Dubovitskii played a significant role in protecting both scientists from any further investigation by vouching for their political loyalty to the KGB.

Almost four decades later, most of my interviewees found it difficult to talk to me about the Liubarskii affair. Some scientists said that they learned about it only later, after the dissident was arrested. Others remembered discussing it with their friends and family back then, but said they had no opinion on the matter, referring me to either Efimov or Liubovskii. Few scientists admitted to having known Liubarskii personally before 1972. Even fewer insisted that, although the trial was unfair, the state had the right to protect itself from opponents who strove to undermine Soviet power in any way, even with verbal assaults. Overall, the attempts of the local administration to silence the

[71] *Kronid*, p. 53.
[72] Interview 1 with Rustem Liubovskii, Chernogolovka, December 2009; Interview 2 with Oleg Efimov, Chernogolovka, March 2011.
[73] Interview 1 with Rustem Liubovskii, Chernogolovka, December 2009; Interview 2 with Oleg Efimov, Chernogolovka, March 2011.

Liubarskii affair proved to be effective. The vast majority of Chernogolovka scientists seemed to agree that Liubarskii was an outsider and his arrest did not concern them personally. "Liubarskii was a dissident before he came to Chernogolovka, and he remained a dissident when he left," an employee of the ICP Branch testified in his interview.[74]

At the same time, Liubarskii's arrest raised some uncomfortable questions about the repressive side of the Soviet system and scientists' participation in it. Was it really a crime to read uncensored literature, or even distribute it among friends and colleagues? Wasn't the free flow of information a cornerstone of scientific knowledge? While many scientists agreed to "play by the rules" to maintain a good working environment, they also believed in behaving decently and preserving their integrity. No one spoke out in defense of Liubarskii at the November party meeting. But many felt relieved they were not forced to denounce the dissident publicly. The ISSP and ICP Branch's administrations arranged for the Liubarskii family to keep their apartment in Chernogolovka.[75] Liubarskii's daughter went on to attend both middle school and high school in the town. She remembered that her teachers and classmates never mistreated her. However, no one mentioned her father's arrest to her, either.[76] Efimov and Liubovskii supported the dissident's family while Liubarskii was in a labor camp. They continue to maintain a good relationship with the family to the present day.

However, no Chernogolovka scientist used his or her authority to publicly defend Liubarskii and his cause. For one thing, they recognized the high price they would have to pay for active dissent. For another, they did not perceive the Liubarskii affair as an assault on their own professional autonomy. If anything, it posed a threat to the local community by attracting the KGB and high-ranking party officials to the town. If scientists' political loyalty was in question, did not they need closer supervision? Could they really be trusted in their professional fields? Most Chernogolovka scientists chose to overlook the Liubarskii affair, as it allowed them to preserve their professional autonomy, instead of striving for what they viewed as unattainable political goals.

The case of Chernogolovka provides valuable insights into the causes of widespread conformity among ordinary scientists in the late Soviet era.[77] It first confirms that scientists were indeed thoroughly integrated into the post-Stalin system, which made it difficult for them to protest against the domestic or foreign violence of the Soviet government. Chernogolovka residents believed in the development of Soviet society on a scientific basis promoted by the

---

[74] Interview 3 with Georgii Manelis, Chernogolovka, December 2009.

[75] Interview 2 with Galina Salova, Moscow, March 2011.

[76] Interview with Veronika Liubarskaia-Hock, Berlin, November 2013.

[77] While it would be too much to claim that this case study is representative of the entire scientific intelligentsia, it is suggestive of a potentially general pattern.

Soviet regime, and happily embraced their new status in society, as well as the privileges that came with it. Many were proud of their closeness to a powerful state that held science in such high esteem, and managed to live and function successfully within the system.

Second, this case study demonstrates that while there existed a wide spectrum of political opinions among the scientific intelligentsia that included people who consented and dissented in part, scientists in Chernogolovka did not use their professional autonomy to demand more political liberties. Instead, they silently accepted "the rules of the game," put in place during the first post-Stalin decade, according to which scientists could enjoy a higher degree of professional autonomy as long as they did not participate in active dissent. Surprisingly, even the most "enlightened" members of the scientific intelligentsia in Chernogolovka found this compromise to be acceptable. Privately criticizing the repressive policies of the Soviet state, they never condemned the State itself, since the latter recognized the importance of scientific development for the Soviet economy. In the post-Soviet period, when state support of science decreased drastically, many of my interviewees lamented the passing of the time when their work was in high demand. "It is better to be needed than free," one of them called his memoirs.[78]

Finally, we should not underestimate the punitive side of the late Soviet system and the effect it had on keeping educated people in line. The slightest manifestations of dissent among Chernogolovka scientists, such as Martemianov's protest against the 1968 invasion of Czechoslovakia, met with harsh criticism and condemnation. Although the state allowed scientists more professional autonomy, it did not tolerate any challenges to its political authority. The Chernogolovka scientific community was well aware of this, and consciously chose professional autonomy over political freedom, acknowledging that they could not have both. At the same time, Chernogolovka scientists maintained that they were able to behave decently and preserve their integrity, since the state no longer required their active participation in what they called "ideological struggles."

---

[78] Merzhanov, *"Luchshe byt' nuzhnym."*

6   Scientists behind the Iron Curtain: Traveling Abroad in the 1960s and 1970s

In early 1972, a Bulgarian scientist who was visiting the Soviet Union took a bus from Moscow to Chernogolovka and unexpectedly appeared at the ICP Branch's control post. He asked a man on duty to call one of the institute's employees, a scientist whom he had met in Sofia not long before. He even had the employee's work number! The visitor was not allowed to enter the institute, but the incident caused a scandal and alarmed the local administration. It was scrutinized at the annual meeting of the ICP Branch's party organization held on June 21, 1972, and was castigated as a blatant violation of the institute's security.[1] The party committee urged all employees to stay vigilant, especially "taking into account the recent increase of foreign intelligence's interest in the political, economic and military life of the Soviet Union."[2]

This minor incident illustrates a bigger dilemma faced by the Soviet authorities: how to reconcile the need for Soviet scientists to engage in international communication and exchange with the Communist Party's compulsion to maintain ideological and political controls? The Soviet leaders answered this question differently at various stages of Soviet history. In the 1920s and early 1930s, government policy was to encourage all forms of scientific, economic, and cultural contact with the outside world, as long as such contact was beneficial to the new state.[3] Soviet scientists and industrial specialists continued to travel abroad during the First Five-Year Plan. By the mid-1930s, however, contacts between Soviet and foreign scientists, and citizens in general, came to a halt, since they came to be regarded as treacherous by the Soviet regime. In September 1934, Petr Kapitsa, a prominent Soviet physicist who had worked at Cambridge University since 1921, was trapped in the USSR during one of his visits there. He was prohibited to leave the country again. During the Stalin era, only a select few from the Soviet intelligentsia were allowed to travel, and only subject to Stalin's personal approval.[4] In the late 1930s – in the

---

[1] TsAOPIM, f. 8099, d. 107, ll. 26–27.   [2] TsAOPIM, f. 8099, d. 107, l. 26.
[3] A. J. Longrigg, "Soviet Science and the Closed Society," *The World Today* 28.5 (1972), p. 216. Consider also Josephson, *Physics and Politics*.
[4] Zubok, *Zhivago's Children*, p. 91; Anne E. Gorsuch, "'There Is No Place Like Home': Soviet Tourism in Late Stalinism," *Slavic Review* 62.4 (2003), pp. 760–761. See also Michael David-

midst of the Great Terror – the Soviet Union turned completely inwards, as the fear of "infection" from foreigners outweighed the benefits of international contact. According to Anne Gorsuch, from 1939 to June 1941 fewer than 3,000 foreign tourists visited the USSR.[5] After a temporary respite during World War II, this isolation reached a new peak in 1947, when Andrei Zhdanov, the high-ranking party official in charge of Soviet cultural policy, launched a notorious campaign against "kowtowing" and "servility before the West." Between 1947 and 1953, domestic travel became the only accessible type of travel for the vast majority of Soviet citizens.[6] These developments were especially detrimental to Soviet scientists, who found themselves isolated from the international scientific community, unable to exchange their work or keep up with the most recent research of their Western colleagues.

All this began to change in the mid-1950s, once Stalin's death introduced a new era in Soviet foreign policy. While Khrushchev largely retained the Manichean outlook of a world sharply divided into mutually hostile camps and believed that the rotten capitalist world was doomed to perish, he rejected the Stalinist thesis of an inevitable clash with capitalism. After the Twentieth Party Congress in 1956, the new Soviet leader embraced a philosophy of "peaceful coexistence," which soon led to a broader engagement with the West and improved East–West relations.[7] This new approach was grounded in Khrushchev's realization that in the nuclear age, any open confrontation with the West would lead to a nuclear disaster. It was also a testament to the First Secretary's new confidence in the viability of the Soviet project, in particular his belief that the Soviet Union could catch up, and even surpass, the United States in the fields of science and technology, consumer goods, and overall living standards.[8] Unlike Stalin, who rarely left the USSR, Khrushchev took a personal interest in discovering the world beyond Soviet borders. In 1954, he went to China; in May 1955, to Yugoslavia; then to India, Burma, and Indonesia.[9] In 1956, Khrushchev traveled to the United Kingdom, inviting Igor' Kurchatov, the head of the Soviet nuclear program, to accompany him on the journey.[10] In 1959, he visited the United States, which made a strong, if mixed, impression on him. As early as April 1955, the Central Committee of

Fox, "Stalinist Westernizer? Aleksandr Arosev's Literary and Political Depictions of Europe," *Slavic Review* 62.4 (2003), pp. 733–759.

[5] Anne E. Gorsuch, *All This Is Your World: Soviet Tourism at Home and Abroad After Stalin* (New York: Oxford University Press, 2011), p. 136.

[6] Gorsuch, *All This Is Your World*, pp. 26–27.

[7] English, *Russia and the Idea of the West*, pp. 50–52; Vladislav Zubok and Constantine Pleshakov, *Inside the Kremlin's Cold War: From Stalin to Khrushchev* (Cambridge: Harvard University Press, 1996), pp. 178, 184.

[8] Eric Shiraev and Vladislav Zubok, *Anti-Americanism in Russia: From Stalin to Putin* (New York: Palgrave, 2000), p. 13.

[9] Zubok and Pleshakov, *Inside the Kremlin's Cold War*, p. 186.

[10] Khrushchev, *Reformator*, p. 324.

the Communist Party accepted a resolution that permitted ordinary Soviet citizens to travel abroad – after more than two decades of isolation. According to a rough estimate, from 1955 to 1964 approximately half a million Soviet tourists traveled to foreign countries, mostly in Eastern Europe.[11] This number continued to grow throughout the 1960s and 1970s.

Soviet scientists benefited tremendously from the policy of "peaceful coexistence" and the country's re-opening to the outside world. Not only did they receive an opportunity to exchange research with their Western colleagues, they could now also travel to international conferences and workshops. Some were even able to work at various Western and Eastern European universities for extended periods of time (usually from one to ten months). Convinced that modern science was the key to the material well-being of the USSR, both Khrushchev and Brezhnev were willing to tolerate international communication as part of their efforts to create room for innovation inside Soviet society. After the Twentieth Party Congress, the Soviet government moved promptly to initiate cultural and scientific exchanges with the West. Cultural agreements were signed with Norway and Belgium in 1956, and with France and the United Kingdom in 1957. In January 1958, the Soviet Union signed a cultural agreement on exchanges with the United States. The latter was for a two-year period only, but it was periodically renegotiated throughout the Cold War.[12]

Obtaining access to Western science and technology was one of the main Soviet objectives in such exchanges. While Soviet authorities remained suspicious of international communication, they reasoned that in this particular area the payoffs were significantly larger than the risks. In the 1960s and 1970s, scientists constituted the majority of Soviet scholars who were permitted to travel abroad, attending international conferences or working in foreign labs for longer periods of time. High priority was usually given to activities that could provide opportunities for scientists and engineers to acquire technological information useful to Soviet development.[13] Besides, scientists appeared to be best equipped to promote the image of the Soviet Union as the equal of the United States. The success of the Soviet nuclear and space programs, including the first Sputnik and Yuri Gagarin's journey to outer space, provided obvious justifications for such high expectations.

In this chapter, I ponder what it meant for Chernogolovka scientists to live in a closed community. Even though by the early 1970s most research institutes in the town had shifted to work on non-military topics, the ICP Branch remained a controlled-access enterprise. This created myriad obstacles to scientific exchanges. One of them was the fact that access to the town was restricted to

[11] Gorsuch, *All This is Your World*, p. 18.
[12] Yale Richmond, *Cultural Exchange and the Cold War: Raising the Iron Curtain* (Pennsylvania: Pennsylvania State University Press, 2003), p. 15
[13] Richmond, *Cultural Exchange and the Cold War*, p. 68.

foreign scholars – from both Eastern European countries and the West – until the late 1980s. In this situation, traveling abroad was the only viable option for local scientists to exchange their work with foreign colleagues. It was also their only chance, apart from brief abstracts published in the reference journals (*referativnyi zhurnal*),[14] to keep in touch with the progress of the international scientific community in their respective fields. In the following pages, I examine the experiences of Chernogolovka scientists by focusing on the following questions. Who could travel abroad in the 1960s and 1970s? What did the process of obtaining an "exit" visa look like in practice? And how did exposure to the outside world affect Chernogolovka scientists' political views? I show that scientists' trips abroad did not undermine their loyalty to the Soviet state. By contrast, many came to realize that they felt much more comfortable in Soviet society, with its emphasis on collective values, socialist equality, and its generous state support of science, than in the capitalist West.

Who Could Travel?

In 1969, Vsevolod Gantmakher, a thirty-four-year-old physicist working at the ISSP in Chernogolovka, applied to join a group of Soviet scientists traveling to a conference in the GDR. The trip was part of Soviet "scientific tourism,"[15] and all group participants had to pay for their own travel expenses. Yet, whether Gantmakher could go or not was for Soviet officials to decide. The fact that he was a well-established scholar spoke in his favor. By the age of thirty-four not only had he defended his "doctor of physical and mathematical sciences" degree, but he also had discovered a new scientific phenomenon named after him – "the Gantmakher effect" – for which he had received the prestigious Lenin Communist Youth League Prize (*Premiia Leninskogo Komsomola*). Both were extraordinary achievements for such a young scientist. He had been abroad before: in 1967, he took part in a similar trip to Poland.[16] Still,

---

[14] Most Soviet libraries were not allowed to subscribe to foreign journals directly. Soviet scientists were kept informed on research conducted abroad primarily by means of an abstract journal (*Referativnyi Zhurnal*), published monthly in sixteen branches of science, and a weekly publication (*Express-Informatsiia*) that specialized in abstracts and summaries of important foreign articles. Both publications were produced by the All-Union Institute of Scientific and Technical Information (VINITI) that subscribed to 15,000 foreign journals and employed 2,500 full-time staff and 22,000 scientists as outside collaborators. See Longrigg, "Soviet Science and the Closed Society," p. 224.

[15] Scientific tourism was a special type of traveling abroad in the USSR. Its main goal was to provide the Soviet scientific intelligentsia with the opportunity to attend international conferences and symposia. Participants usually had to pay for their own travel expenses.

[16] In fact, according to the ISSP annual plan for scientific trips, in 1966 Gantmakher was scheduled to spend a month at the Leipzig University in the GDR and four months at Cambridge University in England conducting research on the electronic structure of metals. It appears that in each case he did not go. See Archive of the ISSP, f. 1, op.1, d. 21, ll. 1–2. For a list of

Gantmakher did not know if he would be allowed to travel to the GDR until the last moment. This was a common practice in the Soviet Union at the time. He had filled out a lengthy application form and received approval from the ISSP director and the Foreign Department of the Presidium of the Soviet Academy of Sciences, as well as a secretary of the ISSP's party organization and the regional committee of the Communist Party. He had even had the required medical exam. Finally, one day prior to his scheduled departure, Gantmakher was invited to the Presidium of the Academy of Sciences to pay for the trip, pick up his foreign passport with an "exit" visa, and go through a mandatory orientation. When he arrived at the Presidium, however, he found out, to his surprise and frustration, that his application had been declined. "My wife was there with me and we decided not to despair," Gantmakher recalled many years later. "Instead we went to a store in Moscow and bought our first TV with the money that I had been saving up for that trip."[17] Gantmakher never found out why his candidacy had been rejected for that particular trip. It took several years before he was permitted to travel again.

Almost fifteen years after Khrushchev partially lifted the Iron Curtain, traveling abroad remained a complicated and strenuous enterprise. It required much patience from a prospective traveler, who had to fill out endless forms and obtain approval from a number of authorities at his or her place of work, including the Komsomol, the CPSU, and the trade union – all for, at best, a faint hope of being allowed to cross the Soviet border and visit a foreign country, even one that was part of the Soviet sphere of influence like the GDR. Yet the post-Stalin leaders seemed to understand that first-class scientific research could not be carried out in isolation from the outside world. From 1956 onwards, they allowed Soviet scientists, including a younger generation, to travel abroad and learn from their foreign counterparts. While there were risks involved in allowing highly educated and intelligent people to travel and to be exposed to different ways of life, the benefits were obvious. For one thing, it was an easy and legal way of getting information about the most recent scientific discoveries outside of the Soviet Union. For another, scientific cooperation was crucial for maintaining the high level of Soviet scientific and technological research. In this respect, Chernogolovka scientists were no exception. A few of them could travel abroad as early as the late 1950s. Others managed to do so in the second half of the 1960s. The number of travelers increased in the 1970s. However, some scientists were not allowed to leave the Soviet Union until Gorbachev's perestroika in the late 1980s. What criteria did the state use to decide who could travel and why?

Gantmakher's trips abroad, see Archive of the ISSP, f. 6122, "Vydvizhenie v chleny-korrespondenty AN SSSR. 1984 god," "Iz lichnogo listka Gantmakhera V.F."
[17] Interview with Vsevolod Gantmakher, Chernogolovka, March 2010.

It appears that the residents of Chernogolovka can be roughly divided into three categories. First, there were scientists who could travel more or less freely, and, moreover, did not feel that their freedom of movement was limited by the Soviet authorities. Second, there were scientists like Gantmakher, who traveled on a regular basis, but usually faced various obstacles along the way. The third category consisted of scientists who traveled outside of the Soviet Union rarely, if at all. The reasons for the latter were numerous, including scientists' participation in classified research or their unreliable political views. Some scientists did not travel abroad simply because they did not want to go through the complicated and stressful process of obtaining an "exit" visa.

Party and scientific authorities used several criteria to judge which of these three categories a scientist belonged to. These criteria included a scientist's prominence in the international scientific community, the nature of one's research (open or classified), and a scientist's loyalty to the Soviet regime, which was gauged, above all but not exclusively, by his or her membership of the Communist Party. Another consideration that often proved crucial in the process of decision-making was the type of institution where a scientist worked. For example, scientists who were employed at the ICP Branch, a controlled-access enterprise engaged indirectly in military-oriented research, had a much harder time obtaining permission to travel than scientists from the ISSP, which focused on fundamental research in solid state physics and materials science. Finally, the determination of a research institute's director to lobby for his employees' travel privileges also played an important role. Many ISSP scientists testified, for example, that Osipyan often went to battle with higher party officials to make sure that scientists at his institute could travel for conferences and scientific exchanges.

Regardless of what category they belonged to, the vast majority of Chernogolovka scientists did not have an opportunity to leave the Soviet Union until the mid-1960s. Aleksandr Shilov, a young chemist working at the ICP Branch, was an exception in this respect. In 1958–1959, he became one of the first scientists from the USSR to work in England for nine months. His trip was extraordinary for that era, and was made possible by his advisor, Nikolai Semenov. In 1956, Semenov shared a Nobel Prize in Chemistry with Sir Cyril Norman Hinshelwood,[18] and nominated Shilov to work with Hinshelwood at Oxford University. Shilov was only twenty-eight years old, and his trip to England made an exceptionally strong impression on him.[19] Since he was one of very few representatives of the Soviet Union at Oxford, everyone was interested in meeting him. "I was from a completely unknown world, which

---

[18] Sir Cyril Norman Hinshelwood (1897–1967) was an English chemist and a professor at the University of Oxford. In 1956 he was jointly awarded the Nobel Prize in Chemistry, with Nikolai Semenov, for his research on the mechanism of chemical reactions.

[19] Interview 3 with Aleksandr Shilov, Chernogolovka, March 2010.

intrigued them," Shilov recollected. "Practically every evening somebody invited me over for dinner, and people asked questions about life in the USSR."[20] A patriot of his country and a Communist believer, Shilov stressed the advantages of life in the Soviet Union and tried to portray things in the most favorable light.[21] He made good progress in his research, and in 1959 he returned to the USSR.

Shilov, without a doubt, belonged to the first category of scientists who could travel more or less freely outside of the Soviet Union. He had all the attributes necessary for that. A well-respected scholar, he also was a loyal member of the Communist Party. Besides, his research in organic chemistry was open to the public. Semenov's patronage helped, too, since he was a prominent figure in the Soviet Academy of Sciences. In one of his interviews with the author, Shilov revealed that after 1959 he went to various socialist and capitalist countries on multiple occasions and never had trouble doing so.[22] Nina Konovalova, who worked at the biological department of the ICP Branch and conducted research on experimental oncology, did not feel the impact of restrictions on foreign travel either. Her first visit abroad was in 1962, to Japan, where she attended the National Cancer Congress and established relations with international scholars working in the same field. According to Konovalova, after that trip she traveled outside of the Soviet Union at least nineteen times, including five more times to Japan, six times to Italy, and two times to Czechoslovakia. "We had collaborative agreements with different institutes in these countries, according to which we had to come and work there. I even managed to go to Cuba twice in 1979–1980," she remembered.[23] She also traveled to international conferences and symposia on comparative oncology. Like Shilov, Konovalova did not recollect encountering any obstacles whenever she needed to travel outside of the Soviet Union.

Several other scientists from Chernogolovka's research institutes enjoyed the same freedom of movement. Gennadii Bogdanov, a young chemist who worked with Konovalova in the field of comparative oncology, traveled to England for two weeks in 1969, which was his first time outside of the Soviet Union. Later that year he visited Bulgaria, and in the 1970s went to East Germany, Czechoslovakia, France, and Japan. "I never had any problems traveling abroad," he maintained. "Only once was I not allowed to go, but I do not suspect any political reasons behind that decision."[24] Evgenii Poniatovskii, a scientist employed at the ISSP, whose research on

[20] Kukushkin, "Celebration of Inorganic Lives," p. 6.
[21] Kukushkin, "Celebration of Inorganic Lives," p. 6; Interview 3 with Aleksandr Shilov, Chernogolovka, March 2010.
[22] Interview 3 with Aleksandr Shilov, Chernogolovka, March 2010.
[23] Interview with Nina Konovalova, Chernogolovka, March 2011.
[24] Interview 3 with Gennadii Bogdanov, Chernogolovka, August 2010.

high-temperature physics was well known in the West, began traveling in 1957. He was twenty-seven years old at the time, and went to Czechoslovakia as a scientific tourist. In 1965, Poniatovskii also spent ten days in the United States; he went there again in 1966, 1977, 1981, and 1983. Among the countries he visited in the 1960s and 1970s were England (1967, 1970, and 1975), West Germany (1968 and 1976), France (1969, 1972, and 1979), Sweden (1978), and Japan (1979).[25] "I traveled abroad on a regular basis, because I received invitations to various conferences and institutes," Poniatovskii explained in his interview:

Once I had all the papers together, I never experienced any problems obtaining an "exit" visa. Besides, after Kurdiumov[26] helped me become a deputy Chair of the All-Union Council of High Physics, I got to know all the people who worked at the Presidium of the Academy of Sciences and its Foreign Department [Inostrannyi otdel]. After this, how could they not let me go?[27]

The second category of travelers was not as distinct and consisted of scientists who managed to go abroad on a regular basis, but who remembered experiencing myriad difficulties every time they left the USSR. Gantmakher, who was refused an "exit" visa to go to East Germany in 1969, was one of them. "I managed to go abroad for the first time in 1967 to Poland," he recollected in his interview. "I must say it was a huge achievement that was largely made possible by Yuri Osipyan, the director of our institute."[28] Gantmakher's personal records indicate that he began to travel more extensively in the 1970s. He went to East Germany in 1970, Hungary (1973), France (1974, 1978), Finland (1975), Italy (1976), Czechoslovakia (1977), Denmark (1977), and England (1979).[29] In his interview, Gantmakher argued that the turning point in his traveling status occurred in 1974, when Osipyan managed to include him in a group of Soviet scholars going to France. "I think Osipyan put titanic efforts into bringing me into that group. As a result I got onto a list of scholars who could travel more or less regularly, and from 1974 onwards I went to different capitalist countries every year or two."[30] Still, during the 1960s and early 1970s, Gantmakher had to turn down dozens of invitations to international conferences and symposia in his field, which had a negative impact on his research. Decades later, he was convinced that traveling could have been much easier for him had he become a party member.

---

[25] Archive of the ISSP, f. 6122, "Vydvizhenie v chleny-korrespondenty. 1984," "Iz lichnogo listka Poniatovskogo E.G."

[26] Georgii Kurdiumov (1902–1996), a prominent Soviet physicist, was the founder of the Institute of Solid State Physics in Chernogolovka. See Chapter 1 for more detail.

[27] Interview with Evgenii Poniatovskii, Chernogolovka, March 2010.

[28] Interview with Vsevolod Gantmakher, Chernogolovka, March 2010.

[29] Archive of the ISSP, f. 6122, "Vydvizhenie v chleny-korrespondenty AN SSSR. 1984 god," "Iz lichnogo listka Gantmakhera V.F."

[30] Interview with Vsevolod Gantmakher, Chernogolovka, March 2010.

Georgii Manelis, who worked at the ICP Branch and who also belonged to the second category, faced difficulties of another kind. His work on combustion, detonation, and solid rocket propellant had direct military applications, and as such was considered classified by the Soviet authorities. "They [party authorities and the KGB] always had a hard time with me," Manelis recalled. "My research was considered to be secret, and they always had to check what types of secrets my colleagues and I had access to, and to make sure we would not give any of them away while traveling."[31] Strangely, Manelis took pride in his special status and was happy to justify extra party and security clearances. Although he did not travel at all in the late 1950s and early 1960s, his first time abroad was in 1964 to England. Since it was a major Western country, it was much harder to obtain permission to go there. He went to Cambridge University to attend a Combustion Symposium, where he met renowned scholars working in the same area. In the late 1960s and 1970s, Manelis went to Czechoslovakia, England, France, the United States, and Japan. "These were all technologically developed, wealthy countries, which could afford investing money in research on combustion, detonation, and solid rocket propellant."[32] Like Gantmakher, Manelis considered international cooperation to be a sine qua non condition for his research.

Finally, there was the third and largest category, which included the vast majority of Chernogolovka scientists: those who rarely went outside of the Soviet Union, if at all. This was a very diverse group which consisted of scientists who did not travel due to the classified nature of their research; scientists who were not allowed to go abroad because of their "unreliable" political views; and those who did not think they had enough credentials to pass the complicated and stressful application process, and therefore did not apply at all. This category also included scientists who had lost their privilege to travel, sometimes for no obvious reason.

Lev Vashin, for example, could not travel because his work on high explosives was considered secret, which made it almost impossible for him to pass security clearance. He went abroad only once, in 1975, to a scientific conference in Poland. "I could not travel, because my research was classified and I was not allowed to report my findings abroad," he recalled. "My colleagues wanted to go, but I did not, because I knew that my research was secret."[33] The language that Vashin used to describe his experiences deserves particular attention: he was not frustrated that he could not share his scientific results with

[31] Interview 5 with Georgii Manelis, Chernogolovka, February 2011. On the Soviet obsession with secrecy, see, for example, Asif A. Siddiqi, "Cosmic Contradictions: Popular Enthusiasm and Secrecy in the Soviet Space Program," in Andrews and Siddiqi, eds., *Into the Cosmos*, pp. 47–76; and Jenks, *The Cosmonaut Who Couldn't Stop Smiling*.

[32] Interview 5 with Georgii Manelis, Chernogolovka, February 2011.

[33] Interview 2 with Lev Vashin, Chernogolovka, April 2010.

foreign scholars. Instead, as a passionate Communist, he thought it was a natural outcome of his participation in classified research. "They [party authorities and the KGB] did not prohibit me from going abroad. I simply did not feel the need to go. My colleagues inside the Soviet Union knew about my results, and that was enough. Why would I care that the Americans did not know about them?"[34] Vashin attempted to go abroad one more time to Czechoslovakia in the late 1970s, but was denied an "exit" visa. He never tried to leave the Soviet Union again. Even after the Soviet collapse, he chose to stay at home.

Oleg Efimov and Rustem Liubovskii did not travel during the 1960s and 1970s either, but for a different reason. Both were involved in the "Liubarskii Affair." After Liubarskii was arrested in January 1972, Efimov and Liubovskii were summoned to the KGB, where they were interrogated about the nature of their relationship with the dissident. Prior to that, Efimov went to Bulgaria only once as a scientific tourist. However, when after the trial he applied to go to Poland, his candidacy was turned down by the regional party organization.[35] Liubovskii, who was a Party member, was more aware of his "sins." His attempt to travel abroad to Czechoslovakia in 1975 to go mountain skiing turned out to be a failure: "People who worked at the October regional party committee simply crossed my name off the list, without any explanations. Later, I was told, in private, that I was guilty of having 'wrong relationships.'"[36]

Those who could not travel responded differently to it. Some felt resentful; they complained that their inability to exchange work with foreign colleagues seriously handicapped their research. Others, such as Vashin, justified the actions of the state apparatus. Many ordinary Chernogolovka residents, though, gradually convinced themselves that traveling was really not that important. One possible reason was that most of them did not realize they lived "behind the barbed wire" until they first went abroad in the 1990s. Another reason was that they knew too well how complicated, and sometimes humiliating, it was to try to obtain an "exit" visa, and preferred to avoid this process altogether.

"A Ticket to Outer Space"

What did the process of obtaining an "exit" visa – or "a ticket to outer space,"[37] as Roald Sagdeev ironically dubbed it – look like in practice? And why did it cause such anxiety among Chernogolovka scientists, and Soviet scientists more

[34] Interview 2 with Lev Vashin, Chernogolovka, April 2010.
[35] Interview 2 with Oleg Efimov, Chernogolovka, March 2011.
[36] Interview 4 with Rustem Liubovskii, Chernogolovka, February 2011.
[37] Roald Sagdeev, *The Making of a Soviet Scientist: My Adventures in Nuclear Fusion and Space from Stalin to Star Wars* (New York: Wiley, 1994), p. 137.

generally? To answer these questions, let us consider a document that I discovered at the Archive of the Russian Academy of Sciences, which can shed light on the peculiarities of the process.

On June 4, 1965, the Presidium of the Soviet Academy of Sciences held an extended meeting to discuss Soviet scientists going abroad. The meeting went on for three hours, and, as a result of it, the Presidium issued a decree called "On instructions determining the order of scientists' traveling abroad."[38] In twenty pages, this document set forth the rules and regulations by which all Soviet scientists going outside of the Soviet Union had to abide. First and foremost, it stated that, like everything else, traveling abroad was part of Soviet central planning: "All employees of the Soviet Academy of Sciences, who go abroad on academic trips, including scientific tourism, travel in strict compliance with yearly and quarterly plans of foreign travel."[39] "These plans," the document clarified, "include events that can significantly contribute to the development of major areas of scientific research in the USSR and raise the international prestige of Soviet science."[40]

Second, the instructions outlined when and in what situations employees of the Academy of Sciences could legitimately go abroad. Scholars were allowed to travel in order to participate in international conferences, congresses, symposia, exhibitions, or to give lectures. They could also go abroad to take part in the work of executive committees of international scientific conferences, to visit major scientific centers, and to participate in events which facilitated international scientific exchanges. Finally, scholars could temporarily leave the Soviet Union to carry out scientific research that was part of Soviet bilateral agreements on scientific exchanges and cooperation, or multilateral cooperation between academies of sciences of socialist countries, as well as to take part in scientific expeditions organized by the Soviet Academy of Sciences and foreign scientific organizations.[41] No other types of traveling were mentioned in the instructions, and thus could not be included in either yearly or quarterly plans.

The process of obtaining an "exit" visa was complicated, and required a lot of planning at each stage. First, a scientific institution where a prospective traveler was employed had to prepare requests (*zaiavki*) for traveling and submit two copies of each request to the Foreign Department (*Inostrannyi otdel*) or the Department of Scientific Relations with Socialist Countries (*Otdel nauchnykh sviazei s sotsialisticheskimi stranami*) at the Soviet Academy of Sciences. These two departments would then send them to the proper scientific

---

[38] The full name of this document is "On instructions determining the order of Soviet scientists' traveling abroad, hosting foreign scientists, and the corresponding documentation," ARAN, f. 2, op. 6, d. 528, l. 15.

[39] ARAN, f. 2, op. 5, d. 528, l. 18.   [40] ARAN, f. 2, op. 5, d. 528, l. 18.

[41] ARAN, f. 2, op. 5, d. 528, ll. 18, 19.

departments at the Academy, which recommended what trips should be included in yearly and quarterly plans. Afterwards, the Presidium of the Academy of Sciences and the Presidium's chief scientific secretary approved of a composite yearly plan. This plan determined how much money, in foreign currency and rubles, the Academy would need during that year. All trips to conferences and symposia had to be part of a quarterly plan, and research institutes had to submit their requests no later than five months before the trip in order to be considered for the upcoming plan.

An ordinary scientist could not do much at this stage of the process. He or she could be corresponding with a foreign scholar and receive a personal invitation to attend a conference or to come and work at a research institute abroad. However, it was for the Presidium of the Academy of Sciences to decide if their trips fit into the plans of the Academy that year, or if they contributed to "the development of major areas of scientific research in the Soviet Union." Once the trip was approved by the Presidium, which usually took up to ten days, a research institute where a particular scientist was employed had to start getting the appropriate documentation ready for each individual scientist. Application materials consisted of a detailed explanation of the purpose of the trip, the complete program of a conference or a scientific assignment abroad, and two copies of a scientist's "exit dossier" (*vyezdnoe delo*).[42] A dossier had to include an application form filled out by a prospective traveler, his or her detailed autobiography, a scientist's health certificate, and an evaluation by his or her superior (*kharakteristika*). "A characteristic had to reflect scientific, social and political activity of a prospective traveler and his or her moral standing (*moral'nyi oblik*)." It had to be signed by a director of a research institute, a secretary of a local party organization, and a head of a local trade union. These evaluations were then sent to a regional committee of the Communist Party for final approval.[43]

Once this stage of the process was complete, the Foreign Department and the Department of Scientific Relations with Socialist Countries contacted respective embassies of foreign countries in the USSR to get foreign passports and visas for prospective travelers. They also took care of scientists' plane or train tickets, provided them with foreign currency, and organized obligatory orientations on how Soviet citizens should behave abroad.[44] In addition to this "open" part of the application process, there were a number of party and security reviews carried out without scientists' direct knowledge or participation. At the end of the day, each scientist, who had been approved for traveling, was summoned to a meeting of a special committee at the regional organization of the CPSU, where he or she was interviewed by senior members of the party.

[42] ARAN, f. 2, op. 5, d. 528, l. 23.   [43] ARAN, f. 2, op. 5, d. 528, l. 23.
[44] ARAN, f. 2, op. 5, d. 528, l. 24.

The goal of the interview was to determine if the candidate for a trip abroad was "politically mature and morally stable." After these hurdles were negotiated, the dossier was passed to the Science Section of the Central Committee, and then to the special "Exit Commission," for approval.[45] A person could be denied a visa at any stage of this tedious process, and usually did not know if he or she would be allowed to travel abroad until the last minute.

Most Chernogolovka scientists remembered this procedure with dismay. While many eventually got used to the bureaucratic side of the process, with its endless paperwork and inspections,[46] many complained about its arbitrariness. Interviews at the local and then regional party committees caused even more frustrations. Manelis, for example, readily accepted a long and complicated application process but found a final interview to be repulsive. He remembered:

At the October regional party organization, we had to be interviewed by a committee which consisted of old party members. These people usually no longer worked anywhere, and were assigned to this job, because they were considered to be "ideologically mature." The kinds of questions they asked were absurd and annoying. These questions usually focused on rigid ideological matters and had nothing to do with science.[47]

In order to pass an interview, it was often crucial for an interviewee to have been involved in some kind of public work (*obshchestvennaia rabota*). While scientists who wanted to go abroad were usually much more educated and intelligent than their interviewers, their candidacies could easily be turned down if he or she did not know an answer to a question, or did not partake in any political seminars or participate in any public work. Like Manelis, many Chernogolovka scientists found the process to be irritating and even humiliating. Some preferred to stay at home rather than try to convince a senior party official that their trip was justified. Efimov, who attempted to go to Poland in the mid-1970s, passed all stages of the application process. However, when it came to an interview at the regional committee, he exploded in anger and rushed out of the room. "They asked me if I knew about some local initiatives of a factory in Poland, which I had never heard of. I said I did not. So they started lecturing me, telling me that I should go read about these initiatives first and then come back for another interview," Efimov recollected. "The whole procedure was revolting! What gave these old people, who were old enough to have met Lenin, the right to tell me off? I was going to Poland to do scientific work, not to propagate Soviet power."[48] Efimov refused to come back for another interview, and eventually had to give up his trip to Poland.

[45] Longrigg, "Soviet Science and the Closed Society," p. 226.
[46] Interview with Alexei Abrikosov, Lemont (Illinois), July 2010.
[47] Interview 5 with Georgii Manelis, Chernogolovka, February 2011.
[48] Interview 2 with Oleg Efimov, Chernogolovka, March 2011.

Other scientists had similar reactions. Liubovskii, who managed to leave the USSR for the first time in 1979 to go to a conference in Hungary, remembered that it took him two years to obtain an "exit" visa:

I still have my evaluation from going abroad back then. It is hard to imagine, but it had thirteen signatures on it! Thirteen different people had to sign this piece of paper, so that I could travel abroad – first, a secretary of our department's party organization, a head of the trade union and the Komsomol organization had to sign it; then, secretaries of the institute's party organization and the institute's director; finally, members of the Academy of Sciences in Moscow had to approve of all these signatures. Most of these people had never seen me before and had no idea who I was, but they put down their signatures anyways.[49]

Rimma Liubovskaia also recollected how humiliating it was to attend an interview at the ICP Branch's party organization, when she tried to go to Poland:

All my life I was engaged in some kind of public work [obshchestvennaia rabota], but at that particular moment I had none, as I was devoting all my time to scientific research. So they asked me why I had not participated in any public work, and then asked who was a leader of some Communist country. I did not know, and a young girl, a member of the committee, began to lecture me, saying that I was not ready to go, and that I would just embarrass myself there. It was such a nightmare. None of them really cared about who the leader of that country was, but they treated me like that.[50]

At the end of the day, Liubovskaia obtained an "exit" visa and went to Poland. Yet, she never forgot the humiliation she went through at that party meeting.

Glimpses Through the Iron Curtain

What did scientists see on the other side the Iron Curtain, once they managed to overcome all the difficulties associated with obtaining permission to travel? And how did these exchanges affect their worldview? While traveling abroad expanded the horizons of Chernogolovka scientists, it did not necessarily make them more critical of the Soviet regime. Nor did it make them more pro-Western, as Yale Richmond argues.[51] It is also unhelpful to project the traveling experiences of several scientists who published memoirs decades later onto the rest of the scientific intelligentsia. For example, few of my interviewees remembered experiencing the "strong shock" from their first encounter with the capitalist world described by Roald Sagdeev.[52] Even fewer scientists

---

[49] Interview 4 with Rustem Liubovskii, Chernogolovka, February 2011.
[50] Interview 2 with Rimma Liubovskaia, Chernogolovka, February 2011.
[51] See Richmond, *Cultural Exchange and the Cold War*, pp. 65, 75. Consider also English, *Russia and the Idea of the West*, p. 75. By contrast, Anne Gorsuch contends that for many Soviet tourists in the 1950s and early 1960s, "enjoying the West did not necessitate a rejection of the Soviet self"; in Gorsuch, *All This is Your World*, p. 166.
[52] Sagdeev, *The Making of a Soviet Scientist*, pp. 71–72.

admitted to having felt overwhelmed by the prosperity and wealth of the Western countries they had visited.[53] By contrast, many Chernogolovka scientists recognized that traveling abroad remained a privilege of a select minority, and highly valued their special status as one of the few "trustworthy" professional groups in the USSR. Most of my interviewees saw trips to international conferences as a unique opportunity to exchange their research with colleagues abroad, and were proud when their scientific results turned out to be on a par with the accomplishments of their Western peers. They also readily embraced the chance to work in technologically advanced laboratories, especially in Western countries, as well as to observe firsthand the organization of science beyond Soviet borders. Overall, for most Chernogolovka scientists, traveling abroad presented an exciting opportunity to feel part of the international scientific community. This was especially valuable to citizens of a closed society like the Soviet one.

The fact that most local scientists did not start traveling until the mid- to late 1960s, without doubt, affected their views of the outside world. By then many were already well-established professionals and mature adults, in their thirties and forties, and they perceived their experiences accordingly. There were a few exceptions, of course, such as Shilov, who spent a year in England in 1958–1959, or Liubovskii, whose father served in the Red Army in Poland during the Second World War and brought his family there in 1945–1947. Yet, the rest of Chernogolovka scientists did not encounter any alternative ways of life until the mid- to late 1960s or even the 1970s, after the launch of the détente.[54]

The context of those trips was crucial, too. Most scientists traveled as part of a Soviet delegation for one to two weeks, and had little free time on their hands. Usually they attended scientific conferences and visited foreign research institutes, met with scholars from other countries at formal gatherings, and talked about their work. They sometimes went on sightseeing tours, organized specifically for them. Few people, however, had a chance to experience the everyday life and culture of a foreign country firsthand. For example, Konovalova, who went to Japan in 1962, remembered her trip fondly: "Apart from the Congress, the Japanese organized wonderful sightseeing tours for us. They took us all over Japan, and it was very interesting." Yet, during her stay there, Konovalova did not talk to any Japanese people outside of the Congress. Nor did she have an opportunity to compare life in Japan with life in the Soviet Union. "We spent all

---

[53] Richmond, *Cultural Exchange and the Cold War*, p. 66; Sagdeev, *The Making of a Soviet Scientist*, p. 71.

[54] There were a few exceptions to that rule, of course: Liubovskaia and Manelis, for example, took part in the 1957 World Youth Festival; Mezhov-Deglin met an American exchange student during his internship at the Kapitsa Institute of Physical Problems. Yet, such encounters were too few and too fragmentary to have a serious impact on scientists' worldviews. For an excellent discussion of the 1957 World Youth Festival and its impact on Soviet youth, see Zubok, *Zhivago's Children*, pp. 100–111.

our time at the Congress, which went on from early morning till late evening. Then the conference organizers took us sightseeing. But that was it. We were always supervised and were never left alone," she recalled.[55] Shekhtman, who went to East Germany in June 1970, managed to spend three days in Dresden without any supervision. He thought it was quite extraordinary: "I had a separate room in a hotel in Dresden, and I walked around the city, visiting places I wanted to see."[56] Gantmakher remembered spending a month in England in 1979, working with a British physicist, Robert Chambers. "I did not see any single Russian person or hear any Russian word for the whole month," he recollected. "When I returned home it took me a while to readjust to speaking Russian and Soviet life in general."[57] Gantmakher did not specify, unfortunately, what he meant by this "readjustment." It is likely that he was referring to the cultural differences between the two countries.

In most cases, though, scientists had little opportunity to interact with ordinary people abroad. Moreover, they were usually not fully equipped to do so. Linguistic barriers were often in the way. While many Chernogolovka scientists knew some English or German and were able to correspond with their foreign colleagues,[58] few could speak these languages fluently. "I knew enough English to be able to give a paper on my research, but I could not really communicate with my foreign colleagues outside of work," Konovalova testified.[59] Other scientists had a hard time even presenting their work in a foreign language. Another problem was that most Chernogolovka scientists who went abroad had little hard currency.[60] Since the Academy of Sciences or the inviting organization usually paid all expenses, including transportation, food, and accommodation, prospective travelers received next to nothing for their everyday expenses, which made it difficult to enjoy the material side of life in the West or even in socialist Eastern Europe.

This might have been one of the reasons why the majority of the interviewed scientists did not remember being overwhelmed by the material affluence and superiority of the countries they visited. Bogdanov, who went to England in 1969, acknowledged that he was surprised by the fact that everything was available there: "You did not have to waste lots of time trying to procure

---

[55] Interview with Nina Konovalova, Chernogolovka, March 2011.
[56] Interview 1 with Veniamin Shekhtman, Chernogolovka, March 2010.
[57] Interview with Vsevolod Gantmakher, Chernogolovka, March 2010.
[58] The Archive of the ISSP, for example, has an extensive collection of letters that were exchanged by the ISSP scientists with their foreign colleagues from the mid-1960 to the mid-1980s.
[59] Interview with Nina Konovalova, Chernogolovka, March 2011.
[60] As noted in *Tourism and Economic Development*, "until recently all currencies of the region were inconvertible. Theoretically they could not be taken out of, or into, their country of origin, and they were worthless elsewhere." See Derek R. Hall, ed., *Tourism and Economic Development in Eastern Europe and the Soviet Union* (London; New York: Belhaven Press, 1991), p. 56.

[*dostavat'*] things. You could simply buy things that you needed."[61] However, the Academy only gave him sixteen English pounds for his two-week stay in England, which was barely enough to enjoy his trip.[62] Besides, even this money came with a clear instruction: save it and return it to the Academy of Sciences, if possible. Liubovskii recollected that when he eventually was allowed to go to Hungary in 1979, he was issued some amount of American dollars. He was told to exchange them into Hungarian currency, but to spend the money only in case of emergency. One time this put Liubovskii into an awkward position. He and his two colleagues – a Portuguese man and a French woman – met outside of the conference to discuss their research: "My French colleague kept suggesting that we continue our conversation at a restaurant," Liubovskii recalled, "and all I could think about was: 'What restaurant? How will I pay for it?' So I insisted that we stay outside, pointing out that it was a beautiful night, and we should enjoy it."[63] Before leaving Hungary, Liubovskii exchanged the money back to dollars, but lost on the exchange rate. "I was terrified by the prospect of explaining what happened at the Administration of External Relations [*Upravlenie vneshnikh sviazei*] at the Academy. As soon as I came back, I returned all the money I had left after the trip; luckily they did not ask any questions."[64] While such restrictions on traveling might seem absurd to us, at the time most of my interviewees accepted them as a norm.

Scientists who traveled abroad in the 1960s and early 1970s remembered that there was an immense interest in Soviet visitors. According to Konovalova, during her trip to Japan in 1962, everyone tried to meet with them and asked questions about Moscow, and about life and work in the Soviet Union. "I never felt any animosity directed at me, in spite of the Cold War," she remembered. "On the contrary, since I was one of a few Russians who could actually go abroad at that time, I was always in the center of attention, particularly during my first trips."[65] Manelis also recalled that during his 1964 visit to Cambridge University, a Soviet delegation was the only group that was invited to a private dinner at the house of Ronald Norrish, an honorary chair of the symposium and a future Nobel Prize laureate.[66]

It is curious that the majority of Chernogolovka scientists contended that they did not feel culturally isolated during their trips. Many emphasized that they had been familiar with the cultures of the countries they visited long before embarking on their trips, regardless of any "iron curtains." Manelis, for example, recalled that when he and his colleagues were taken sightseeing around

[61] Interview 2 with Gennadii Bogdanov, Chernogolovka, December 2009.
[62] Interview 2 with Gennadii Bogdanov, Chernogolovka, December 2009.
[63] Interview 4 with Rustem Liubovskii, Chernogolovka, February 2011.
[64] Interview 4 with Rustem Liubovskii, Chernogolovka, February 2011.
[65] Interview with Nina Konovalova, Chernogolovka, March 2011.
[66] Interview 5 with Georgii Manelis, Chernogolovka, February 2011.

London during one of the breaks at the 1964 symposium, they discovered that they knew the city quite well from the books they had read. "We read Dickens, Wells, Conan Doyle and other British writers, and were well familiar with London and its geography. When we arrived at Hyde Park, we already knew about the Speaker's Corner." Manelis boasted, in fact, that sometimes it seemed to him that the Soviet delegation of scientists knew more about the history and culture of London that their English hosts.[67] Whether that was true is, of course, a different question.

Poniatovskii, who grew up in Moscow, and since a young age was a frequent visitor to the Tretyakov Gallery and other Moscow museums, echoed Manelis. "I never experienced any cultural shock going to the West," he testified. "I was used to being surrounded by art museums and beautiful architecture. Moscow is Moscow after all. Besides, the Russian intelligentsia always took interest in Western culture." Poniatovskii explained that he was always fascinated by Gothic architecture, and used to spend hours at Notre Dame Cathedral in Paris, whenever he visited there, admiring the stained glass and the organ music. "Of course, I had read 'The Hunchback of Notre Dame,' and had imagined it before I went there, but to see all this with my own eyes was different."[68] In this respect, Chernogolovka scientists were typical representatives of the well-read and erudite audience that Eleonory Gilburd described in her chapter on "Books and Borders." Most of them were educated professionals who grew up reading Charles Dickens, John Galsworthy, and Victor Hugo, and who had started "visiting" the main European capitals, such as London or Paris, long before they were physically able to do so.[69]

European literature was only one point of reference for scientists who traveled abroad. Soviet propaganda was another. Despite the policies of peaceful coexistence, and then détente, ideological indoctrination remained a significant part of Soviet citizens' everyday lives. The small community in Chernogolovka was no exception. Soviet foreign policy and the USSR's relations with the outside world were recurring themes on the agenda of the meetings of local party organizations, which every member of the Communist Party was expected to attend. While the tone of these discussions shifted depending on the changing international environment, certain aspects remained invariable. Following the official party line, institutes' employees were constantly reminded that they lived in a world sharply divided into mutually hostile camps. In this world, capitalist countries were doomed to perish, while socialist

---

[67] Interview 5 with Georgii Manelis, Chernogolovka, February 2011.
[68] Interview with Evgenii Poniatovskii, Chernogolovka, March 2010.
[69] Eleonory Gilburd, "Book and Borders: Sergei Obraztsov and Soviet Travels to London in the 1950s," in Anne E. Gorsuch and Diane Koenker, eds., *Turizm: The Russian and Eastern European Tourist under Capitalism and Socialism* (Ithaca: Cornell University Press, 2006), pp. 228, 237.

countries, led by the Soviet Union, were about to gain ultimate victory. Let us turn to the proceedings of the meetings of local party organizations for illustration.

On July 17, 1963, the ICP Branch's party organization held a general meeting, during which its members talked about the need to intensify propaganda among Soviet people in order to counteract the "ideological battle" launched by the imperialists. "We have recently witnessed a radical shift in the balance of power in favor of the socialist system," the discussion went on. "The rapid pace of the economic development of the world socialist system, and the Soviet Union above all, leaves imperialists no hope to win in a peaceful economic competition. The imperialists, therefore, place all their hopes in winning the battle of ideas. Their main goal is 'to cut into the very heart of the Communist ideology.'"[70] The Communist Party's response, the discussants suggested, should be to educate Soviet scientists as true Communists and to heighten their political vigilance. The record specified that this implied "cultivating feelings of patriotism, collectivism, love of labor, and other qualities that distinguish a Soviet person and a constructor of Communism from the people of the corrupt capitalist world."[71] At all party meetings, the Soviet Union was invariably presented as a peace-loving country, seeking détente and stability in the face of constant threats of military and ideological aggression coming from the capitalist world.[72]

While most Chernogolovka scientists were skeptical of this forceful indoctrination, many admitted that it was often difficult to distinguish truth from lies. Even Oleg Efimov, whom I described as a "passive dissident" in Chapter 5, recalled that after the Soviet invasion of Czechoslovakia in 1968 he and his friends had a hard time trying to figure out what really happened and which information was correct. "We would listen to both the official propaganda and to western radio stations, but we did not know what to make out of it, especially since we did not know the perspective of the Czechs themselves."[73] Some of Efimov's colleagues refused to listen to Western broadcasting at all, either because they were not interested in hearing an alternative point of view or because they were afraid this could get them in trouble.

Traveling abroad made it possible for Chernogolovka scientists to reconsider their image of the outside world. What they noticed, however, often reflected their preconceived ideas and the extent of scientists' political indoctrination. Some were stunned to find out that Soviet propaganda did not lie about homeless people in the West. "When I began going abroad," Bogdanov remembered, "I saw homeless people there for the first time in my life. I saw them on the

---

[70] TsAOPIM, f. 8099, op. 1, d. 46, l. 146.   [71] TsAOPIM, f. 8099, op. 1, d. 46, l. 146.

[72] For a detailed analysis of Chernogolovka scientists' responses to the Soviet invasion of Czechoslovakia in 1968, see Chapter 5.

[73] Interview 2 with Oleg Efimov, Chernogolovka, March 2011.

subway, sleeping on newspapers. At least in the Soviet Union the majority of people did not have to experience such striking poverty."[74] Manelis had a similar reaction during his trip to London in 1964. "One day we decided to visit the poor suburbs of London," he recollected. "And we saw a person there looking for food in a garbage can. It was absolutely unbelievable. Of course, we had heard about it from the Soviet media, and there were many very poor people in the Soviet Union after the war, too. But none of us could have imagined this kind of scene in our own country."[75] The fact that both scientists came from a closed and privileged community certainly spared them from witnessing the extreme cases of poverty in the USSR.

Those scientists who had been critical of the Soviet political and economic order prior to their trips usually paid attention to the negative contrasts between the USSR and the West. For example, Mezhov-Deglin had an eye-opening experience coming back from his two-week trip to the United States in 1977:

When my plane was flying over America, I could see lines of cars and illuminated cities below. Then I came back to my native land. Looking down out of the plane window, I saw a barren, absolutely desolate country. I remember I had to take a bus from Moscow to Chernogolovka, and on my way home, I noticed drunken men at a village store, a woman carrying a sack of potatoes . . . I saw two different kinds of lives, and I thought to myself: "It is fine that I have to live in this country, but what about my children, what have they done wrong?"[76]

Of course, none of these personal observations found their way into the reports that scientists had to write upon their return from foreign travels. The reports typically contained information about research institutes and laboratories that scientists had visited, work they had accomplished, and ways in which this new data could contribute to Soviet scientific and technological development.[77] It appears that scientists working at the ISSP were especially well integrated into the international community. As early as the mid-1960s, young employees of the ISSP began traveling for extended periods of time (up to ten months) to conduct research at leading Western institutions, such as Cambridge, Oxford, and Birmingham Universities and the National Physics Laboratory in England; École Normal Supérieure in France; and New York University, Columbia University, and the Massachusetts Institute of Technology in the United States.[78] Scientists' reports, meticulously

[74] Interview 3 with Gennadii Bogdanov, Chernogolovka, August 2010.
[75] Interview 5 with Georgii Manelis, Chernogolovka, February 2011.
[76] Interview 2 with Leonid Mezhov-Deglin, Chernogolovka, March 2010.
[77] The Archive of the ISSP, for example, has an extensive collection of such reports.
[78] Archive of the ISSP, f. 1, op. 1, d. 50, l. 1, "Otchet o poezdke v SShA gruppy sotrudnikov AN SSSR (30.1. – 7.2.1968 goda)"; f. 1, op. 1, d. 37, l. 1 "Otchet o nauchnoi komandirovke v Angliiu mladshego nauchnogo sotrudnika Instituta fiziki tverdogo tela AN SSSR B.K. Tkachenko (13.12.1966 – 19.09.1967)"; f. 1, op. 1, d. 66, l. 78, "S.T. Mileiko, Otchet o komandirovke v Angliiu (dekabr' 1968 – oktiabr' 1969 g.)."

preserved at the ISSP archive contain references to dozens of research facilities they visited during their trips, most of them located in Western and Eastern Europe, the United States, or Japan. Such tight integration was characteristic of specific fields of study. In this case, the fact that the Soviet Union had one of the largest communities working in the field of solid state physics, together with the United States and England, made scientific cooperation more likely and desirable. The high level of research carried out at the Landau Institute of Theoretical Physics facilitated, in its turn, foreign traveling for the ITP employees.[79]

Chernogolovka scientists who went abroad in the 1960s and 1970s did not simply travel around "sucking up scientific and technological data like vacuum cleaners."[80] According to their reports, visitors usually gave papers on their recent scientific results and delivered public lectures on the state of their respective fields in the Soviet Union. Scientists also carried out joint research experiments with their hosts, making good use of advanced lab equipment.[81] Many of my interviewees maintained that they were proud of Soviet scientific accomplishments and were able to communicate with their foreign colleagues as equals. Although they thought highly of Western scientific achievements, Chernogolovka scientists were confident that Soviet science was in no way inferior to Western science. "They were superior in some areas, we were superior in others," Manelis recollected. "But at the end of the day we could learn from each other. My colleagues and I did not feel the need to emulate them."[82] At the same time, numerous reports indicate that Soviet visitors were interested not only in exchanging scientific results, but also in learning about the general organization of research abroad. This was especially true for scientists who occupied top administrative positions, like Yuri Osipyan. Many reports praised the high level of scientific research in the West, as well as the efficient set-up of various universities and departments. Sometimes, though, the reports pointed to certain negative trends, such as the cutting down of research funding and scientists' salaries at British universities as a result of the economic recession of the mid-1970s.[83]

Remarkably, while most scientists recognized the importance of international communication, their trips abroad made them realize that their own lives and work were irrevocably linked to the Soviet Union. For one thing, life at

---

[79] Khalatnikov, *Dau, Kentavr i drugie*, pp. 110, 122, 144–148.

[80] Richmond, *Cultural Exchange and the Cold War*, p. 74.

[81] Archive of the ISSP, f. 1, op. 1, d. 80, l. 56, "Otchet o poezdke vo Frantsiiu starshego nauchnogo sotrudnika Instituta fiziki tverdogo tela AN SSSR Vol'skogo E.P. (9.02 – 9.05 1970 g.)."

[82] Interview 5 with Georgii Manelis, Chernogolovka, February 2011.

[83] Archive of the ISSP, f. 1, op. 1, d. 203, l. 126, "Otchet o nauchnoi komandirovke v Angliiu na mesiats (20 aprelia – 18 maia 1975 g.) zaveduiushchego laboratoriei fiziki vysokikh davlenii Instituta fiziki tverdogo tela AN SSSR, doktora fiziko-matematicheskikh nauk E.G. Poniatovskogo."

home was familiar. Having spent their childhood and young adulthood in a country that had a highly centralized economic system, many could not imagine how they could carry out their research without the generous and steady support of science by the Soviet state. The high status of scientists in Soviet society, as well as the privileges that came with it, was yet another factor in favor of the USSR. For another, the rapid advances of Soviet science in the 1950s, 1960s, and early 1970s not only allowed my interviewees to travel and exchange their work, but also further convinced them that the Soviet Union was moving in the right direction. Children of war, they could not help but feel proud of the postwar Soviet scientific achievements, and saw their own research as part of the Soviet success in this area. Even though the USSR was lagging behind advanced capitalist countries in a number of scientific and economic spheres, its physicists and chemists produced first-class research in certain, if limited, scientific fields.

Living in a closed community did not make Chernogolovka scientists feel more isolated from the outside world. In fact, it made traveling abroad easier for a wide number of scientists whose work was not considered classified. In the 1960s and 1970s, select employees of the ISSP, the ICP Branch, and the Landau ITP traveled to France, England, the United States, Sweden, and Japan, as well as numerous Eastern European countries. Some went for one or two weeks to attend international conferences and learn about the most recent results in their respective fields of study. Others traveled for extended periods of time (from one to ten months) to visit different scientific facilities and work in research laboratories of leading US, Western, and Eastern European universities. While the Soviet authorities retained the right to deny permission to travel to any Soviet citizen, they were more lenient toward the scientific intelligentsia. Both Khrushchev and Brezhnev considered the benefits of scientific exchanges for Soviet development to largely outweigh the risks. They also trusted that scientists were less likely to "turn into enemies of the Soviet regime" after their exposure to the West. After all, the post-Stalin state invested tremendous financial and human resources to create favorable conditions for the develop-ment of modern science in the USSR. As I argued in Chapter 5, most Chernogolovka scientists readily accepted the "rules of the game" set by the Soviet regime for the chance to do science.

It is not entirely accurate to assume that scientists' trips abroad made them more pro-Western or helped them realize "how far their country lagged behind."[84] The first Cold War generation of Soviet scientists still had a lot of confidence in the Soviet Union and its ability to catch up with the United States,

---

[84] Richmond, *Cultural Exchange and the Cold War*, pp. 65, 75; Robert G. Kaiser, *Why Gorbachev Happened: His Triumph and His Failure* (New York: Simon and Shuster, 1991), pp. 403–404.

as well as other Western countries.[85] Their confidence was based on the rapid economic reconstruction of Soviet society after the Great Patriotic War. It was further reinforced by the massive state investments in the expansion of the scientific enterprise in the late 1940s, 1950s, and 1960s. How could scientists feel differently, when the ultimate economic, military, and technological success of the USSR largely depended on their work and research? This was not mere propaganda, but an important part of the modernizing and enlightening mission of the Soviet intelligentsia. At the time, many of my interviewees readily embraced this belief. Trips abroad allowed Chernogolovka scientists to join the international academic community, and to receive valuable information about many recent developments in their fields of study.

Last but not least, scientists' exposure to the outside world contributed to the diversity of thinking among the scientific intelligentsia. Few people were converted: there were no incidents of Chernogolovka scientists defecting. Yet, many were able to compare what they saw with their own eyes to the information that came from the official Soviet media. For example, witnessing firsthand the material abundance of Western European grocery and department stores impelled some of my interviewees to reflect on the repeated failure of the Soviet economy to provide enough food supplies and consumer goods to Soviet people. By the same token, engaging in informal conversations with their Hungarian colleagues helped scientists realize that the Soviet portrayal of the Hungarian Uprising of 1956 had been heavily distorted. These snapshot revelations led some of the more critically minded individuals to search for alternative sources of information. The end result was a more complex picture of the world that existed outside the Soviet borders.

---

[85] Interestingly, Anne Gorsuch also concludes that for many privileged Soviet travelers during the Khrushchev era, it was possible to admire Western consumer goods and still believe in the future of Soviet socialism. See Gorsuch, *All This Is Your World*, pp. 166–167.

Conclusion

"Perhaps you would like my narrative to be more dramatic, but here in Chernogolovka we never felt the urgency of political reforms." So stated one of my interviewees when asked to reflect on the final years of the Soviet Union. "Many of my friends supported Gorbachev's perestroika," he continued, "but our discontent with the system was not political, and it was fairly subdued." The scientist went on to admit that by the mid-1980s he and his colleagues could not help but notice the constant food shortages and other economic failings of the Soviet system. Yet, they also recognized that they lived in a relatively favorable environment, where they could do science and were spared from the rigid ideological dictates of the party.[1]

The case study of Chernogolovka is enlightening because it helps us to better understand the transition of Soviet society from the Stalinist system to a more humane model of socialism under Khrushchev and Brezhnev. In the 1960s and 1970s, the small scientific community in Chernogolovka came to represent the best of what mature socialism had to offer. Residents of the town received generous and steady state funding. Many were able to have successful careers at local research institutes and to fulfill themselves professionally, all while pursuing their scientific interests. In comparison to the vast majority of the Soviet population, scientists enjoyed relative material prosperity. Free modern housing, better health care, and higher quality education for their children were some of the most attractive spotlights of mature socialism, readily available to select professional groups in the late USSR. Although local residents did not experience the affluence promised by Khrushchev in 1961, they did live in a privileged community, where their basic needs were mostly met.

For people who grew up in the 1930s and survived the hardships and desolation of the Great Patriotic War and the immediate postwar years, these were important and tangible accomplishments. They fueled scientists' faith in the strong state that had defeated Nazi Germany, as official Soviet propaganda claimed, and now provided them with opportunities to have a normal life. These accomplishments also indicated that, overall, their country was going in

---

[1] Interview 2 with Veniamin Shekhtman, Chernogolovka, March 2010.

the right direction. At the time, few scientists were alarmed by the high cost that the rest of Soviet society was asked to pay to support the privileged status of academic towns and the scientific intelligentsia in general.[2] Traveling abroad was yet another privilege that contributed to the general contentment of the scientific intelligentsia residing in closed academic communities such as Chernogolovka.[3]

The fact that in the post-Stalin era scientists' professional interests largely overlapped with the interests of the state was even more significant, as it contributed to scientists' idealism and enhanced their commitment to the Soviet project. Most of my interviewees could readily identify with Khrushchev's promise to revitalize socialism through science. They were eager to participate in building a more efficient and humane model of socialism. Unlike members of the cultural intelligentsia, who perceived the central agenda of the Thaw as saving socialism through culture, the scientific intelligentsia saw the Thaw as an opportunity to implement their scientific visions through working with the Soviet state. Many shared the regime's belief that science would play a crucial role in spurring the economic growth and vitality of the Soviet Union.[4] They were also convinced that the post-Stalin system created the most favorable conditions for the advancement of modern science. "If I were 30 years old now and I had the same research idea that led me to my Nobel Prize discovery," Zhores Alferov admitted in one of his interviews, "I do not think I would have been able to successfully finish my research, because I would have spent most of my time looking for funding."[5] The first Cold War generation of Chernogolovka scientists shared Alferov's sentiment. The withdrawal of state funding from science in the 1990s, they argued, was one of the major causes of the economic problems facing present-day Russia.

Remarkably, the vast majority of the late Soviet scientific intelligentsia, with the exception of a few prominent dissidents, considered the liberalization of the cultural and political spheres to be a desirable, yet secondary goal. At the end of the day, they were willing to overlook the repressive side of the Khrushchev and Brezhnev regimes in the name of scientific progress, which they believed

---

[2] Loren Graham contends that the financial burden on the Soviet Union to maintain its enormous scientific establishment was great. In fact, it was incommensurate with the size of the Soviet economy. See Graham and Dezhina, *Science in the New Russia*, pp. 2–5.

[3] Kate Brown also argues that residents of Ozersk were content to live in a closed, privileged community. See Brown, *Plutopia*, pp. 266–267.

[4] Remarkably, many of their Western colleagues also subscribed to the view that advancing science and technology was a sine qua non condition for maintaining the economic vitality of states. See, for example, Norman Hackerman and Kenneth Ashworth, *Conversations on the Uses of Science and Technology* (Denton, Texas: University of North Texas Press, 1996), pp. 10, 32–33.

[5] *Vremia novostei*, July 18, 2008. For a comprehensive portrait of Zhores Alferov, see Paul R. Josephson, *Lenin's Laureate: Zhores Alferov's Life in Communist Science* (Cambridge: The MIT Press, 2010).

the post-Stalin leadership helped promote. This was one of the main reasons why the disillusionment with the Soviet project was not as widespread among the scientific intelligentsia as it was among writers, artists, poets, and enlightened apparatchiks. Unlike their literary peers, who lost their autonomy after the political crackdown in the late 1960s, scientists continued to enjoy many of the privileges granted to them under Khrushchev. They recognized that they could only enjoy these privileges as long as they did not openly challenge the Soviet system. Many found this compromise to be acceptable, especially since the price for violating the officially set "rules of the game" was extremely high, and very few scientists were ready to pay it. The scientific community in Chernogolovka proved their loyalty to the Soviet regime with passive participation in the system and overall conformity.

Their general contentment with the late Soviet regime notwithstanding, my interviewees welcomed the economic and political reforms launched by the new General Secretary Mikhail Gorbachev in the mid-1980s. What part of Gorbachev's perestroika did scientists find attractive, and why? The fact that "a man of our generation" had come to power elicited widespread enthusiasm among the first Cold War generation of Chernogolovka scientists. After years of political inertia during Brezhnev's rule, the ascendance of the fifty-four-year old Gorbachev – full of energy, reformist idealism, and hopes for building a better socialist society – was perceived as a positive change. Gorbachev's "new thinking" in foreign policy, especially his promise of gradual rapprochement with the West, was also appealing to the scientific intelligentsia. Having lived through the Great Patriotic War, many Chernogolovka residents were convinced that avoiding another large-scale military confrontation should be a top priority for the Soviet government. In light of this, many viewed disarmament and Soviet security cooperation with the West, both part of Gorbachev's rapprochement, as highly valuable international goals.

Scientists' main concern, however, was the economic stagnation of the Soviet system. Indeed, by 1985 economic growth had declined to 2 percent a year, down from the 6 percent of the early 1960s.[6] The scientific intelligentsia welcomed Gorbachev's coming to power, because the new General Secretary began by recognizing that the economy was in sharp decline. In December 1984, several months before his ascendance to power, Gorbachev declared that the remedy for this economic slowdown was a rapid transition to "intensive" economic development, "increased labor productivity," and a "breakthrough ... of scientific-technological progress."[7] This was the language with which Chernogolovka scientists could readily identify. Many of

---

[6] Josephson, *Lenin's Laureate*, p. 178.
[7] Martin Malia, *The Soviet Tragedy: A History of Socialism in Russia, 1917–1991* (New York: The Free Press, 1994), p. 412.

my interviewees believed that addressing economic problems, particularly the persistent decline in production rates, was the most urgent task of the new government. Curiously, scientists had different interpretations of the severity of the economic crisis. Some thought that radical reforms were necessary to avoid the imminent economic collapse; others maintained that limited reforms were needed to simply increase the efficiency of Soviet central planning. Both groups expected that Gorbachev's perestroika would help reinvigorate the economy and infuse new life into the Soviet project. Many also hoped that fundamental science would play a crucial role in achieving these goals. In a sense, Chernogolovka scientists looked back to one of the central promises of Khrushchev's Thaw – the promise to revitalize the Soviet model of socialism through scientific development and innovation – hoping that it was still applicable to their own time. In the late 1980s, however, scientists no longer enjoyed the prestige and public admiration they had mastered during the Thaw.[8] Very few, in fact, would form the intellectual vanguard of perestroika.

While most residents of the town did not feel the urgency of political reforms, they viewed positively the limited political liberalization and democratization that began under Gorbachev. A small group of my respondents admitted they had thought that the introduction of free elections and the gradual democratization of Soviet society would help improve the political, social, and, eventually, economic situation in the country. In 1988–1989, these scientists actively participated in promoting the candidacy of the historian Yuri Afanasiev to the newly convened national assembly, the Congress of People's Deputies. Shortly after his election, Afanasiev would move on to denounce the very foundations of the Soviet state and society.[9] Yet, his early Chernogolovka supporters were not ready to follow him down this radical path. At the same time, only three of my interviewees openly disapproved of perestroika when it began. Years later, they admitted that they resented Gorbachev's confusing and inconsistent policies, which, they thought, betrayed the Soviet model of socialism, as well as many "honest Communists."

The failure of perestroika and the subsequent collapse of the Soviet Union confirmed the worst fears of these few skeptical scientists. But it also led to widespread disillusionment among the rest of the local intelligentsia. Scientists' complete dependence on the Soviet state proved to be a serious challenge. This became especially obvious, when the social and economic structure of Soviet society began to crumble in the early 1990s. Towns like

---

[8] After the Chernobyl disaster there was a public backlash against scientists, especially nuclear scientists, in the Soviet Union. See Zubok, *Zhivago's Children*, p. 340.

[9] Zubok, *Zhivago's Children*, p. 344.

Chernogolovka, Dubna, or Akademgorodok, it turned out, could exist only as long as the Soviet state made the advancement of science its main priority. In the context of the highly centralized command economy, the regime was able to redirect resources into scientific towns and maintain a higher quality of life there. However, once science lost the support of state ideology, the level of state funding declined dramatically, which had an immediate negative impact on scientific towns. According to the early post-Soviet estimates, from 1985 to 1995 state funding of science in Russia decreased to 7 percent of its pre-perestroika level.[10] In the early post-Soviet era, hundreds of advanced research laboratories and institutes across the country went bankrupt.[11]

For most of my interviewees, the degradation of Soviet science in the 1990s became the most challenging – even depressing – part of their professional careers. Struggling to survive, many institutes across the new Russia redirected their meager budgets to maintaining scientists' salaries at the expense of buying new materials and equipment.[12] Chernogolovka was no exception. This allowed the "Thaw generation" of scientists to stay employed at the local research institutes. But it became increasingly hard, and sometimes impossible, for them to maintain dynamic research agendas without updated equipment and necessary materials at their disposal. Scientists' material conditions also deteriorated significantly. In the 1960s, the mean salary of a scientist in the Soviet Union was three-and-a-half to five times higher than the average salary across the country.[13] In the 1990s, the government did not even try to maintain a minimum living standard for scientific researchers.[14] Although all of my respondents managed to keep their state-owned apartments, and eventually to privatize them, they had a hard time maintaining any decent quality of life.

An equally painful transition for the scientific intelligentsia was the loss of their privileged status, and the decline in prestige of the scientific profession in post-Soviet Russia. Dire financial conditions spurred some scientists of the "Thaw generation" to emigrate (admittedly, a much higher number of their younger colleagues who came of age under Brezhnev chose emigration). They went mostly to the United States and Western Europe, where they could continue their scientific research. The vast majority of my interviewees, however, thought it was too late for them to start their lives from scratch in a foreign country: after all, they were already in their mid-sixties. Many focused on the simple pleasures of daily life, their families, children, and

---

[10] *Migratsionnye protsessy i rossiiskii nauchno-tekhnicheskii potentsial: Sotsial'no-ekonomicheskie posledstviia migratsii nauchnykh kadrov*, ed. by S.I. Nizhniaia(Moskva: Institut, 1996), p. 30.
[11] Zubok, *Zhivago's Children*, p. 352; Josephson, *Lenin's Laureate*, p. 213.
[12] Graham and Dezhina, *Science in the New Russia*, p. 22.   [13] *Migratsionnye protsessy*, p. 13.
[14] Graham and Dezhina, *Science in the New Russia*, p. 18.

grand children. They kept working at the same research institutes, but struggled to readjust to the new environment wherein they had to compete for meager funding with their colleagues. With science in deep crisis, the first Cold War generation of Chernogolovka scientists looked back at their youth and Khrushchev's promise to revitalize socialism through scientific development and innovation with a bitter blend of fondness, regret, and nostalgia for a time long gone.

Biographical Notes

Abrikosov, Alexei Alexeevich (1928–2017). Theoretical physicist; doctor of physical and mathematical sciences; member of the Russian Academy of Sciences. Graduated from Moscow State University in 1948. From 1948 until 1964, he worked at the Institute of Physical Problems (under directorship of Petr Kapitsa); his scientific advisor was a prominent Soviet physicist Lev Landau. In 1964, he became one of the founders of the Landau Institute of Theoretical Physics in Chernogolovka, where he worked from 1964 to 1988. He never joined the Communist Party. He was awarded a prestigious Lenin Prize in 1966 and the USSR State Prize in 1982. He emigrated from the Soviet Union in 1991 to work at the Argonne National Laboratory, and became a US citizen. In 2003, he received the Nobel Prize in Physics (jointly with Vitaly L. Ginzburg and Anthony J. Leggett) "for pioneering contributions to the theory of superconductors and superfluids."

Bogdanov, Gennadii Nikolaevich (born in 1934). Chemist; candidate of chemical sciences. Graduated from the Department of Chemistry at MGU in 1959. He moved to Chernogolovka in 1962 to work at the Branch of the ICP (currently, the Institute of Problems of Chemical Physics). In 1973, he established his own laboratory at the ICP Branch. He is currently a senior research fellow at the Institute of Problems of Chemical Physics. He joined the Communist Party in 1964.

Chernozemova, Valentina Nikolaevna. Graduated from the Institute of Marxism and Leninism in Moscow. She was appointed the director of the House of Scientists of the Noginsk Scientific Center in Chernogolovka in 1967, and held this position until 2014.

Efimov, Oleg Nikolaevich (born in 1936). Chemist; candidate of chemical sciences. Graduated from the Mendeleev Institute of

Four of my interviewees requested that I refer to them by pseudonyms and not use their real names.

Chemical Technology in 1959. He moved to Chernogolovka in 1962 to work at the Branch of the ICP. In 1983, he became head of laboratory at the ICP Branch. He is currently a senior research fellow at the same institute. He was one of the two scientists in Chernogolovka who were friends with Kronid Liubarskii, a dissident who lived in the town from 1967 to 1972. He never joined the Communist Party.

Enman, Vladimir Karlovich (born in 1928). Engineer. Graduated from Riga River College in 1950 and from the Leningrad Institute of Water Transport Engineers in 1955. From 1956 to 1959, he worked at the Kaliningrad Branch of the Laboratory of Engines of the Soviet Academy of Sciences. He moved to Chernogolovka in 1959 to work as a senior engineer at the Branch of the ICP. He was promoted to the main engineer of the testing ground in 1961, and appointed head of the Machine Shop of the ICP Branch in the late 1960s. He joined the Communist Party in 1968.

Gantmakher, Vsevolod Feliksovich (1935–2015). Physicist; doctor of physical and mathematical sciences; member of the Russian Academy of Sciences. Graduated from the Moscow Physical-Technical Institute (Fiztech) in 1959. From 1959 to 1964, he worked at the Kapitsa IPP in Moscow. In 1964, he moved to Chernogolovka to work at the Institute of Solid State Physics. In 1972, he established his own laboratory at the ISSP. He is best known for his contributions to condensed matter physics: the Gantmakher effect and Gantmakher-Kaner oscillations. He never joined the Communist Party.

Khalatnikov, Isaak Markovich (born in 1919). Theoretical physicist; doctor of physical and mathematical sciences; member of the Russian Academy of Sciences. Graduated from the Department of Physics at Dnepropetrovsk State University in 1941. He served in the Red Army during the Great Patriotic War. From 1945 to 1964, he worked at the Kapitsa IPP in Moscow. In 1964, he became one of the founders and the first director of the Landau ITP in Chernogolovka, which he directed until 1992. Received multiple state awards, including a prestigious Stalin Prize in 1953. He joined the ranks of the Communist Party in 1944.

Khrushchev, Sergei Nikitich (born in 1935). Son of Nikita Sergeevich Khrushchev, the First Secretary of the CPSU from 1953 to 1964 and Chairman of the Council of Ministers from 1958 to 1964. Engineer; doctor of technical sciences. Graduated from the Moscow Electric Power Institute in 1958. From 1958 to

1968, he worked as an engineer, then deputy section head in charge of guidance systems for missile and space design, at the design bureau directed by Vladimir Chelomei. From 1968 to 1991, he worked at the Control Computer Institute in Moscow. He emigrated from the Soviet Union to the United States in 1991. He is currently a Senior Fellow at the Watson Institute for International Studies at Brown University and resides in Cranston, Rhode Island.

Konovalova, Nina Petrovna (born in 1930). Biologist; doctor of biological sciences. Graduated from the Tashkent Medical Institute in 1954. She then moved to Moscow, where her husband, Georgii Manelis, studied at the graduate school of the ICP. In 1957, she began working at the ICP, too. She moved to Chernogolovka in 1962, and became head of laboratory at the Branch of the ICP in 1973. She joined the Communist Party in 1968.

Liubovskaia (maiden name **Stepanova**), Rimma Nikolaevna (born in 1937). Chemist; doctor of chemical sciences. Graduated from the Mendeleev Institute of Chemical Technology in 1959. From 1961 to 1964, she studied at the graduate school of the Institute of Organic Chemistry in Moscow. She moved to Chernogolovka in 1964 to work at the ICP Branch, where she has worked ever since. In 1993, she became head of laboratory at the same institute. She was never a member of the Communist Party.

Liubovskii, Rustem Bronislavovich (born in 1938). Physicist; doctor of physical and mathematical sciences. Graduated from Fiztech in 1963. He came to Chernogolovka in 1963 to work at the Branch of the ICP, where he has worked ever since. He joined the Communist Party in 1968. He was one of two scientists in Chernogolovka who were friends with the dissident Kronid Liubarskii.

Manelis, Georgii Borisovich (1930–2015). Chemist; doctor of chemical sciences; corresponding member of the Russian Academy of Sciences; deputy director of the Institute of Problems of Chemical Physics. After graduating from the Department of Chemistry at Central Asian State University (renamed Tashkent State University in 1960) in 1953, he studied at the graduate school at the ICP in Moscow. In 1960, he was transferred to Chernogolovka, where he became head of laboratory at the ICP Branch. He was awarded the prestigious USSR State Prize in 1976 and 1986. He is best known for his contribution to combustion science and chemical kinetics. He joined the ranks of the CPSU in 1972.

Merzhanov, Aleksandr Grigor'evich (1931–2013). Physicist; doctor of physical and mathematical sciences; member of the Russian

Academy of Sciences. Graduated from the Physico-Mathematical Department of Rostov State University in 1954. From 1954 to 1960, he worked at the ICP in Moscow. In 1960, he was transferred to the ICP Branch in Chernogolovka, where he became head of laboratory. In 1987, he founded and became the first director of the Institute of Structural Macrokinetics and Materials Science in Chernogolovka. He is best known for his contribution to the discovery of Self-Propagating High-Temperature Synthesis (SHS). He joined the CPSU in the late 1980s.

Mezhov-Deglin, Leonid Pavlovich (born in 1937). Physicist; doctor of physical and mathematical sciences. Graduated from Fiztech in 1963, and was employed at the ISSP in Chernogolovka. He became head of laboratory at the ISSP in 1989. He was never a member of the Communist Party.

Mileiko, Sergei Tikhonovich (born in 1935). Engineer; doctor of technical sciences. Graduated from the Mechanical Department of the Moscow Institute of Aviation and Technology in 1958. From 1958 to 1964, he worked at the Institute of Hydrodynamics in Akademgorodok. He moved to Chernogolovka in 1964 to work at the ISSP. In 1976, he became head of laboratory at the ISSP. He joined the CPSU in 1962.

Mironova, Emma Pavlovna (born in 1932). Designer and engineer. She moved to Chernogolovka in 1959 to work as a designer at GIPRONII, a major research institute of the Academy of Sciences responsible for designing new facilities.

Nikiforov, Sergei Ivanovich (born in 1937). Physicist; doctor of physical and mathematical sciences. Graduated from the Physico-Mathematical Department of Odessa State University in 1959. From 1959 to 1962, he studied at the graduate school of the Institute of Crystallography in Moscow. He moved to Chernogolovka in 1963 to work at the ISSP. In 1972, he became head of laboratory at the ISSP. He joined the Communist Party in 1974. He is currently employed at the National Institute of Standards and Technology in the United States. He is also a senior research fellow at the ISSP.

Poniatovskii, Evgenii Genrikhovich (born in 1930). Physicist; doctor of physical and mathematical sciences. Graduated from the Physico-Chemical Department of the Moscow Institute of Steel and Alloys (MISiS) in 1954. From 1959 to 1965, he worked at the Institute of Metal Physics under directorship of Georgii Kurdiumov. In 1965, he was invited to become head of laboratory at the ISSP in Chernogolovka. He has worked in this position since then. In 1980 he was awarded the State Prize of the Council of Ministers of the USSR. He joined the Communist Party in 1964.

Salova, Galina Il'inichna (born in 1934). Graduated from the Mechanical and Mathematical Department of MGU in 1956. Wife of Kronid Liubarskii, a Soviet dissident scientist, who lived in Chernogolovka from 1967 to 1972. Her husband was arrested in 1972 and sentenced to five years in the Gulag. She and their daughter, Veronika Liubarskaia, continued to live in Chernogolovka until 1977, when the Liubarskii family was forced to emigrate from the Soviet Union.

Sedykh, Vera Dmitrievna (born in 1944). Physicist; doctor of physical and mathematical sciences. Graduated from the Department of Physics of MGU in 1968. From 1968 to 1970, she studied at the graduate school of the Department of Physics at MGU. In 1971, she moved to Chernogolovka to work at the ISSP, where her husband, Ernest Suvorov, had been employed since 1967. She has worked at the ISSP ever since. She was never a member of the Communist Party.

Shekhtman, Veniamin Sholomovich (born in 1929). Physicist; doctor of physical and mathematical sciences. Graduated from the Physico-Chemical Department of MISiS in 1952. From 1956 to 1963, he worked at the Institute of Metallurgy and Materials Science. He moved to Chernogolovka in 1963 to work as a senior research fellow at the ISSP. In 1976, he was appointed head of laboratory at the ISSP. He joined the ranks of the Communist Party in 1956.

Shibaeva, Rimma Pavlovna (born in 1935). Physicist; doctor of physical and mathematical sciences. Graduated from the Physico-Mathematical Department of Gor'kii State University (present-day Nizhnii Novgorod State University) in 1958. From 1958 to 1961, she studied at the graduate school at the Institute of Crystallography in Moscow. In 1962, she came to Chernogolovka to work at the Branch of the ICP. From 1990 to the present day, she has been employed at the ISSP.

Shilov, Aleksandr Evgen'evich (1930–2014). Chemist; doctor of chemical sciences; member of the Russian Academy of Sciences. Graduated from the Department of Chemistry of Kiev State University in 1952. From 1952 to 1955, he studied at the graduate school of the ICP under directorship of Nikolai Semenov. In 1962, he was transferred to the Branch of the ICP in Chernogolovka, where he became head of laboratory, and then head of a scientific department. He is best known for his discovery of the nitrogen fixation. He joined the Communist Party in 1954.

Suvorov, Ernest Vital'evich (born in 1937). Physicist; doctor of physical and mathematical sciences. Graduated from the Department of Physics of Tashkent State University in 1960. From 1964 to 1967, he studied at the graduate school of the Department of Physics at MGU. In 1967, he came to Chernogolovka to work at the ISSP. From 1980 to 2003, he was head of laboratory at the ISSP. He is currently a senior research fellow at the ISSP.

Timirbaev, Al'bert Ravil'evich (born in 1941). Geologist. Graduated from the Geology Department of MGU in 1965. In 1969, he co-founded the informal cinema club "Kaleidoscope" in Chernogolovka.

Tolmachev, Vladimir Alekseevich (1931–2011). Main architect of Chernogolovka. Graduated from the Moscow Institute of Architecture in 1954; worked in Alma-Ata, Kazakhstan, for eleven years. In 1965, he came to Chernogolovka to work at the branch of GIPRONII, a major research institute of the Soviet Academy of Sciences responsible for designing new facilities.

Ukrainka, Lana Antonovna (born in 1938). Physicist; doctor of physical and mathematical sciences. Graduated from the Department of Physics of MGU in 1962. From 1962 to 1965, she studied at the Physics Institute of the Academy of Sciences (FIAN). She moved to Chernogolovka in 1965 to work at the laboratory of spectroscopy of defect structures headed by Yuri Osipyan at the ISSP. She has worked at the ISSP since then. She never joined the Communist Party.

Vashin, Lev Nikolaevich (1929–2015). Physicist; doctor of physical and mathematical sciences. Graduated from the Physico-Technical Department (future Fiztech) of MGU in 1951. He was employed at the ICP in 1952. In 1960, he was transferred to the Branch of the ICP in Chernogolovka, where he became head of laboratory. Most of his publications on combustion and detonation were classified. He joined the Communist Party in 1954.

Zakharov, Vladimir Evgen'evich (born in 1939). Mathematician and theoretical physicist; doctor of physical and mathematical sciences; corresponding member of the Russian Academy of Sciences. He studied at the Moscow Power Engineering Institute and Novosibirsk University, where he graduated from in 1963. From 1963 to 1974, he worked at the Institute of Nuclear Physics in Akademgorodok under directorship of Gersch Budker. He moved to Chernogolovka in 1974 to work at the Landau ITP. He was awarded the prestigious USSR State Prize in 1987 and the

Dirac Medal for his contributions to the theory of turbulence in 2003. He is currently a professor of mathematics at the University of Arizona in the United States and the head of the Mathematical Physics sector at the Lebedev Physical Institute in Moscow. He is also a poet: a collection of his poetry in an English translation, called *Paradise for Clouds*, was published in 2009.

Bibliography

Archival Collections

Arkhiv Rossiiskoi Akademii Nauk – ARAN (Archive of the Russian Academy of Sciences)

> fond 2 – Presidium of the Academy of Sciences
> fond 342 – N.N. Semenov Institute of Chemical Physics
> fond 434 – Moscow House of Scientists
> fond 579 – Main Administrative Board on Foreign Affairs of the Academy of Sciences
> fond 1647 – A.N. Nesmeianov
> fond 1654 – I.E. Tamm
> fond 1729 – M.V. Keldysh
> fond 1916 – A.P. Aleksandrov
> fond 2046 – A.I. Shal'nikov

Rossiiskii gosudarstvennyi arkhiv noveishei istorii – RGANI (Russian State Archive of Contemporary History)

> fond 5 – Central Committee of the Communist Party of the Soviet Union
> > op. 17 – Department of Science and Higher Education (1951–1952, 1952–1953, 1953–1955)
> > op. 30 – General Department (1953–1966)
> > op. 32 – Department of Administrative Party Work (1965–1966)
> > op. 35 – Department of Science and Higher Education (1955–1956, 1956–1962, 1965–1966)
> > op. 37 – Department of Science and Higher Education (1956–1962, 1964–1966)
> > op. 55 – Department of Ideology (1962–1965)
> > op. 58–90 – Departments of the Central Committee (1966–1984)

Tsentral'nyi arkhiv obshchestvenno-politicheskoi istorii Moskvy – TsAOPIM (Central Archive of Social and Political History of Moscow)

> fond 8099 – Party Organization of the Institute of Chemical Physics of the Soviet Academy of Sciences
> fond 1281 – Party Organization of the Institute of Solid State Physics of the Soviet Academy of Sciences
> fond 4491 – Party Organization of the Landau Institute of Theoretical Physics of the Soviet Academy of Sciences

fond 78 – October Regional Committee of the Communist Party of the Soviet Union

fond 128 – Noginsk Regional Committee of the Communist Party of the Soviet Union

Arkhiv Instituta Problem Khimicheskoi Fiziki (Archive of the Institute of Problems of Chemical Physics – Former Archive of the Branch of the Institute of Chemical Physics)

fond 1 – Scientific Archive of the Institute of Problems of Chemical Physics

Decrees of the Presidium of the Academy of Sciences (1953–2005)

Newsletter (*stengazeta*) of the Branch of the Institute of Chemical Physics

Orders and Resolutions of the ICP Branch

Photo Archive of the IPCP

Reports on Scientific Travels (1967–1982)

Trade Union Records of the ICP Branch

Arkhiv Instituta Fiziki Tverdogo Tela (Archive of the Institute of Solid State Physics)

fond 1 – Scientific Archive of the Institute of Solid State Physics

Newsletter (*stengazeta*) of the Institute of Solid State Physics

Photo Archive of the ISSP

Reports on Scientific Travels

Trade Union Records of the ISSP (1968–2006)

Arkhiv Doma Uchenykh Nauchnogo Tsentra RAN v Chernogolovke (Archive of the House of Scientists at the Scientific Center of the Russian Academy of Sciences in Chernogolovka)

Cinema Club "Kaleidoscope"

Decrees of the Presidium of the Academy of Sciences (1967, 1972, and 1988)

Photo Archive of the House of Scientists

Proceedings of the Meetings of the House of Scientists (1971–1987)

Reports on the Work of the House of Scientists (1981–1987)

Statute of the House of Scientists

Arkhiv Mezhdunarodnogo obshchestva "Memorial" (Archive of the International Society Memorial)

fond 103 – Biographical Materials: K. Liubarskii

fond 156 – The Collection of Periodicals

Forschungsstelle Osteuropa (Archive of the Research Center for East European Studies)

fond 42 – K.A. Liubarskii

fond 86 – Raisa Orlova's Interviews

Newspapers and Periodicals

Chernogolovskaia gazeta
Pravda
Vestnik Akademii Nauk SSSR
Vremia novostei

Memoirs and Published Source Collections

Akademiia Nauk v resheniiakh Politbiuro TsK RKP(b)-VKP(b)-KPSS, 1922–1991. Tom 2: 1952–1958, ed. by V.D. Esakov. Moskva: ROSSPEN, 2010.

Alexeyeva, Ludmilla and Paul Goldberg. *The Thaw Generation: Coming of Age in the Post-Stalin Era*. Pittsburgh: University of Pittsburgh Press, 1993.

Doklad Pervogo sekretaria TsK KPSS tov. N.S. Khrushcheva XX s'ezdu Kommunisticheskoi Partii Sovetskogo Soiuza "O kul'te lichnosti i ego posledstviiakh." Moskva: Novaia gazeta, 2008.

Dubovitskii, F.I. *Institut Khimicheskoi Fiziki (Ocherki istorii)*. Chernogolovka: Tipografiia IKhFCh RAN, 1992.

Nauchnyi Tsentr RAN v Chernogolovke. Chernogolovka: Izdatel'skii otdel IPKhF RAN, 1999.

O proshlom (Avtobiograficheskii ocherk). Chernogolovka: Tipografiia IKhFCh RAN, 1994.

"A prozhito nemalo . . . " Chernogolovka: Izdatel'stvo "Borei," 2013.

XX s'ezd Kommunisticheskoi Partii Sovetskogo Soiuza (14–25 fevralia 1956). Stenograficheskii otchet. Tom 1. Moskva: Gosudarstvennoe izdatel'stvo politicheskoi literatury, 1956.

XXII s'ezd Kommunisticheskoi Partii Sovetskogo Soiuza (17–31 oktiabria 1961 goda). Stenograficheskii otchet. Tom 3. Moskva: Gospolitizdat, 1962.

Gol'danskii, Vitalii I. *Essays of a Soviet Scientist: A Revealing Portrait of a Life in Science and Politics*. Woodbury: American Institute of Physics, 1997.

Hackerman, Norman and Kenneth Ashworth. *Conversations on the Uses of Science and Technology*. Denton, Texas: University of North Texas Press, 1996.

Institut Fiziki Tverdogo Tela: 40 let, ed. by L.P. Mezhov-Deglin. Moskva: Nauka, 2004.

Kapitsa, Tamm, Semenov: v ocherkakh i pis'makh, ed. by A.F. Andreev. Moskva: Vagrius, 1998.

Khalatnikov, I.M. *Dau, Kentavr i drugie (Top nonsecret)*. Moskva: Fizmatlit, 2009.

Khrushchev, N.S. *O kontrol'nykh tsifrakh razvitiia narodnogo khoziaistva SSSR na 1959–1965 gody*. Moskva: Gospolitizdat, 1959.

Razvitie ekonomiki SSSR i partiinoe rukovodstvo narodnym khoziaistvom. Moskva: Gospolitizdat, 1962.

Sotsializm i kommunizm. Moskva: Izdatel'stvo literatury na inostrannykh iazykakh, 1963.

Vospominania: Vremia. Liudi. Vlast'. Tom 4. Moskva: Moskovskie novosti, 1999.

Khrushchev Remembers: The Glasnost Tapes, ed. and trans. by Jerrold Schechter and Viacheslav Luchkov; with a foreword by Strobe Talbott. Boston: Little, Brown, 1990.

Khrushchev, Sergei. *Nikita Khrushchev: Trilogiia ob ottse*. Tom 1: *Reformator*. Moskva: Vremia, 2010.

Nikita Khrushchev: Trilogiia ob ottse. Tom 2: *Rozhdeniie sverkhderzhavy*. Moskva: Vremia, 2010.

Kronid: Izbrannye stat'i Kronida Liubarskogo, ed. by G.I. Salova. Moskva: RGGU, 2001.

Kukushkin, Vadim Yu. "Celebration of Inorganic Lives: Interview with A.E. Shilov," *Coordination Chemistry Reviews* 251 (207): 1–11.

Lenin, V.I. *Polnoe sobranie sochinenii*. Tom 36, 38. Moskva: Gosizdatel'stvo politicheskoi literatury, 1962.

Matthews, Owen. *Stalin's Children: Three Generations of Love, War, and Survival*. New York: Walker & Company, 2008.

Merzhanov, A.G. *"Luchshe byt' nuzhnym, chem svobodnym . . . "* Chernogolovka: Territoriia, 2005.

Narodnoe obrazovanie, nauka i kul'tura v SSSR: Statisticheskii sbornik, ed. by G. M. Kharat'ian. Moskva: Izdatel'stvo "Statistika," 1971.

Nikita Sergeevich Khrushchev. Dva tsveta vremeni: Dokumenty iz lichnogo fonda Khrushcheva v 2-kh tomakh, ed. by N.G. Tomilina. Tom 2. Moskva: Mezhdunarodnyi fond "Demokratiia," 2009.

Orlov, Yuri. *Opasnye mysli: memuary iz russkoi zhizni*. Moskva: Zakharov, 2008.

Osipyan, Yu. A. *Moi vospominaniia*. Moskva: "Mezhdunarodnye otnosheniia," 2006.

Pimenov, R.I. *Vospominaniia*. Moskva: "Panorama," 1996.

Prezidium TsK KPSS, 1954–1964. Tom 1: *Chernovye protokol'nye zapisi zasedanii. Stenogrammy*, ed. by A.A. Fursenko. Moskva: ROSSPEN, 2003.

Programma Kommunisticheskoi Partii Sovetskogo Soiuza. Moskva: Izdatel'stvo "Pravda," 1961.

Raleigh, Donald J., ed. *Russia's Sputnik Generation: Soviet Baby Boomers Talk about Their Lives*. Bloomington: Indiana University Press, 2006.

Raushenbakh, Boris. *Postskriptum*. Moskva: Agraf, 2002.

Sagdeev, Roald. *The Making of a Soviet Scientist: My Adventures in Nuclear Fusion and Space from Stalin to Star Wars*. New York: Wiley, 1995.

Sakharov, A.D. *Vospominania*. Tom 1, 2. Moskva: Vremia, 2006.

Semenov, N.N. *Izbrannye trudy*. Tom 2: Gorenie i vzryv. Moskva: Nauka, 2005.

Izbrannye trudy. Tom 4: O vremeni i o sebe. Moskva: Nauka, 2006.

Nauka i obshchestvo: Stat'i i rechi. Moskva: Izdatel'stvo "Nauka," 1973.

Shikheeva-Gaister, Inna. *Deti vragov naroda: Semeinaia khronika vremen kul'ta lichnosti*. Tenafly, N.J.: Hermitage Publishers, 2003.

Tsukerman, Veniamin and Zinaida Arzakh. *Arzamas-16: Soviet Scientists in the Nuclear Age: a Memoir*, ed. by Michael Pursglove; transl. by Timothy Sergay. Nottingham: Bramcote Press, 1999.

Turchin, V.F. *The Inertia of Fear and the Scientific Worldview*. New York: Columbia University Press, 1981.

Vashin, Lev. *Autobiography* (unpublished manuscript). Chernogolovka, 2004.

Vavilov, S.I. *Sovetskaia nauka na novom etape*. Moskva: Izdatel'stvo Akademii Nauk SSSR, 1946.

Vospominaniia o Ia.I. Frenkele, ed. by V.M. Tuchkevich. Leningrad: Nauka, 1976.

Vospominaniia ob akademike Nikolae Nikolaeviche Semenove, ed. by A.E. Shilov. Moskva: Nauka, 1993.

Secondary Sources

Adams, Mark B. "Networks in Action: The Khrushchev Era, the Cold War, and the Transformation of Soviet Science," in Garland E. Allen and Roy M. MacLeod, eds., *Science, History, and Social Activism: A Tribute to Everett Mendelsohn.* Dordrecht: Kluwer Academic Publishers, 2001.

Adler, Nanci. *The Gulag Survivor: Beyond the Soviet System.* New Brunswick: Transaction Publishers, 2002.

Agirrechu, A.A. *Naukogrady Rossii: istoriia formirovaniia i razvitiia.* Moskva: Izdatel'stvo Moskovskogo Universiteta, 2009.

Ailes, Catherine P. and Francis W. Rushing. *The Science Race: Training and Utilization of Scientists and Engineers, US and USSR.* New York: Crane Russak, 1982.

Aksiutin, Iurii. *Khrushchevskaia "ottepel'" i obshchestvennye nastroeniia v SSSR v 1953–1964 gg.* Moskva: ROSSPEN, 2010.

Alexeyeva, Liudmila. *Istoriia inakomysliia v SSSR.* Vil'nius-Moskva: Vest', 1992.

Andrews, James T. *Science for the Masses: The Bolshevik State, Public Science, and the Popular Imagination in Soviet Russia, 1917–1934.* College Station: Texas A&M University Press, 2003.

Andrews, James T. and Asif A. Siddiqi, eds. *Into the Cosmos: Space Exploration and Soviet Culture.* Pittsburgh: University of Pittsburgh Press, 2011.

Applebaum, Anne. *Gulag: A History.* New York: Doubleday, 2003.

Attwood, Lynne. *Gender and Housing in Soviet Russia: Private Life in a Public Space.* Manchester: Manchester University Press, 2010.

Bailes, Kendall E. *Science and Russian Culture in an Age of Revolutions: V.I. Vernadsky and His Scientific School, 1863–1945.* Bloomington: Indiana University Press, 1990.

Technology and Society under Lenin and Stalin: Origins of the Soviet Technical Intelligentsia, 1917–1941. Princeton: Princeton University Press, 1978.

Barber, John and Mark Harrison, eds. *The Soviet Defence-Industry Complex from Stalin to Khrushchev.* London: Macmillan Press/New York: St. Martin's Press, 2000.

Barghoorn, Frederick C. "Cultural Exchanges between Communist Countries and the United States," *Annals of the American Academy of Political and Social Sciences* 372, Realignments in the Communist and Western Worlds (1967): 113–123.

Bastrakova, M.S. *Stanovlenie sovetskoi sistemy organizatsii nauki (1917–1922).* Moskva: Izdatel'stvo "Nauka," 1973.

Beevor, Antony. *Stalingrad.* New York: Viking, 1998.

Bergman, Jay. *Meeting the Demands of Reason: The Life and Thought of Andrei Sakharov.* Ithaca: Cornell University Press, 2009.

Berkhoff, Karel. *Harvest of Despair: Life and Death in Ukraine under Nazi Rule.* Cambridge: The Belknap Press of Harvard University Press, 2004.

Bertaux, Daniel, Paul Thompson, and Anna Rotkirch, eds. *Living through the Soviet System.* New Brunswick: Transaction Publishers, 2004.

Bezborodov, A.B. *Fenomen akademicheskogo dissidentsva v SSSR.* Moskva: RGGU, 1999.

Birnstein, Vadim. *The Perversion of Knowledge: The True History of Soviet Science.* Cambridge: Westview Press, 2001.

Bittner, Stephen V. *The Many Lives of Khrushchev's Thaw: Experience ad Memory in Moscow's Arbat*. Ithaca: Cornell University Press, 2008.

Boobbyer, Philip. *Conscience, Dissent and Reform in Soviet Russia*. London/New York: Routledge, 2005.

"Truth-telling, Conscience and Dissent in Late Soviet Russia: Evidence from Oral Histories," *European History Quarterly* 30.4 (2000): 568–571.

"Vladimir Bukovskii and Soviet Communism," *The Slavonic and East European Review* 87.3 (2009): 452–487.

Bren, Paulina and Mary Neuburger, eds. *Communism Unwrapped: Consumption in Cold War Eastern Europe*. Oxford: Oxford University Press, 2012.

Brent, Jonathan. *Stalin's Last Crime: The Plot against the Jewish Doctors*. New York: Perennial, 2004.

Breslauer, George W. *Khrushchev and Brezhnev as Leaders: Building Authority in Soviet Politics*. London: George Allen & Unwin, 1982.

Brooks, Jeffrey. *Thank you, Comrade Stalin!: Soviet Public Culture from Revolution to Cold War*. Princeton: Princeton University Press, 2000.

Brown, Kate. *Plutopia: Nuclear Families, Atomic Cities, and the Great Soviet and American Plutonium Disasters*. New York: Oxford University Press, 2013.

"Utopia Gone Terribly Right: Plutonium's 'Gated Communities' in the Soviet Union and United States," in Paulina Bren and Mary Neuburger, eds., *Communism Unwrapped: Consumption in Cold War Eastern Europe*. Oxford: Oxford University Press, 2012.

Bystrova, I.V. *Voenno-promyshlennyi kompleks SSSR v gody kholodnoi voiny (Vtoraia polovina 40-kh – nachalo 60-kh godov)*. Moskva: Institut Rossiiskoi Istorii RAN, 2000.

Churchward, L.G. *The Soviet Intelligentsia: An Essay on the Social Structure and Roles of Soviet Intellectuals during the 1960s*. London: Routledge & Kegan Paul, 1973.

Chutkerashvili, E.V. *Razvitie vysshego obrazovaniia v SSSR*. Moskva: Gosudarstvennoe izdatel'stvo "Vysshaia shkola," 1961.

Cohen, Stephen. *Victims Return: The Survivors of the Gulag after Stalin*. London: I.B. Tauris, 2011.

Conquest, Robert. *Great Terror: A Reassessment*. New York: Oxford University Press, 1990.

David-Fox, Michael. "Stalinist Westernizer? Aleksandr Arosev's Literary and Political Depictions of Europe," *Slavic Review* 62.4 (2003): 733–759; Special issue: Tourism and Travel in Russia and the Soviet Union.

Davies, Sarah. *Public Opinion in Stalin's Russia: Terror, Propaganda, and Dissent, 1934–1941*. New York: Cambridge University Press, 1997.

Derluguian, Georgi M. *Bourdieu's Secret Admirer in the Caucasus: A World-System Biography*. Chicago: University of Chicago Press, 2005.

De Witt, Nicholas. *Education and Professional Employment in the USSR*. Washington DC: National Science Foundation, 1961.

DiMaio, Alfred John. *Soviet Urban Housing: Problems and Policies*. New York, Praeger Publishers, 1974.

Dobson, Miriam. *Khrushchev's Cold Summer: Gulag Returnees, Crime, and the Fate of Reform after Stalin*. Ithaca: Cornell University Press, 2009.

Dorofeeva, V.B. and V.V. Dorofeev *Vremia, uchenye, sversheniia*. Moskva: Politizdat, 1975.

Dyker, David A. *Restructuring the Soviet Economy*. London/New York: Routledge, 1992.

Eaton, Katherine B. *Daily Life in the Soviet Union*. Westport: Greenwood Press, 2004.

Ellman, Michael. "The 1947 Soviet Famine and the Entitlement Approach to Famines," *Cambridge Journal of Economics* 24.5 (2000): 603–630.

Emeliantseva, Ekaterina. "The Privilege of Seclusion: Consumption Strategies in the Closed City of Severodvinsk," *Ab Imperio* 2 (2011): 1–21.

English, Robert. *Russia and the Idea of the West: Gorbachev, Intellectuals, and the End of the Cold War*. New York: Columbia University Press, 2000.

Evans, Jr., Alfred B. *Soviet Marxism-Leninism: The Decline of an Ideology*. Westport: Praeger, 1993.

Fediukin, S.A. *Sovetskaia vlast' i burzhuaznye spetsialisty*. Moskva: Izdatel'stvo "Mysl'," 1965.

Field, Deborah. *Private Life and Communist Morality in Khrushchev's Russia*. New York: Peter Lang, 2007.

Figes, Orlando. *The Whisperers: Private Life in Stalin's Russia*. New York: Metropolitan Books, 2007.

Filtzer, Donald. "Standard of Living versus Quality of Life: Struggling with the Urban Environment in Russia during the Early Years of Post-war Reconstruction," in Juliane Fürst, ed., *Late Stalinist Russia: Society between Reconstruction and Reinvention*. London/New York: Routledge, 2006.

Finkel, Stuart. *On the Ideological Front: The Russian Intelligentsia and the Making of the Soviet Public Sphere*. New Haven & London: Yale University Press, 2007.

Firsov, B.M. *Raznomyslie v SSSR 1940–1960-e gody: Istoriia, teoriia i praktika*. Sankt-Peterburg: Izdatel'stvo Evropeiskogo universiteta v Sankt-Peterburge: Evropeiskii Dom, 2008.

Fitzpatrick, Sheila, *Education and Social Mobility in the Soviet Union, 1921–1934*. New York: Cambridge University Press, 1979.

  Everyday Stalinism: Ordinary Life in Extraordinary Times: Soviet Russia in the 1930s. New York: Oxford University Press, 1999.

  Tear off the Masks! Identity and Imposture in Twentieth-Century Russia. Princeton: Princeton University Press, 2005.

Fortescue, Stephen. *Science Policy in the Soviet Union*. New York: Routledge, 1990.

  The Communist Party and Soviet Science. Baltimore: The Johns Hopkins University Press, 1986.

Frierson, Cathy A. and Semyon S. Vyslensky. *Children of the Gulag*. New Haven: Yale University Press, 2010.

Fürst, Juliane, ed. *Late Stalinist Russia: Society between Reconstruction and Reinvention*. London/New York: Routledge, 2006.

  Stalin's Last Generation: Soviet Post-war Youth and the Emergence of Mature Socialism. Oxford: Oxford University Press, 2010.

Gerovitch, Slava. *From Newspeak to Cyberspeak: A History of Soviet Cybernetics*. Cambridge: The MIT Press, 2002.

"Stalin's Rocket Designers' Leap into Space: The Technical Intelligentsia Faces the Thaw," in Michael Gordin, Karl Hall, and Alexei Kojevnikov, eds., *Intelligentsia Science: The Russian Century, 1860–1960, Osiris* 23. Chicago: University of Chicago Press, 2008.

Gilburd, Eleonory. "Book and Borders: Sergei Obraztsov and Soviet Travels to London in the 1950s," in Anne E. Gorsuch and Diane Koenker, eds., *Turizm: The Russian and Eastern European Tourist under Capitalism and Socialism*. Ithaca: Cornell University Press, 2006.

Glazyrina, Viktoriia. "Krasnoiarsk-26: A Closed City of the Defence-Industry Complex," in John Barber and Mark Harrison, eds., *The Soviet Defence-Industry Complex from Stalin to Khrushchev*. London: Macmillan Press/New York: St. Martin's Press, 2000.

Gorelik, Gennadii. *Andrei Sakharov: Nauka i Svoboda*. Moskva: Vagrius, 2004.

Gorsuch, Anne E. *All This Is Your World: Soviet Tourism at Home and Abroad after Stalin*. New York: Oxford University Press, 2011.

"From Iron Curtain to Silver Screen: Imaging the West in the Khrushchev Era," in Gyorgy Peteri, ed., *Imagining the West in Eastern Europe and the Soviet Union*. Pittsburgh: University of Pittsburgh Press, 2010.

"'There Is No Place like Home': Soviet Tourism in Late Stalinism," *Slavic Review* 62.4 (2003): 760–785.

Gorsuch, Anne E. and Diane Koenker, eds. *Turizm: The Russian and Eastern European Tourist under Capitalism and Socialism*. Ithaca: Cornell University Press, 2006.

Graham, Loren R., ed. *Science and the Soviet Social Order*. Cambridge: Harvard University Press, 1990.

Science in Russia and the Soviet Union: A Short History. New York: Cambridge University Press, 1993.

Science, Philosophy, and Human Behavior in the Soviet Union. New York: Columbia University Press, 1987.

The Ghost of the Executed Engineer: Technology and the Fall of the Soviet Union. Cambridge: Harvard University Press, 1993.

The Soviet Academy of Sciences and the Communist Party, 1927–1932. Princeton: Princeton University Press, 1967.

What Have We Learned about Science and Technology from the Russian Experience? Stanford: Stanford University Press, 1998.

Graham, Loren and Irina Dezhina. *Science in the New Russia: Crisis, Aid, Reform*. Bloomington: Indiana University Press, 2008.

Gronow, Jukka. *Caviar with Champagne: Common Luxury and the Ideals of Good Life in Stalin's Russia*. Oxford: Berg, 2003.

Grushin, B.A. *Chetyre zhizni Rossii v zerkale oprosov obshchestvennogo mneniia. Ocherki massovogo soznaniia rossiian vremen Khrushcheva, Brezhneva, Gorbacheva i El'tsina. Zhizn' 1-a: Epokha Khrushcheva*. Moskva: Progress-Traditsiia, 2001.

Gvishiani, D.M., S.R. Mikulinsky, and S.A. Kugel, eds. *The Scientific Intelligentsia in the USSR: Structure and Dynamics of Personnel*, transl. by Jane Sayers. Moscow: Progress Publishers, 1976.

Hall, Derek R., ed. *Tourism and Economic Development in Eastern Europe and the Soviet Union*. London/New York: Belhaven Press, 1991.

Hanson, Philip. *The Consumer in the Soviet Economy*. Evanston: Northwestern University Press, 1968.

The Rise and Fall of the Soviet Economy. London: Longman, 2003.

Hargittai, Istvan. *Buried Glory: Portraits of Soviet Scientists*. New York: Oxford University Press, 2013.

Candid Science: Conversations with Famous Chemists. London: Imperial College Press, 2000.

Harris, Steven E. *Communism on Tomorrow Street: Mass Housing and Everyday Life after Stalin*. Washington DC: Woodrow Wilson Center Press, 2013.

Hellbeck, Jochen. *Revolution on My Mind: Writing a Diary under Stalin*. Cambridge: Harvard University Press, 2006.

Stalingrad: The City that Defeated the Third Reich, transl. by Christopher Tauchen. New York: PublicAffairs, 2015.

Hessler, Julie. *A Social History of Soviet Trade: Trade Policy, Retail Practices, and Consumption, 1917–1953*. Princeton: Princeton University Press, 2004.

Holloway, David. *Stalin and the Bomb: The Soviet Union and Atomic Energy, 1939–1956*. New Haven: Yale University Press, 1994.

Hopkins, Mark. *Russia's Underground Press: The Chronicle of Current Events*. New York: Praeger, 1983.

Hornsby, Robert. *Protest, Reform and Repression in Khrushchev's Soviet Union*. New York: Cambridge University Press, 2013.

Ideologiia i nauka: Diskussii sovetskikh uchenykh serediny XX veka, ed. by A.A. Kas'ian. Moskva: Progress-Traditsiia, 2008.

Ilic, Melanie, Susan E. Reid, and Lynne Attwood, eds. *Women in the Khrushchev Era*. London: Palgrave Macmillan, 2004.

Inkeles, Alex and Raymond A. Bauer. *The Soviet Citizen: Daily Life in a Totalitarian Society*. Cambridge: Harvard University Press, 1959.

Ivanova, L.V. *Formirovanie sovetskoi nauchnoi intelligentsii (1917–1927 gg.)*. Moskva: Izdatel'stvo "Nauka," 1980.

Jenks, Andrew. *The Cosmonaut Who Couldn't Stop Smiling: The Life and Legend of Yuri Gagarin*. DeKalb: NIU Press, 2012.

Johnson, Priscilla. *Khrushchev and the Arts: The Politics of Soviet Culture, 1962–1964*. Cambridge: The MIT Press, 1965.

Johnson, Vidad T. and Graham Petrie. *The Films of Andrei Tarkovskii: A Visual Figure*. Bloomington: Indiana University Press, 1994.

Jones, Polly. *Myth, Memory, Trauma: Rethinking Stalinist Past in the Soviet Union, 1953–1970*. New Haven: Yale University Press, 2013.

ed. *The Dilemmas of De-Stalinization: Negotiating Cultural and Social Change in the Khrushchev Era*. London: Routledge, 2006.

Joravsky, David. *Soviet Marxism and Natural Science, 1917–1932*. New York: Columbia University Press, 1961.

The Lysenko Affair. Cambridge: Harvard University Press, 1970.

Josephson, Paul R. "Atomic-Powered Communism: Nuclear Culture in the Postwar USSR," *Slavic Review* 55.2 (1996): 297–324.

Lenin's Laureate: Zhores Alferov's Life in Communist Science. Cambridge: The MIT Press, 2010.

New Atlantis Revisited: Akademgorodok, the Siberian City of Science. Princeton: Princeton University Press, 1997.

Physics and Politics in Revolutionary Russia. Berkeley: University of California Press, 1991.

"'Projects of the Century' in Soviet History: Large Scale Technologies from Lenin to Gorbachev," *Technology and Culture* 36.3 (1995): 519–559.

"Rockets, Reactors, and Soviet Culture," in Loren R. Graham, ed., *Science and the Soviet Social Order*. Cambridge: Harvard University Press, 1990.

"Soviet Scientists and the State: Politics, Ideology, and Fundamental Research from Lenin to Gorbachev," *Social Research* 59.3 (1992): 589–614.

Totalitarian Science and Technology. New York: Humanity Books, 2005.

Kaiser, Robert G. *Why Gorbachev Happened: His Triumph and His Failure*. New York: Simon and Shuster, 1991.

Karlov, N.V. *Povest' drevnikh vremen, ili predystoriia Fiztekha*. Moskva: Tsentr gumanitarnogo obrazovaniia MFTI "Petr Velikii," 2004.

Katuntseva, N.M. *Rol' rabochikh fakul'tetov v formirovanii intelligentsii SSSR*. Moskva: Nauka, 1966.

Katz, Milton, Mac Lane Saunders, Robert McC. Adams and Robert R. Wilson. "Scientific Exchanges with the Soviet Union," *Bulletin of the American Academy of Arts and Sciences* 34.1 (1980): 6–19.

Kelly, Catriona. *Children's World: Growing up in Russia, 1890–1991*. New Haven: Yale University Press, 2007.

Kneen, Peter. *Soviet Scientists and the State: An Examination of the Social and Political Aspects of Science in the USSR*. New York: SUNY, 1984.

Kochetkova, Irina. *The Myth of the Russian Intelligentsia: Old Intellectuals in the New Russia*. London: Routledge, 2010.

Koenker, Diane P. "Travel to Work, Travel to Play: On Russian Tourism, Travel, and Leisure," *Slavic Review* 62.4 (2003): 657–665.

Kojevnikov, Alexei. *Stalin's Great Science: The Times and Adventures of Soviet Physicists*. London: Imperial College Press, 2004.

Kol'tsov, A.V. *Lenin i stanovlenie Akademii Nauk kak tsentra sovetskoi nauki*. Leningrad: Nauka, 1969.

Komaromi, Ann. *Uncensored: Samizdat Novels and the Quest for Autonomy in Soviet Dissidence*. Evanston: Northwestern University Press, 2015.

Kotkin, Stephen. *Magnetic Mountain: Stalinism as a Civilization*. Berkeley: University of California Press, 1995.

Kozlov, Denis. *The Readers of Novyi Mir: Coming to Terms with the Stalinist Past*. Cambridge: Harvard University Press, 2013.

Kozlov, Denis and Eleonory Gilburd, eds. *The Thaw: Soviet Society and Culture during the 1950s and 1960s*. Toronto: University of Toronto Press, 2013.

Kozlov, Vladimir A. *Mass Uprising in the USSR: Protest and Rebellion in the Post-Stalin Years, transl.* and ed. by Elaine McClarnand MacKinnon. New York: M.E. Sharpe, 2002.

Kozlov, Vladimir A., Sheila Fitzpatrick, and Sergei Mironenko, eds. *Sedition: Everyday Resistance in the Soviet Union under Khrushchev and Brezhnev.* New Haven: Yale University Press, 2011.

Krementsov, Nikolai. *Stalinist Science.* Princeton: Princeton University Press, 1997.

Kudrov, V.M. *Ekonomika Rossii v mirovom kontekste.* Sankt-Peterburg: Aleteiia, 2007.

Kulavig, Erik. *Dissent in the Years of Khrushchev: Nine Stories of Disobedient Russians.* New York: Palgrave Macmillan, 2002.

Kurakov, I.G. *Science, Technology and Communism: Some Questions of Development.* Oxford: Pergamon Press, 1966.

Lappo, G.M. and P.M. Polian, "Naukogrady Rossii: vcherashnie zapretnye i poluzapretnye goroda – segodniashnie tochki rosta," *Mir Rossii* 17.1 (2008): 20–49.

Lebina, N.B. and A.N. Chistikov. *Obyvatel' i reformy: Kartiny povsednevnoi zhivni gorozhan.* S.-Peterburg: Dmitrii Bulanin, 2003.

Lewis, Robert. *Science and Industrialization in the USSR.* New York: Holmes and Meier, 1979.

Linz, Susan J., ed. *The Impact of World War II on the Soviet Union.* New Jersey: Rowman & Allanheld, 1985.

Livschiz, Ann. "Children's Lives after Zoia's Death: Order, Emotions and Heroism in Children's Lives and Literature in the Post-war Soviet Union," in Juliane Fürst, ed., *Late Stalinist Russia: Society between Reconstruction and Reinvention.* London/New York: Routledge, 2006.

Longrigg, A.J. "Soviet Science and the Closed Society," *The World Today* 28.5 (1972): 216–228.

Lourie, Richard. *Sakharov: A Biography.* Hanover: Brandeis University Press, 2002.

Lovell, Steven. *The Shadow of War: Russia and the USSR, 1941 to the Present.* Chichester; Malden: Wiley-Blackwell, 2010.

Lubrano, Linda L. and Susan Gross Solomon, eds. *The Social Context of Soviet Science.* Boulder: Westview Press, 1980.

Malia, Martin. *The Soviet Tragedy: A History of Socialism in Russia, 1917–1991.* New York: The Free Press, 1994.

Manley, Rebecca. *To the Tashkent Station: Evacuation and Survival in the Soviet Union at War.* Ithaca: Cornell University Press, 2009.

Martin, Sean. *Andrei Tarkovsky.* Harpenden: Pocket Essentials, 2005.

Matiushkin, Vladimir. *Povsednevnaia zhizn' Arzamasa-16.* Moskva: Molodaia gvardiia, 2008.

McCauley, Martin. *The Khrushchev Era, 1953–1964.* London: Longman, 1995.

McClelland, James C. *Autocrats and Academics: Education, Culture, and Society in Tsarist Russia.* Chicago: University of Chicago Press, 1979.

Medvedev, Roi. *Nikita Khrushchev: Otets ili otchim sovetskoi "ottepeli."* Moskva: "Iuza," "Eksmo," 2006.

Medvedev, Zhores. *Soviet Science.* Oxford: Oxford University Press, 1979.

Merridale, Catherine. *Ivan's War: The Red Army, 1939–1945.* London: Faber, 2005.

   Night of Stone: Death and Memory in Twentieth-Century Russia. New York: Viking, 2000.

Migratsionnye protsessy i rossiiskii nauchno-tekhnicheskii potentsial: Sotsial'no-ekonomicheskie posledstviia migratsii nauchnykh kadrov, ed. by S.I. Nizhniaia. Moskva: Institut, 1996.

Millar, James R., ed. *Politics, Work, and Daily Life in the USSR: A Survey of Former Soviet Citizens*. Cambridge: Cambridge University Press, 1987.

Nathans, Benjamin. "The Dictatorship of Reason: Aleksandr Vol'pin and the Idea of Rights under 'Developed Socialism,'" *Slavic Review* 66.4 (2007): 630–663.

Nauka Soiuza SSR: K 50-letiiu obrazovaniia Soiuza Sovetskikh Sotsialisticheskikh Respublik: 1922–1972, ed. by M.V. Keldysh and G.D. Komkov. Moskva: Izdatel'stvo "Nauka," 1972.

Neumann, Matthias. *The Communist Youth League and the Transformation of the Soviet Union, 1917–1932*. New York: Routledge, 2011.

Nove, Alec. *An Economic History of the USSR, 1917–1991*. London: Penguin Books, 1992.

Novikov, Vladimir. *Vysotskii: Zhizn' zamechatel'nykh liudei*. Moskva: Molodaia gvardia, 2008.

Organizatsiia nauki v pervye gody sovetskoi vlasti (1917–1925): sbornik dokumentov, ed. by K.V. Ostrovitianov. Leningrad: Nauka, 1974.

Orlov, I.B. *Sovetskaia povsednevnost': istoricheskii i sotsiologicheskii aspekty stanovleniia*. Moskva: Izdatel'skii dom Gosudarstvennogo universiteta – Vysshei shkoly ekonomiki, 2010.

Osokina, Elena. *Our Daily Bread: Socialist Distribution and the Art of Survival in Stalin's Russia, 1927–1942*, transl. and ed. by Kate Transchel. New York: M.E. Sharpe, 2001.

Overy, Richard. *Russia's War: Blood upon the Snow*. New York: Penguin Putnam, 1997.

Peteri, Gyorgy, ed. *Imagining the West in Eastern Europe and the Soviet Union*. Pittsburgh: University of Pittsburgh Press, 2010.

Podvlastnaia nauka? Nauka i sovetskaia vlast', ed. by S.S. Neretina and A.P. Ogurtsov. Moskva: Izdatel'stvo "Golos," 2010.

Pohl, Michaela. "From White Grave to Tselinograd to Astana: The Virgin Lands Opening, Khrushchev's Forgotten First Reform," in Denis Kozlov and Eleonory Gilburd, eds., *The Thaw: Soviet Society and Culture during the 1950s and 1960s*. Toronto: University of Toronto Press, 2013.

Pollock, Ethan. *Stalin and the Soviet Science Wars*. Princeton: Princeton University Press, 2006.

Popovskii, Mark. *Manipulated Science: The Crisis of Science and Scientists in the Soviet Union Today*. New York: Doubleday, 1979.

Pyzhikov, Aleksandr. *Khrushchevskaia "ottepel'."* Moskva: Olma-Press, 2002.

Raleigh, Donald J. *Soviet Baby Boomers: An Oral History of Russia's Cold War Generation*. New York: Oxford University Press, 2012.

Randall, Amy E. *The Soviet Dream World of Retail Trade and Consumption in the 1930s*. London: Palgrave Macmillan, 2008.

Rapoport, Louis. *Stalin's War against the Jews: The Doctors' Plot and the Soviet Solution*. New York: Free Press, 1990.

Read, Christopher. *Culture and Power in Revolutionary Russia: The Intelligentsia and the Transition from Tsarism to Communism*. New York: St. Martin's Press, 1990.

Reddaway, Peter, transl. and ed. *Uncensored Russia: Protest and Dissent in the Soviet Union*. New York: American Heritage Press, 1972.

Reid, Susan E. "Cold War in the Kitchen: Gender and De-Stalinization of Consumer Taste in the Soviet Union under Khrushchev," *Slavic Review* 61.2 (2002): 211–252.

"The Khrushchev Kitchen: Domesticating the Scientific-Technological Revolution," *Journal of Contemporary History* 40.2 (2005): 289–316.

"Who Will Beat Whom? Soviet Popular Reception of the America National Exhibition in Moscow, 1959," *Kritika: Explorations in Russian and Eurasian History* 9.4 (2008): 855–904.

Richmond, Yale. *Cultural Exchange and the Cold War: Raising the Iron Curtain*. Pennsylvania: Pennsylvania State University Press, 2003.

Roberg, Jeffrey. *Soviet Science under Control: The Struggle for Influence*. New York: St. Martin's Press, 1998.

Rothberg, Abraham. *The Heirs of Stalin: Dissidence and the Soviet Regime, 1953–1970*. Ithaca: Cornell University Press, 1972.

Rubenstein, Joshua. *Soviet Dissidents: Their Struggle for Human Rights*. Boston: Beacon Press, 1980.

Ruffley, David L. *Children of Victory: Young Specialists and the Evolution of Soviet Society*. London: Praeger, 2003.

Schattenberg, Susanne. "'Democracy' or 'Despotism'? How the Secret Speech was Translated into Everyday Life," in Polly Jones, ed., *The Dilemmas of De-Stalinization: Negotiating Cultural and Social Change in the Khrushchev Era*. London: Routledge, 2006.

Semenova, Viktoria. "Equality in Poverty: The Symbolic Meaning of *Kommunalki* in the 1930s-50s," in Daniel Bertaux, Paul Thompson, and Anna Rotkirch, eds., *Living through the Soviet System*. New Brunswick/London: Transaction Publishers, 2005.

Shatz, Marshall S. *Soviet Dissent in Historical Perspective*. New York: Cambridge University Press, 1980.

Shchuka, A.A. *Fiztekh i fiztekhi*. Izd. 3-e. Moskva: Fiztekh-poligraf, 2010.

Shiraev, Eric and Vladislav Zubok. *Anti-Americanism in Russia: From Stalin to Putin*. New York: Palgrave, 2000.

Shlapentokh, Vladimir. *Public and Private Life of the Soviet People: Changing Values in Post-Stalin Russia*. Oxford: Oxford University Press, 1989.

Soviet Intellectuals and Political Power: The Post-Stalin Era. Princeton: Princeton University Press, 1990.

Strakh i druzhba v nashem totalitarnom proshlom. Sankt-Peterburg: Izdatel'stvo zhurnala "Zvezda," 2003.

Shnol', S.E. *Geroi, zlodei, konformisty otechestvennoi nauki*. Izd. 4-e. Moskva: Knizhnyi dom "LIBROKOM," 2010.

Shubin, A.V. *Dissidenty, neformaly i svoboda v SSSR*. Moskva: "Veche," 2008.

Siddiqi, Asif A. *The Red Rockets' Glare: Spaceflight and the Soviet Imagination, 1857–1957*. New York: Cambridge University Press, 2010.

Sputnik and the Soviet Space Challenge. Gainesville: University Press of Florida, 2000.

Sillince, J.A.A., ed. *Housing Policies in Eastern Europe and the Soviet Union*. London: Routledge, 1990.

Simonov, N.S. *VPK SSSR: Tempy ekonomicheskogo rosta, struktura, organizatsiia proizvodstva, upravlenie*. Izd. 2-e. Moskva: Universitet Dmitriia Pozharskogo, 2015.

Smith, Mark B. *Property of Communists: The Urban Housing Program from Stalin to Khrushchev*. DeKalb: Northern Illinois University Press, 2010.

Spechler, Dina R. *Permitted Dissent in the USSR: Novyi Mir and the Soviet Regime*. New York: Praeger, 1982.

Taubman, William. *Khrushchev: The Man and His Era*. New York: W.W. Norton, 2003.

Taubman, William, Sergei Khrushchev, and Abbott Gleason, eds. *Nikita Khrushchev*. New Haven: Yale University Press, 2000.

Tokes, Rudolf L., ed. *Dissent in the USSR: Politics, Ideology, and the People*. Baltimore: Johns Hopkins University Press, 1975.

Toren, Nina. *Science and Cultural Context: Soviet Scientists in Comparative Perspective*. New York: Peter Lang, 1988.

Tromly, Benjamin. "Intelligentsia Self-Fashioning in the Postwar Soviet Union: Revol't Pimenov's Political Struggle, 1949–57," *Kritika: Explorations in Russian and Eurasian History* 13.1 (2012): 151–176.

  Making the Soviet Intelligentsia: Universities and Intellectual Life under Stalin and Khrushchev. New York: Cambridge University Press, 2014.

Tucker, Robert C. *The Soviet Political Mind: Stalinism and Post-Stalin Change*. New York: W.W. Norton & Company, 1971.

Tumarkin, Nina. *The Living and the Dead: The Rise and Fall of the Cult of World War II in Russia*. New York: Basic Books, 1994.

Turovskaya, Maia. *7 ½ ili Fil'my Andreia Tarkovskogo*. Moskva: Izdatel'stvo "Iskusstvo," 1991.

Urban, Paul K. and Andrew I. Lebed, eds. *Soviet Science, 1917–1970. Part I: Academy of Sciences of the USSR*. New Jersey: The Scarecrow Press, Inc., 1971.

Usdin, Steven T. *Engineering Communism: How Two Americans Spied for Stalin and Founded the Soviet Silicon Valley*. New Haven: Yale University Press, 2005.

"Vegetarianskaia epokha." Moskva: Nezavisimoe izdatel'stvo "Pik," 2003.

Vodichev, Evgenii. *Siberia's Academic Complex: The History of an Experiment*. Washington DC: Woodrow Wilson Center, Kennan Institute for Advanced Russian Studies, 1995.

Volkov, S.V. *Intellektual'nyi sloi v sovetskom obshchestve*. Sankt-Peterburg: Fond "Razvitie," 1999.

Vucinich, Alexander. *Empire of Knowledge: The Academy of Sciences of the USSR (1917–1970)*. Berkeley: University of California Press, 1984.

Weaver, Kitty. *Russia's Future: The Communist Education of Soviet Youth*. New York: Praeger, 1981.

Weiner, Amir. *Making Sense of War: The Second World War and the Fate of the Bolshevik Revolution*. Princeton: Princeton University Press, 2001.

Weiner, Douglas R. *A Little Corner of Freedom: Russian Nature Protection from Stalin to Gorbachev*. Berkley: University of California Press, 1999.

Yanovky, R.G. *Formirovanie lichnosti uchenogo v usloviiakh razvitogo sotsializma*. Novosibirsk: Izdatel'stvo "Nauka," 1979.

Yurchak, Alexei. *Everything Was Forever Until It Was No More: The Last Soviet Generation*. Princeton: Princeton University Press, 2006.

Za "zheleznym zanavesom:" mify i realii sovetskoi nauki, eds. by Manfred Heinemann and E.I. Kolchinskii. S.-Peterburg: Izdatel'stvo "Dmitrii Bulanin," 2002.

Zima, V.F. *Golod v SSSR 1946–1947 godov: proiskhozhdenie i posledstviia*. Moskva: Institut Rossiiskoi Istorii RAN, 1996.

Zubkova, Elena. *Russia after the War: Hopes, Illusions, and Disappointments, 1945–1957*, transl. and ed. by Hugh Ragsdale. New York: M.E. Sharpe, 1998.

Zubok, Vladislav. *Zhivago's Children: The Last Russian Intelligentsia*. Cambridge: The Belknap Press of Harvard University Press, 2009.

Zubok, Vladislav and Constantine Pleshakov. *Inside the Kremlin's Cold War: From Stalin to Khrushchev*. Cambridge: Harvard University Press, 1996.

Index

Abdrashitov, Vadim, 104
Abrikosov, Alexei
    on anti-Semitic campaign, 113
    education, 66
    Nobel Prize in Physics, 47, 66n88
    parents, 66
    political views, 137–138
    reaction to Khrushchev's "secret
        speech," 117
    scientific career, 46
Academy of Sciences
    decree on building scientific
        center, 25
    decree on House of Scientists,
        99–100
    funding of Chernogolovka, 10
    scientific centers, 80–81n28
    travel policy, 162, 167
Afanasiev, Yuri, 178
Akademgorodok
    construction of, 2, 10, 32
    food supply, 87
    historiography, 16
    housing and infrastructure, 76
    Khrushchev's visits to, 29
    party organization, 111
    state support, 28–29
    young specialists in, 36
Akulov, Nikolai, 30n30
Alferov, Zhores, 176
All-Union Institute of Scientific and Technical
        Information (VINITI), 155n14
Antonioni, Michelangelo, 104
Apin, Al'fred, 36, 38
Arzamas-16 (Sarov), 9, 76

Babkin, Gennadii, 101, 105
Bailes, Kendall, 15, 131
Barshai, Rudolf, 101
Beliaev, Aleksandr, 36
Beria, Lavrentii, 2
Bidulia, Pavel, 70

biomedical research, 40
Bogdanov, Gennadii
    on absence of crime in Chernogolovka, 93
    awareness of Stalinist repressions, 56–57
    childhood, 56
    on collective identity, 96
    on Doctors' Plot, 113
    education, 39, 70–71
    foreign travel experience, 158, 167–168,
        170–171
    impact of Stalin's death on, 114
    on involvement in public work, 128
    at meeting on invasion of
        Czechoslovakia, 139
    member of party organization, 120, 123
    on movie repertoire, 104–105
    on population of Chernogolovka, 42
    scientific career, 40, 75
    student life in Moscow, 70–71
    war memories, 60–61, 63
Bronstein, Matvei, 30n30
Broude, Vladimir, 99, 105
Brown, Kate, 16, 106, 132
Bykov, Rolan, 104

Calvin, Melvin, 145
Chambers, Robert, 167
Chemical Evolution (Calvin), 145
Chernogolovka. See also Noginsk Scientific
        Center; testing ground project
    absence of crime, 92–93
    arrival of first employees, 1
    biomedical research, 40
    chemical research, 40
    classified research, 39
    combustion science, 4, 39
    construction of, 23–24
    decline of, 107, 175, 179
    development of polymer science, 40
    directors of laboratories, 39
    Dubovitskii's role in development of, 78
    fundamental research, 10, 12

Chernogolovka (cont.)
  historical context, 3
  landscaping, 93, 94
  living conditions, 106, 175
  local grocery store, 19
  location, 23
  non-military research, 39
  organizational structure, 36
  original settlement, 23–24
  population growth, 75
  recreational facilities, 93, 94–96
  restriction of visitors, 152
  school, 94
  scientific community, 1, 2, 10–11, 20, 25,
    45–46
  social and cultural life, 21
  state funding, 15
  status of scientists, 4, 16–17
  transformation into scientific center, 1, 2, 25
Chernogolovka scientists. *See also* cultural life;
    everyday life; foreign travels; housing
  access to foreign media, 141
  affiliation with Communist party, 110, 123
  anti-Semitic campaign and, 113
  awareness of Stalinist repressions, 56
  career choice, 66, 70
  challenges of postwar period, 64
  collective identity, 53, 57, 58, 72, 96, 109
  Communist believers, 135, 137
  conformity among, 143, 150–151
  educational background, 73, 112, 169
  emigration, 179
  fundamental research, 68
  Gorbachev's reforms and, 175, 177–178
  Great Terror and, 55
  ideological views, 109, 129, 136
  impact of popular science on, 71–72
  international community and, 171–172
  involvement in public work, 78, 93–94,
    96, 128
  living standards, 106–107
  loyalty to Soviet regime, 22, 106, 109, 112,
    138, 157, 176–177
  material conditions, 175, 179
  optimism of, 73
  participation in *subbotniks*, 93–94
  "passive participation," 21, 110, 126, (*See
    also* "privilege of passive participation")
  "playing by the rules," 124, 129
  political opinions, 21–22, 129, 133,
    134–135, 137, 151
  pride of Soviet science, 172–173
  as products of the Khrushchev era, 74, 110,
    117–118
  professional autonomy of, 151

scientific exchanges, 154–155
shared memories and values, 65
social backgrounds of, 53, 56, 68–69
Soviet invasion of Czechoslovakia and, 121,
    125, 141
Soviet propaganda and, 111–112, 169–170
Stalin's death and, 115
war memories, 59–60, 61
World War II and formation of, 50, 63–64
Chernozemova, Valentina, 99–100, 103
Chronicle of Current Events, The (samizdat
    periodical), 145, 146
Chugunova, Maria, 102
Cold War
  prestige of science during, 20, 67
  professional opportunities for scientists,
    50–51, 66, 74
Communist Party of the Soviet Union
  20th Congress, 110
  21st Congress, 7
  22nd Congress, 7–8, 27
  control of people's life, 108
  membership priority, 122
  organizational structure, 108
  qualities of true Communist, 112
communist party organization in
    Chernogolovka
  affiliation with October regional committee,
    111, 121
  growth of membership, 120
  jurisdiction of Noginskii gorkom, 109
  philosophical and ideological seminars,
    124–125, 129
  primary party organizations (PPO), 111,
    119, 120
  recruitment into, 120
  relationship with scientists, 108–109, 120,
    124, 128
  "rules of the game," 124n86, 124–125
  topics of party meetings, 126–128
  workers and staff as members of, 123, 124
Communist Youth League (*Komsomol*), 112
Council of Ministers of the USSR, 1, 25, 32, 36
cultural life
  access to film repositories, 104, 105–106
  cinema club "Kaleidoscope," 101, 104
  concerts, 101, 103
  development of, 97–98
  film repertoire, 102, 104–105
  guest lecturers, 98
  hobby groups (*kruzhki*), 101
  intellectual freedom, 105
  local performances, 99, 100–101
  movie theater, 98–99
  poetry association, 101

Tarkovskii's visit, 102
theater studio, 100
trips to Moscow to concert halls, 99
Vysotskii's concerts, 98, 103

de-Stalinization, 1, 24, 110
dissent
    Chernogolovka scientists and, 105, 134–135,
        137, 151
    definition, 131n3
    in the USSR, two pillars of, 132
dissident movement, 131, 133n14, 134, 145
Dolukhanova, Zara, 101
Dremin, Anatolii, 39
Dubček, Alexander, 139
Dubna physics center, 10
Dubovitskii, Fedor
    as administrator, 36, 76
    food supply management, 87, 89
    housing distribution, 81, 83–84
    on involvement of scientists in
        construction, 95
    Liubarskii Affair, 148–149
    participation in cultural life, 103
    primary party organization and, 120,
        135–136
    recruitment of researchers, 41
    role on development of Chernogolovka, 20,
        32, 78
    search for construction organization, 81
    on sports facilities, 95

Efimov, Oleg
    attendance of Stalin's funeral, 114–115
    education, 72
    friendship with Liubarskii, 145–146
    grocery shopping, 89
    impact of popular science on, 72
    invitation to join Communist party, 123
    Liubarskii Affair and, 149
    on official propaganda, 170
    political views, 137, 138
    reaction to Khrushchev's "secret
        speech," 117
    relations with mother, 58
    research interests, 40
    restriction on foreign travels, 161, 164
    samizdat movement and, 146
    on staff of public organizations, 124
    support of Soviet regime, 85
    war memories, 62, 64
Emanuel', Nikolai, 39, 120
Enman, Vladimir
    birth, 58
    childhood, 54

on collective identity of scientists, 96
description of Chernogolovka, 23
on difficulties of everyday life, 41
education, 72–73
on grocery shopping, 87
housing, 78–79
impact of Great Terror on, 54
job offer, 23
member of Communist party, 108
scientific career, 108
Stalin's death and, 115
war memories, 62
work at auto-repair factory, 62
Eremenko, Leonid, 90, 95
Esenin-Vol'pin, Aleksandr, 134, 145
everyday life. See also cultural life; food
        supplies; housing
    cultural center, 76
    health care, 75
    infrastructure, 75
    lack of basic comforts, 75
    sports activities, 95
Experimental Factory of Scientific
    Instrumentation, 84

Fellini, Federico, 105
Fock, Vladimir, 30n30
food supplies
    assortment of food in stores, 90, 91
    during Brezhnev era, 106
    changing situation with, 87, 92
    delivery of, 91–92
    Dubovitskii's management of, 89
    farmer's market, 91
    food rationing system, 89, 90, 92
    gardening, 88
    lack of complaints about, 92
    opening of "Gastronom," 85, 87, 90–91
    provision of vegetables, 90
    travels for groceries, 87
foreign travels
    access to hard currency, 167, 168
    application approval procedure, 163
    benefits for science, 156, 174
    communication with Western scientists
        during, 167
    familiarity of scientists with Western
        culture, 168
    instructions of the Academy of Sciences
        on, 162
    interest in Soviet visitors abroad, 168
    interview process, 164
    obtaining travel documents, 163
    organization of, 166
    professional activities during, 172

foreign travels (cont.)
    reports about, 171
    restrictions on, 159, 160, 161
    scientists' perception of, 165–166,
        167, 170
    security reviews, 163–164
    selection criteria for, 157
    Soviet practice of, 156
    statistics of, 156
    visa obtaining process, 161–163
Fürst, Juliane, 50, 109

Galich, Aleksandr, 136
Gantmakher, Feliks, 70
Gantmakher, Vsevolod
    awards, 155
    board member of the House of
        Scientists, 100
    on collective identity of scientists,
        96–97
    on Communist Party and science, 124
    decline of party membership, 122
    foreign travels, 155–156, 159
    on intellectual freedom, 105
    living conditions, 84
    reaction to Khrushchev's "secret
        speech," 117
    research interests, 45–46
    scientific career, 45
    trip to England, 167
Gantmakher effect, 45–46, 155
Gerovitch, Slava, 132
Gilburd, Eleonory, 169
GIPRONII, 33
Glavspetsstroi (contractor), 34, 81
Gol'danskii, Vitalii, 34
Gorbachev, Mikhail, 177
Gor'kov, Lev, 99
Gorsuch, Anne, 153, 174n85
Graham, Loren, 15, 132, 176n2
Great Patriotic War
    destruction of infrastructure, 59
    formation of Soviet scientists and, 50
    German attack of Stalingrad, 58–59
    human losses, 59
    patriotic sentiments after, 63
    postwar years, 65, 173–174
    suffering and survival during, 58
    urban housing stock, 79
Great Terror, 57, 111–112

Hinshelwood, Cyril Norman, 157n18
Hornsby, Robert, 124n86, 131n3
House of Scientists (Dom Uchenykh), 98,
    99–100

housing
    average apartment in Chernogolovka, 81
    during Brezhnev era, 84
    decline of residential construction, 84
    dormitory, 84
    government investment in, 79–80
    individual cottages, 81
    Khrushchev's program to improve, 80, 82
    priority of scientists, 82–84, 85
    in the Soviet Union, shortage of, 79
Hungarian Uprising, 118, 174

Iakir, Petr, 145
Institute of Chemical Physics (ICP)
    archival collections, 19
    construction of testing ground, 1, 32
    creation of, 24, 30
    dissolution of Political Department, 118
    role in Soviet science, 24
Institute of Chemical Physics (ICP) Branch
    creation of, 1
    development of polymer industry, 44
    foreign travels, 173
    meeting on Czechoslovakia invasion, 139,
        140–141
    primary party organization, 19, 118, 120
    reception on grocery store opening, 85
Institute of New Chemical Problems
    (INCP), 44
Institute of Physical Problems (IPP), 45
Institute of Solid State Physics (ISSP)
    archival collections, 19–20
    creation of, 10, 44
    early development of, 44–45
    foreign travels, 155–156
    meeting on Czechoslovakia invasion, 141–142
    number of employees, 122
    primary party organization, 19, 121, 122
    recruitment of scientists, 45–46
    research agenda, 44
    research facilities, 46
    scientific trips, 155n16
Institute of Theoretical Physics (ITP)
    creation of, 10, 46
    foreign travels, 173
    housing for scientists, 83–84
    research agenda, 47
intelligentsia, 13–14
Ioffe, Abram, 30n27

Joravsky, David, 15
Josephson, Paul, 16, 26, 68, 111, 132

Kaidanovskii, Aleksandr, 104
Kapitsa, Petr, 27, 45, 73, 152

Karabasov, Iurii, 121
Kawalerowicz, Jerzy, 104
Keldysh, Mstislav, 35, 43
Kelly, Catriona, 52
Khalatnikov, Isaak, 46
Khariton, Yulii, 30, 38
Khristianovich, Sergei, 27
Khrushchev, Nikita
    on Communism, 75
    on construction of socialism, 6
    creation of Scientific Council, 26
    denunciation of the cult of personally,
        115–116
    domestic policy, 6
    expectations for Soviet youth, 37
    foreign travels, 153–154
    ideological views, 5, 6, 7
    on improving the living conditions, 80
    personality, 5–6
    removal from power, 4
    science policy, 2, 12, 19, 26, 27, 47
    scientific intelligentsia and, 8
    "secret speech," 2, 5, 110, 115–116
    support of Semenov, 34
    Virgin Lands campaign, 7
    visits to Akademgorodok, 29
Khrushchev, Sergei, 34
Kieślowski, Krzysztof, 104
Konovalova, Nina
    arrival in Chernogolovka, 39
    awareness of Stalinist terror, 56
    childhood, 55
    on cultural life, 97
    education, 69
    foreign travel experience, 158, 166–167, 168
    member of Communist party, 120
    research interests, 40
    war memories, 63
Korsunskii, Moisei, 72
Kozakov, Mikhail, 98, 99
Krasnoiarsk-26, 76, 86–87
Kurchatov, Igor', 27
Kurdiumov, Georgii, 44, 46

Landau, Lev, 30n30, 45
Lavrentiev, Mikhail, 2, 26, 28–29
Lavrentieva, Tatiana, 99
Ledogorov, Igor', 100
Ledogorova, Stal', 100
Lenin, Vladimir, 8
Leningrad Physico-Technical Institute, 30
libraries' subscription to foreign periodicals,
    155n14
Liubarskii, Kronid
    arrest, 134, 147

    circle of friends, 145
    connection with dissidents, 145
    education, 143–145
    engagement in samizdat, 145
    family, 143–144, 147, 150
    political views, 135, 137, 143–144
    prosecution of, 21, 139
    status among scientists, 144
    student activist, 144
Liubarskii Affair
    administration of Chernogolovka and,
        148
    background, 143
    impact on science community, 148, 150
    interviews about, 149–150
    KGB investigation, 149
    party organization meetings on, 147–148
    trial and sentence, 147, 148–149
Liubovskaia, Rimma
    birthday, 111
    childhood, 71
    education, 71
    foreign travels, 165, 166n54
    on life during repressions, 57
    on postwar period, 64–65
    scientific career, 49
    war memories, 49, 60
Liubovskii, Rustem
    on construction of recreational park,
        94–95
    foreign travels, 98, 161, 165, 168
    friends, 145, 146–147
    housing, 83
    invasion of Czechoslovakia and, 141, 142
    Liubarskii Affair and, 149
    member of Communist party, 121
    political views, 137, 146–147
    on relation between generations, 57
    samizdat movement and, 146–147
    war experience, 62–63
    year of birth, 59
Lovell, Stephen, 58n44
Lysenko, Trofim, 28, 30n30
Lysenko Affair, 134n16

Manelis, Georgii
    affiliation with Communist party, 120
    age, 38
    awareness of Stalinist terror, 56
    chairman of the House of Scientists, 100
    on collective identity, 96
    comparison of Soviet and Western
        scientists, 172
    criticism of food assortment, 91
    on cultural life, 103–104

Manelis, Georgii (cont.)
    education, 69
    foreign travels, 160, 164, 166n54, 168–169
    on grocery shopping, 88
    on homeless and poverty in the West, 171
    housing, 81
    Komsomol member, 112
    on life during repressions, 57
    on living conditions in Chernogolovka, 65
    on new school in Chernogolovka, 94
    on optimism of postwar generation, 50
    reaction to Khrushchev's "secret
        speech," 117
    research interests, 39
    scientific career, 38–39
    war memories, 63
Martemianov, Vladimir
    affiliation with Communist party, 121
    dispute on invasion of Czechoslovakia, 140
    reputation, 140
    violation of the "rules of the game," 141
Medvedev, Zhores, 133n14, 134
Merridale, Catherine, 54, 58n44
Merzhanov, Aleksandr, 39, 138
Mezhov-Deglin, Leonid
    age, 59
    education, 73
    family, 51–52
    foreign travels, 166n54, 171
    hardship of childhood, 51–52
    impact of Great Terror on, 51–52
    political opinions, 52, 137
    scientific career, 46, 73
    war experience, 61–62
    on work of local party organization, 128
Mileiko, Sergei
    affiliation with Communist party, 123
    memories of Stalin's death, 115
    on mission of postwar generation, 65
    war memories, 58–59
military–industrial complex, 4, 5, 25, 51
Ministry of Medium Machine-Building, 10, 32
Mironova, Emma, 90
Mitta, Aleksandr, 104
Moscow Physical-Technical Institute (Fiztech),
    51, 68
Moscow State University (MGU)
    Chemistry Department, 39
    Physical and Technical Department, 51
    Physics Department, 66, 71

Nesmeianov, Aleksandr, 27, 28
nitrogen fixation research, 40
Noginsk Scientific Center. *See also*
    Chernogolovka

atmosphere of the Thaw and, 48
creation of, 35, 44
government funding, 44
population, 44
renaming, 35n49
research institutes, 47
Norrish, Ronald, 168
nuclear project
    first nuclear reactor, 11
    launch of, 9
    publication of scientific papers, 30n28
    test of atomic and hydrogen bombs, 11, 67

October regional committee (*Oktiabr'skii
    raikom*), 109, 121, 122
Oistrakh, David, 101
Okudzhava, Bulat, 98, 136
oral history methodology, 18–19
Orlov, Yuri, 134
Osipyan, Yuri
    assistance in foreign travels, 157, 159
    deputy director of the Institute of Solid State
        Physics, 44, 73
    KGB surveillance of, 126
    participation in cultural life, 103, 104
    recruitment of scientists, 45
    scientific career, 44–45
Osokina, Elena, 87n54
Ozersk (Cheliabinsk-40)
    comparative study of, 16
    emergence of, 9
    food supply, 87
    plutonium production, 9, 76
    as socialist paradise, 106

Pasolini, Pier Paolo, 104
"passive dissidents," 133, 136–137
"peaceful coexistence" doctrine, 153
Pervukhin, Mikhail, 31
Petinov, Vladimir, 121
Pimenov, Revol't, 134
Pioneer movement, 112
Pod'iapol'skii, Grigorii, 145
Pokhil, Pavel, 36
Poliakov, Iurii, 101
Poniatovskii, Evgenii
    affiliation with Communist party, 123
    childhood, 54–55
    education, 45
    foreign travels, 158–159, 169
    impact of Great Terror on, 54–55
    political opinions, 136
Prague Spring, 139
Presidium of the Academy of Sciences, 35, 37,
    44, 46, 99–100, 163

primary party organizations (PPO), 108–109, 111, 123
"privilege of passive participation," 21, 110, 126, 141
Pushchino biological center, 10, 28

Reddaway, Peter, 132
Richmond, Yale, 165
Romanov, Aleksei, 104
Rothberg, Abraham, 132

Sagdeev, Roald, 161, 165
Sakharov, Andrei, 49, 74n123, 131, 132
Salova, Galina, 145
samizdat publications, 145, 146
Sarov (Arzamas-16), 9, 76
Scientific Council (Sovet po nauke), 26
scientific intelligentsia
    childhood experience, 49
    conformity of, 176–177
    Khrushchev's view of, 8
    participation in work of Communist Party, 124
    privileges of, 3, 77–78, 107, 110–111, 172–173, 176–177
    relations with Soviet regime, 11, 26
    Thaw and, 15, 48
scientific tourism, 155n15
scientific towns
    decline of, 178–179
    distribution of funds, 80–81n28
    emergence of, 9, 27
    privileges of living in, 3, 76
scientists
    Cold War generation, 17
    environmental and health-related issues, 134n16
    foreign travel policy, 22, 152–154, 165, 173
    idealism of, 14, 20
    increasing number of, 74
    individual initiatives, 25
    international communications, 152–153, 154
    local party organizations and, 21
    memoirs, 138
    oral history, 18
    as part of Soviet intelligentsia, 13
    political and ideological beliefs, 21, 173–174, 174n85
    in postwar period, opportunities for, 51
    primary sources, 18–20
    professional opportunities for, 20, 74
    reaction to Gorbachev's perestroika, 22
    social status of, 3, 8, 86, 131
    studies of, 12, 17

support of Soviet regime, 8–9, 14–15, 132, 133–134
"Thaw generation" of, 25
Sedykh, Vera, 101
Semenov, Nikolai
    advocate of young generation of scientists, 37, 73
    on building scientific towns, 29
    on challenges of modern science, 35
    Chernogolovka project, 20, 23, 25, 32, 35
    correspondence with Petr Kapitsa, 23, 30–31, 47
    on cultivation of scientists, 35
    on decentralization of science, 29
    disagreements with Nesmeianov, 34
    idea of housing for scientists, 81
    interpretation of the Thaw, 48
    Khrushchev and, 34
    Nobel Prize award, 1, 29–30, 34
    opposition to Lysenko, 30n30
    on power of science, 1, 12
    prosecutions of physicists and, 30n30
    relations with Soviet authorities, 29, 34
    on science and socialism, 30
    scientific career, 9, 24, 26, 29–30, 31
    support of de-Stalinization, 118
    testing ground idea, 24, 31
Semenov's "kindergarten," 39
Shatz, Marshall, 132
Shchegolev, Igor', 142
Shekhtman, Veniamin
    affiliation with Communist party, 123, 142–143
    education, 69–70
    effect of anti-Semitic campaign on, 113–114
    foreign travels, 167
    "passive participation," 143
    political opinions, 136
    reaction to Khrushchev's "secret speech," 117
    scientific career, 45, 69–70, 100
shestidesiatniki, 145
Shibaeva, Rimma, 56, 84–85
Shilov, Aleksandr
    arrival in Chernogolovka, 40
    education, 69
    foreign travels, 157, 158
    political opinions, 119–120, 135
    reaction to Khrushchev's "secret speech," 117
    recollections of childhood, 55
    scientific career, 69
    Semenov's patronage, 158
    war experience, 63
    work in local party organization, 135–136, 142

Shilov, Evgenii, 55
Shukshin, Vasilii, 104
solid state physics, 46, 171–172
Soviet invasion of Czechoslovakia
    criticism of, 140, 141–142
    crush of the Prague Spring, 139
    party meeting discussions on, 139, 140–141
    scientists' reaction to, 138–139
Soviet science
    concentration of scientific institutes, 28
    emergence of new disciplines, 28
    fundamental research, 27, 35
    funding, 67–68, 176n2, 179
    major accomplishments, 2
    patronage networks, 29
    political shift in, 26
    politics of decentralization, 28
    scholarship on, 4, 15
Soviet Union
    alienation of intellectuals and state, 14
    anti-Semitic campaign, 69, 113
    consumer culture, 85–86
    cult of science, 12, 68
    cultural agreement on exchanges with
        US, 154
    defeat of anti-party group, 118
    de-Stalinization, 1–2
    dissident trials, 14
    economic development, 77, 177
    foreign policy, 169–170
    higher education, 50–51, 67
    housing shortage, 79–80
    individual initiatives, 87n54
    investment in consumer-oriented
        industries, 77
    lack of debate on Great Terror, 58n44
    legacy of the Stalin era, 5
    living standards, 106
    military–industrial complex, 12n34
    myth of a "happy childhood," 52, 53n14
    popular science in, 71
    postwar period, 64–65
    propaganda, 169–170
    student population, 67
    urban living space, 79
Stalin, Joseph, 1, 8–9, 114
Stepanov, Nikolai, 49
Stepanova, Rimma, 83. See also Liubovskaia,
    Rimma
Suvorov, Ernest
    on distribution of housing, 128
    education, 72
    Great Terror experience, 56
    head of party organization, 121
    impact of popular science on, 72

    life in Tashkent, 64
    recollections of Stalin's death, 115
    on situation with food supply, 92

Tarkovskii, Andrei, 102, 104
testing ground project
    beginning of construction, 33, 36
    budget, 32
    closeness to nature, 42
    communication with government officials,
        31, 43
    contractors, 33, 34
    Council of Ministers' resolution on, 25, 32
    government funding, 37
    hardship of first decades, 42
    independent laboratories, 38
    infrastructure, 43
    Keldysh's visit, 43
    living conditions, 41
    optimism of the first residents, 41–42
    population of, 43
    recruitment of researchers, 32, 36–37, 41
    research on nitrogen fixation, 40
    residential housing, 1
    selection of construction site, 32
    Semenov's idea of, 31
    spending on infrastructure, 43
    transformation into scientific center, 41
Thaw
    "children of enemies of people," 72
    development of science and technology,
        9, 11
    historiography, 12–13, 14
    scientific intelligentsia and, 48, 176
    Soviet science policy, 26
Third Program of the Communist Party, 27, 77,
    78n11, 86
Timirbaev, Al'bert, 101, 103, 104, 105
Troitsk, 10
Tromly, Benjamin, 15, 66–67
Tsentrakademstroi, 33, 81
Tukhachevskii, Mikhail, 54n19

Ukrainka, Lana
    on crisis in Czechoslovakia, 141
    education, 71
    impact of Stalin's death on, 114
    life in postwar Ukraine, 64

Vashin, Lev
    affiliation with Communist party, 119,
        135–136
    age, 58
    childhood, 56
    dispute with Martemianov, 140

experience of Great Terror, 58
housing, 81
ideological views, 119
on invasion of Czechoslovakia, 141
on Liubarskii, 144
political opinions, 135
reaction to Khrushchev's "secret speech," 116
research interests, 39
restriction on foreign travels, 160–161
scientific career, 38, 100
war memories, 61
Vishnevskaia, Galina, 101
Vladimir Pomerantsev

"On Sincerity in Literature," 144
Vysotskii, Vladimir, 98

Wajda, Andrzej, 104
Weiner, Douglas, 11, 132

Zakharov, Vladimir, 57
Zel'dovich, Yakov, 30, 38
Zelenograd, 10, 76
Zernov, Pavel, 43
Zhdanov, Andrei, 153
Zheleznogorsk (Krasnoiarsk-26), 76, 86–87
Zubok, Vladislav, 6, 11, 73–74